TABLE OF CONTENTS

ACKNOWLEDGMENTS	5
ABOUT LIVING FREE	7
MEMO OF UNDERSTANDING	9
SEMESTER I: LAYING FOUNDATIONS	11
Lesson One: Getting Started	13
Lesson Two: Your Hardest Spirit-filled Work	21
Lesson Three: Your Future & Current Direction	27
Lesson Four: The FASTER Scale	35
Lesson Five: True Accountability—Situational Awareness	47
Lesson Six: Personal Promises	57
Lesson Seven: Matrix of Addiction	65
Lesson Eight: Battle Plan	75
Lesson Nine: Survival	85
Lesson Ten: Limbic Holiday	93
Semester I Commitment	99
SEMESTER II: BUILDING SOBRIETY	101
Lesson Eleven: Committing to Your Team	103
Lesson Twelve: Identifying the Pain	111
Lesson Thirteen: Self-care	121
Lesson Fourteen: Hot Buttons	131
Lesson Fifteen: Facing Your Wounds	137
Lesson Sixteen: Get Up Off The Floor	149
Lesson Seventeen: Arousal Template—Part One	159
Lesson Eighteen: Arousal Template—Part Two	165
Lesson Nineteen: What's Next?	173
Semester II Commitment	179
APPENDIX I: THE NEUROCHEMISTRY OF ADDICTION	181
APPENDIX II: TOOLS FOR RECOVERY	191
Check-in	191
Commitment to Change	192
The FASTER Scale	193
Accountability Phone Calls	196
Relapse Analysis	197
APPENDIX III: CLINICAL TESTS	201
FACES Test	201
PTSI Test	205
SAST Test	214

ACKNOWLEDGMENTS

To every man who has fallen prey to the bondage of sexual sin,
To every man who has, at times, felt defeated, hopeless, and at a loss for answers,
To every man who has been wounded by others,
To every man who has resorted to coping with pain in life through his own means,
To every man who wants greater intimacy with Jesus, his friends, and family,
To every man who needs healing in the depths of his soul,
There is hope through Jesus Christ.
This is for you.

The foundations of this workbook were taken directly from the Word of God and what the Holy Spirit has revealed to the three of us through our relationships with Jesus Christ. Some might say that the observations concerning the Word of God were original to us, but the truth is that all of the biblical wisdom found in these pages came from the Holy Spirit. We either recognized the truths through our fellowship with Jesus, our own recovery journeys, or in the middle of a recovery group meeting or counseling session.

Additionally, the clinical insights are not original to us. Dr. Patrick Carnes has been Dr. Ted's mentor for years. This nationally known researcher and clinician has been so gracious in pouring his wisdom and insights into the lives of many.

> *The sting of death is sin, and the power of sin is the law. But thanks be to God,*
> *who gives us the victory through our Lord Jesus Christ.*
> 1 Corinthians 15:56-57 (ESV)

Thanks be to You, Jesus, for You have met our deepest needs by forgiving us of our rebellion toward You, restoring us to a right standing and relationship with You, by Your grace alone through Your life, death, and resurrection. Thanks be to You, Jesus, that You set the captive free, heal our wounds, gives us victory over the enslaving bondage of sin, and restore us to newness of life through a relationship with You. This is for You.

Thank you to the many men and women that God placed in all of our lives who took part in our healing journeys.

GRACE & PEACE,

Ben Bennett
Brett Butcher
Dr. Ted Roberts

ABOUT LIVING FREE

Living Free is a two semester, gospel-centered sexual purity curriculum developed in partnership between two staff members of Cru (formerly Campus Crusade for Christ) and Pure Desire. Pure Desire has been helping men and women break free from sexual addiction for over 20 years. In a group setting, the Living Free process helps men who have become addicted to sexual behavior, which is harmful to their social, family, and spiritual well-being, find healing. God is using the theological and clinical concepts in this process to set men free from sexual sin, so they can walk in the abundant life that Christ promised His people.

Living Free was developed in response to an overwhelming need for an effective resource for college-aged men that is clinically and biblically sound. Throughout this resource, you'll find true solutions to this struggle. Because sexual sin is ultimately not about sex, but about dealing with pain and stress in life, a large part of this process is focused on helping individuals find healing from this pain. It's also important to note that this is a process and not a quick fix solution. Sexual sin often starts out as a series of immoral decisions, but quickly leads to an addiction, which is any sexually-related, compulsive behavior that interferes with normal living and causes severe stress on family, friends, loved ones, and one's work environment.[1] Whether you are battling sexual sin infrequently, habitually, or have moved into the realm of addiction, you will find this resource helpful.

Throughout this process, men will work through the devastating effects that the addiction has had on their social, family, and spiritual life. Because most addictions negatively impact and rewire the brain (see The Neurochemistry of Addiction in Appendix I), this resource focuses on renewing the mind through biblical principles. This process will take you through understanding sexual addiction, its effects on the brain, where addiction comes from, what areas of the soul have been wounded and have led individuals to medicate their pain through sexual sin and other coping behaviors, and how individuals can live fully free.

This process is based on the experiences of Ben Bennett, Brett Butcher, the clinical findings of Dr. Ted Roberts, and many Pure Desire groups that have seen thousands of individuals set free from sexual addiction. Ben and Brett have been leading groups through the healing process for years and have spent significant time working with Dr. Ted Roberts, the founder of Pure Desire. Dr. Ted Roberts was trained under Dr. Patrick Carnes and received his Pastoral Sexual Addiction Professional (PSAP) certification years ago.

This workbook is a compilation of what these three men have learned through their combined decades of working with Christian men who are struggling with sexual addictions in their lives. The principles you will learn are based on the Word of God and have been proven to be effective. Clinical studies have shown that if an individual begins to walk in these principles and begins to incorporate these disciplines into his life within the first year, his relapse rate will drop significantly! It is imperative that your group is structured and run the way outlined in Lesson One. Many of us may want to adapt a resource like this to our own style, but it is critical to the healing process that the group follows all of the criteria listed.

This workbook will take you approximately two semesters to work through with your Living Free group. If group members follow the structure outlined in Lesson One, diligently apply themselves, and incorporate the concepts from this resource into their lives, they will find freedom from that insane cycle of relapsing and promising God to never do it again. There is hope, and many have found it through this process!

---

1. www.sexhelp.com/faq

IMPORTANCE OF THE GROUP FORMAT

Because sexual sin happens in isolation, it's critical that individuals go through *Living Free* in a group setting with at least three and no more than five individuals in order to see healing. This is not a battle that individuals can win on their own. The number one priority is to break the isolation. Curriculum is important, but only if isolation ceases. Breaking isolation means committing to a life without any more secrets, as well as keeping group members aware of how others in the group are doing and in touch with each other. Choose to invest in the men in your group with a commitment of being honest and open. The job of each member is to make sure the group is a safe place to be transparent. Isolation allows the individual to have control that, in turn, allows him to keep his thoughts and behaviors secret. Don't get caught in the trap of thinking that the right curriculum by itself will bring healing. Isolation must be broken before members of your group can truly move forward in healing.

Living Free is a two semester curriculum; we highly recommend starting groups in the fall semester. It's much more beneficial and easier to have a group begin in August or September and end in May or June, given colleges normally have a shorter winter break than summer break. This allows the group to avoid a long break where individuals may be tempted to isolate or their healing may take a back seat.

Also, be sure each member has the willingness to work hard and walk through the healing process. Some men are not ready to face the pain and it would be a disservice to everyone to place them in a group. If men are not willing to commit to meetings, homework completion, and making accountability contacts outside of group time through phone calls, they are not ready to join or continue in a group.

STARTING A GROUP

Before starting a group, you'll first identify a group leader. Ideally, your group leader has been free from masturbation, pornography, and sexual acts outside of the marriage covenant for at least six months. We've found that if an individual can see six months of sobriety, his relapse rate drops significantly and he is much more likely to continue on in freedom. Your leader can only help people see healing if he has experienced it himself.

So if you have identified a group leader, or you will be that leader, pick up the *Living Free Leader's Guide*, which is a comprehensive resource to leading individuals through this workbook. It will give you crucial information, such as navigating difficult issues that arise in group.

TOPICS COVERED IN THE LEADER'S GUIDE:

» Necessary qualifications for a leader
» How to advertise and get a group started
» An in-depth explanation of the tools the group members will need to master
» How to help group members identify trauma in their lives
» How to handle difficult scenarios in the group and legal issues that may arise
» Answers to frequently asked questions

Once you pick up the *Leader's Guide* and learn the ins and outs of leading a group, get a group together and prepare to see God work in the lives of men!

MEMO OF UNDERSTANDING

Living Free Group Participants: Please read and sign this Memo of Understanding, indicating that you have read and understand the purpose and parameters of Living Free groups and the moral and ethical obligations of leaders.

I understand that every attempt will be made to guard my anonymity and confidentiality in this group, but that anonymity and confidentiality cannot be absolutely guaranteed in a group setting.

- I realize that the group coordinator or leader cannot control the actions of others in the group.
- I realize that confidentiality is sometimes broken accidentally and without malice.

I understand that the group coordinator or leader is morally and ethically obligated to discuss with me any of the following behaviors, and that this may lead to the breaking of confidentiality and/or possibly intervention:

- I communicate anything that may be interpreted as a threat to self-inflict physical harm.
- I communicate an intention to harm another person.
- I reveal ongoing sexual or physical abuse.
- I exhibit an impaired mental state.
- I share any illegal activity.

I understand that the Living Free group coordinator or leader may be a mandatory reporter to authorities of sexual conduct that includes minor children, the elderly, or the disabled.

I have been advised that the consequences for communicating the above types of information may include reports to the proper authorities—the police, suicide units, or children's protective agencies, as well as to any potential victims.

I further acknowledge that if I am on parole or probation and I engage in wrongful behavior in violation of my parole or probation, part of my healing and recovery may include notifying the appropriate authorities.

I understand that this is a Christ-centered group that integrates recovery tools with the Bible and prayer, and that all members may not be of my particular church background. I realize that the Bible may be discussed more (or less) than I would like it to be.

I understand that this is a support group and not a therapy group and that the leader is qualified by "life experience" and not by professional training as a therapist or counselor. The leader's role in this group is to create a climate where healing may occur, to support my personal work toward recovery, and to share his own experience, strength, and hope.

My Name _____ **Date** _____

Signature _____

Witness: Living Free Group Leader's Name _____

Living Free Group Leader's Signature _____

LESSON ONE
GETTING STARTED

I am so excited that you picked up this resource and that you desire to see victory over sin, healing, and most importantly, a deeper relationship with Jesus Christ. My prayer is that by committing to this process, you will understand, identify, and heal from the underlying factors that create and reinforce sexually addictive behavior. I pray that in your journey, you will "grasp how wide and long and high and deep is the love of Christ" (Ephesians 3:18 NIV) as you heal through the power of the Holy Spirit and the implications of the gospel in your life.

Throughout this resource, we will be using the term "addiction" frequently. Although this term may bring to mind intense images of chemical dependency or entrapment to substances, sexual addiction can be defined as any sexually-related compulsive behavior which interferes with normal living and causes severe stress on family, friends, loved ones, and one's work environment. So, whether you are battling sexual sin occasionally, habitually, or have moved into the addictive realm, I pray that you will find healing through this resource.

So, let's get started. I used to have significant problems with authority, structure, and following rules. I often thought that my way was better in many situations. Bending rules, cutting corners, and doing what I wanted was my lifestyle. I wanted to do things my way so that I could be in control and ultimately feel safe. It was a defense mechanism to protect myself. Over the years, I learned more and more that my way wasn't always the best way. I learned that many others had more experience and expertise than me. I gained experiences with healthy authority figures who didn't use their position of power for their gain, but to bless me. I had new experiences of following structures that actually worked and helped me grow. These experiences began to change my views on authority and structure.

Your group will ideally be led by an individual who has been free from relapsing, or returning, to masturbation, pornography, and sexual acts outside of the marriage covenant for at least six months. Returning to any of these behaviors would constitute a relapse. If an individual can see six months of sobriety, his relapse rate drops significantly and he is much more likely to continue on in freedom. Your group leader can only help you see healing if he has experienced it himself.

Following structure can seem stale, rigid, or useless at times, but know that everything in this process is here for a reason. It is imperative that your group is structured and run the way outlined in this lesson in order for your group to experience healing.

LIVING FREE GROUP STRUCTURE

Note: Additional information for leaders about legal concerns and issues is included in the "Living Free Leader's Guide" and the resources provided on the Pure Desire website at puredesire.org.

40-60-20 MEETING PLAN

The minimum time for the weekly Living Free group meeting is two hours. Each section is absolutely crucial to the process, so use a timer or stopwatch to stay on track. There should be a minimum of three and no more than five men in your group so that everyone has enough time to participate fully in each aspect of the meeting. We encourage all groups to make time for a meeting that lasts two full hours; 90 minutes is just not enough time.

40 MINUTES: The first 40 minutes is a review of each person's behavior and emotional state from the previous week. Here, each individual will share their Check-in, which covers their past week. The purpose of this review is to help you become more aware of the addictive and healing processes that are at work in your life. Prior to filling out this worksheet, be sure to fill out the FASTER Scale Exercise, which you'll use as a reference. More information about the FASTER Scale can be found in Lesson Four of this workbook. The FASTER Scale and Check-in can be found in Appendix II and in the *Living Free Journal*. Both worksheets should be filled out within 24 hours of the group meeting.

60 MINUTES: The next 60 minutes is reserved for reviewing the reading from the lesson and the homework. As a group, spend 10 minutes discussing the reading and making comments about what you highlighted, underlined, and enjoyed. Spend the next 50 minutes taking turns sharing responses to the homework. Encourage one another and give insights after each member shares. You should come to group with your homework and lesson reading completed. If you do not have your Check-in or homework done you can listen, but cannot share answers. If you have not taken the time to do the homework, responses during group time are off-the-cuff and no internal processing has taken place.

Additionally, you will need to spend a minimum of 30 minutes a day, five days a week on recovery work. This includes homework assignments and utilizing tools which will be explained later in the process like Personal Promises, deep breathing, and the FASTER Scale. All homework assignments should be worked on throughout the week, not in one sitting, so that there is plenty of time for the information to sink in and be processed. Each week's homework assignments should be worked on for a minimum of an hour and a half. If you finish the assignments in a shorter period of time, spend more time praying through the assignments and adding whatever else comes to mind.

20 MINUTES: The last 20 minutes is spent going over the Commitment to Change, which should be filled out prior to the group meeting. The purpose of the Commitment to Change is to put laser focus toward responding to a challenge in the coming week. This worksheet should be filled out within 24 hours of the group meeting. The Commitment to Change can be found in the Appendix II of this workbook.

Without your Living Free group and their support, you will have a slim chance of making it to freedom. So many men have tried to win this battle on their own, but have found themselves back in their addiction. They seldom or never make calls to their group members during the week, and don't really open up in group meetings. They then wonder why they keep relapsing. A lack of situational awareness goes along with isolation. I always tell guys when they go into isolation, passivity, and withdrawal that they are kissing the snake. At some point you are going to get bit, bad.

The number one priority is to break the isolation that has allowed the struggle to continue. Breaking isolation means committing to living without any secrets and keeping other group members aware of how you are doing. It also means inviting others in when you are struggling or hurting, rather than after the temptation or pain has passed.

This group will be extremely important in your healing process. Because we are wounded in the context of relationships, we must be healed in the context of relationships. Relationships are God's idea. God has eternally existed as one in essence, but three in person, which we refer to as the trinity. God Himself is a perfect community and He created the idea of relationships. He didn't create us to live life like Rambo, as a loner trying to take on the world. He created us to live with individuals in our lives who will walk alongside us and be in the fight for healthy sexuality with us at all times. This is war and the enemy is passionate about seeing you stay in sexual sin. So allow the men in this group to battle alongside you.

You need the group to survive the powerful nature of sexual bondage. In bondage, there exists both behavioral and thought-life secrets. You may have tried to survive by protecting your secrets that are threatening to you because they make you vulnerable. But it's time for the secrets to stop so that shame can be broken and you can experience the tangible acceptance and love of Christ through group members.

CHECK-IN

The Check-in is a set of questions that review each person's behavior and emotional state from the previous week. As mentioned, going over the Check-in takes up the first 40 minutes of each group meeting. The purpose of the review is to help you become more aware of the addictive and healing processes that are at work in your life. The Check-in also includes the use of the FASTER Scale and CTC, which all can be found in Appendix II and the *Living Free Journal*. These questions should be filled out within 24 hours of the weekly group meeting. Below, you will find good examples of answers to each question. Blank copies are provided in Appendix II and the *Living Free Journal*.

① What is the lowest level you reached on the FASTER Scale this week? (If there was a relapse be sure to fill out a Relapse Analysis, found in Appendix II. At a minimum, any of the following would constitute as a relapse: masturbation, pornography, or sexual acts outside of marriage. Depending on where you are in your recovery journey or what your struggle is, you may want to consider other behaviors as a relapse as well. This could include any other ways that you tend to cope when you're at the end of your rope. Some examples include overeating, sleeping in really late, drinking too much alcohol, or exploding in anger. If you are struggling consistently with sexual sin at this point in your journey, hold off on considering other behaviors a relapse for now.)

The lowest level I reached this past week was Ticked Off. I was supposed to meet a friend for lunch, and drove 15 minutes to meet him, but he canceled right when I got there, so I saw it as a huge waste of time.

② What level did you find yourself predominantly living in?

I lived in Anxiety this week. I've constantly been worrying about a big test I have next week because I may fail the class if I don't get an A on the test. I've been living in fear and having trouble concentrating on other important things in life.

③ What was the double bind you were dealing with in question one? In question 2? How could you have practically implemented the harder choice? (Remember, there is always an easier choice and a harder choice. Moving toward health usually involves the harder choice. Check out Lesson Five for more info.)

Being Ticked Off at my friend: I got angry due to my fear of feeling disrespected and rejected. I greatly fear feeling rejected because I experienced that so much from my Dad and friends growing up. The harder choice in this double bind was to: ask God for forgiveness for my anger, call a group member to process my emotions and remind myself of the truth, deal with my feelings of rejection by reminding myself that God loves me, is proud of me, and accepts me because I am His son. I could have also reminded myself that my friend most likely wasn't trying to reject me or disrespect me, something important had just come up last minute.

Living in Anxiety: I worried so much this past week about my upcoming test because it will cost a lot of money and disappoint my parents if I fail this class. Rather than constantly worrying, the harder choice would have been to: call a group member to break isolation, address my fears of being a failure, tell myself how God views me and my true identity, and take steps to study and get out of Anxiety.

④ Where are you on your Commitment to Change from our last meeting?

It was to study for my upcoming test every day for 30 minutes. Each day, I reminded myself that God has gifted me with intelligence and a good memory. I followed through on studying although it was difficult. I also texted with Joe and Jake at 9 am each day when I began studying like I committed to doing.

⑤ Have you lied to anyone this week either directly or indirectly? Why?

Yes, someone asked me how I was really doing and rather than talking about my fears of the upcoming test I lied and said I was doing great. I wanted to isolate and avoid my feelings.

⑥ What positive things have you done to move toward sexual and relational health in your life this week?

I spent time with the Lord every day to grow with Him. I took a girl out on a date, encouraged her, and asked her questions about herself.

COMMITMENT TO CHANGE

A Commitment to Change (CTC) is simply a commitment that is developed through answering a set of questions each week that helps one move toward health. As mentioned previously, going over your CTC each week takes up the last 20 minutes of the group meeting. A CTC allows you to put laser focus on a challenge in the coming week. This challenge could center around a stressful situation that needs to be resolved or that you will be facing. It could be steps that need to be implemented to get back to Restoration on the FASTER Scale (Appendix II, Lesson Four, the *Living Free Journal*), or it could be implementing a certain healthy activity into daily life, such as going to the gym to exercise several days a week. These questions should be filled out within 24 hours of the weekly group meeting.

You will hold each other accountable to following through on each other's CTC throughout the week; it is often something difficult to do that would be easier to avoid or not put energy toward. You need the help of the group to follow through on your commitments of living in reality and restoration.

The battle of renewing the mind must be fought and won in the power of the Holy Spirit on a daily basis, and can't be won alone. Without a battle plan of healthy behaviors, you will default to old unhealthy coping behaviors, so you will need to develop new healthy ways to live. Below are the questions you will answer each week to create your CTC. An example of good responses is given as well. A blank copy is also provided in Appendix II.

1. What area do you need to change or what challenge are you facing next week?
I need to stop procrastinating on studying for a test I have next week. I really need to get an A on the test or I may fail the class, so I have been really worried.

2. What will it cost you emotionally if you do change?
I will have to face my fears of failure if I work hard and get a bad grade on the test. I will have to be disciplined and ask for help from others.

3. What fear do you feel with what you have chosen to change?
I fear getting a bad grade on the test and feeling worthless. I fear not having what it takes to get a good grade even if I work hard.

4. What will it cost you if you don't change?
I will probably get stressed out and angry the night before the test due to studying like crazy, which will lead me down the FASTER Scale to Relapse. I won't do the best I can do and see that I probably am smart enough to get a good grade if I work hard. I will also probably fail the class if I don't study hard.

5. What is your plan to maintain your restoration regarding these changes?
I will study for 30 minutes each day at 9 am until the day of the test. Before studying, I will remind myself that God has gifted me with intelligence and a good memory.

6. Who will keep you accountable to this commitment? What are the details of your accountability for this week? What questions should they ask you?
Joe and Jake from my Living Free group will text me at 9 am each day when I begin studying for the test and encourage me. If I don't hear from them, I will text them to let them know I began studying. They can ask me if I have been studying each day at 9 am for 30 minutes and what fears I've been processing that may be driving the desire to procrastinate.

ACCOUNTABILITY PHONE CALLS

As part of recovery, you must commit to initiating at least three phone calls, not text messages, with other people in your group on different days throughout the week to break isolation and check in about your current status on the FASTER Scale (Appendix II, Lesson Four, the *Living Free Journal*), double binds (Lesson Five), and current status on fulfilling your Commitment to Change. Since sexual sin happens in secrecy, it's crucial for you to develop a lifestyle of constant vulnerability throughout the week. Phone calls are a great opportunity to process what's going on in life and ask for help in living a life of restoration.

If you call another member and they don't pick up, leave a voicemail sharing what is going on. Take the opportunity to begin to process and break isolation, but don't count this as one of your three calls for the week.

Phone calls typically last anywhere from five minutes to thirty minutes depending on time available and what is going on in each others' lives. If you're limited by time, be sure to tell the other person how much time you have to talk. If your conversation is cut short and you need to process more that is going on in your life, call another group member. Use the following five questions to check in with one another.

1. **Where are you on the FASTER Scale?**

2. **What double bind are you facing? How can you practically make the harder choice?**
(Remember, there is always an easier choice and a harder choice. Moving toward health usually involves the harder choice.)

3. **Where are you on your Commitment to Change you made at the end of our last meeting?**

4. **What challenges are you facing this week? Who will you allow to help you face them?**

5. **What is your plan to maintain your restoration regarding these challenges? Is the plan you chose at group still applicable? If not, what do you need to pay attention to right now?**

GROUP GUIDELINES[1]

Guidelines are essential to create a safe environment for open and honest conversations during group time. Read through the guidelines together, briefly discuss what each means, and get verbal buy-in from everyone. The guidelines should also be reviewed when anyone new joins the group. Some groups will read the guidelines out loud quarterly, some once a month, some weekly. You may want to also print them on a sheet of paper and display them during group meetings as a reminder of how the group operates. These guidelines are straightforward and give you the basics that allow you and the other men to have a great group experience.

LIVING FREE GROUP GUIDELINES

CONFIDENTIALITY IS ESSENTIAL!
What's said in the group is not shared outside the group.

SELF-FOCUS
Speak only for yourself. Avoid giving advice unless given permission.

BE PRESENT
Refrain from texting, being on your phone, or using your computer for things unrelated to the group meeting.

LIMIT SHARING
We want everyone to have a chance to share.

RESPECT OTHERS
Let everyone find his own answers.

REGULAR ATTENDANCE
Meetings should only be missed in the event of an emergency. Let your leader or co-leader know if you can't attend a meeting.

COMMITMENT TO ACCOUNTABILITY
Make a minimum of three phone call contacts a week; if you have relapsed in the last week, then a daily contact is recommended.

LISTEN RESPECTFULLY
No side conversations.

TAKE OWNERSHIP AND BE RESPONSIBLE
If you feel uncomfortable with anything, talk with your leader or co-leader, or your group.

STAY ON THE SUBJECT/QUESTIONS
Avoid off-topic conversations and comments.

HOMEWORK COMPLETION
Allow 30 minutes per day to complete homework. If you don't do your homework, you won't see healing, and you won't be able to participate while the group is processing their homework.

LET GOD WORK! HE WILL NOT REST UNTIL THE WORK HE HAS STARTED IN YOU IS COMPLETED.

---

1. Roberts, Dr. Ted. *Seven Pillars of Freedom Workbook.* 4th ed., Gresham, OR, Pure Desire, 2015. 22.

COVENANT TO CONTEND

The Covenant to Contend is a commitment of accountability, which states why you have chosen to join a Living Free group and what you are committed to do in order to win your battle with sexual addiction. At the bottom of the page you will notice a place for you and one other person to sign and date. This is to help you understand this is a public commitment. Take the signing of this document seriously. Read it monthly to yourself as a reminder.

COVENANT TO CONTEND:
THE COURAGEOUS FIGHT FOR HEALTHY SEXUALITY

There is a battle going on within me. As much as it pains me to admit it, that battlefield is my sexuality. I realize the outcome of this battle not only holds my life in its hands, but the lives of those I love and care for. I now choose to participate in the battle for godly character and integrity, not only for my soul, but also for my family, friends, brothers and sisters in Christ, and above all else, God.

I am beginning to understand I cannot win this battle myself. I am coming to see the biblical truth that we are one body in Christ (Romans 12:5). Therefore, I surrender to God's wisdom, turn to the leadership above me, and submit myself to the process of the daily renewing of my mind.

THINGS I CAN DO:
- Attend the group weekly.
- Complete the Commitment to Change and Check-in each week.
- Submit to God's values because they supersede mine; therefore, I will contend to live life on His terms instead of my own or the culture around me.
- Pay close attention to what I look at, what I listen to, and what I set my mind on.
- Take responsibility for my thoughts and actions.
- Verbally describe my feelings.
- Make contact with a group members at least three times, between group meetings.

I CAN ACCEPT:
- Healing is a miraculous process over time.
- Healing requires feeling pain and learning from it.
- I am very capable of retreating back into the addictive lifestyle.
- A relapse does not stop the healing process, but it will have consequences.
- I have become skilled at lying to myself and others.
- I do not really live in isolation; my choices affect others.
- My secrecy keeps me in bondage to my sin.

I WILL COMMIT TO:
- A willingness to change—and following through with my plans
- Total confidentiality: I will discuss only my experiences outside the group
- Rigorous honesty with God, my group, myself, and eventually to my friends and family
- Building my knowledge base (books, CDs, DVDs, videos, and seminars)
- Reading Scripture and praying
- A biblical standard of sexual purity in my life
- A goal of moving toward sobriety that is living life God's way
- Giving my hardest Spirit-filled work to this process

Signature _____ **Date** _____

Witnessed _____

Now you know the structure of the group, the guidelines for group operation, and you have made a commitment to contend for your healing. This is an epic journey of transformation and I am excited for your healing.

CHECKLIST FOR A HEALTHY GROUP

Lastly, you'll want to look at the checklist below and see if your group meets these qualifications affirmatively. Be sure to read these out loud in your group meeting. Remember, it's imperative that all of these qualifications are in place for you to get the most out of this process. Revisit these questions monthly in addition to the Covenant To Contend.

1. **Is the leader in a healthy position to lead? Ideally, he has been free from masturbation, pornography, and sexual acts outside of the marriage covenant for a minimum of six months.**

2. **Are we going to be following the 40-60-20 format?**

3. **Are we going to be making a minimum of three phone calls per week to other group members?**

4. **Will we be doing our Check-in and Commitment to Change each week?**

5. **Will we do the reading and homework assignments before coming to the group each week?**

6. **Will we implement natural consequences as outlined in the *Leader's Guide*?**

7. **Is each member committed to working hard at recovery (completing homework assignments, making calls, fulfilling their Commitment to Change, doing their Check-in)?**

8. **Are there a minimum of three and no more than five members in my group?**

9. **Is the group leader using the *Leader's Guide*?**

ASSIGNMENTS FOR NEXT TIME

1. **Re-read through this lesson and become more familiar with each aspect of the process.**

2. **Define what a relapse will be for you and share it with your group at your next meeting.**

3. **Spend time in prayer for your healing and the healing of other members.**

4. **Begin making a minimum of three calls per week to other group members.**

5. **Fill out a Commitment to Change, FASTER Scale Exercise, and Check-in before the next group meeting. The Check-in should be completed within 24 hours of the next group meeting.**

There is one blank copy of each worksheet that you will use on a weekly basis in Appendix II. You can either make photo copies of these to fill out each week, write your responses on a separate piece of paper, or use the *Living Free Journal*, which includes all the copies of the worksheets you'll need throughout this process.

LESSON TWO
YOUR HARDEST SPIRIT-FILLED WORK

*I worked harder than any of them, though it was not I,
but the grace of God that is with me.*
1 Corinthians 15:10b (ESV)

Several years ago, I had an experience in my life where I said, "Enough is enough." I was hanging out with some of my guy friends and we were talking about exercising and weightlifting. For some reason, one of my friends decided to pull out a scale and see what he weighed. You may be thinking, "What kind of guys weigh themselves when they hang out together?" I know, I know, it was weird, but it happened. So I hesitantly decided to get on the scale. I knew I had gained quite a bit of weight over the past six years since high school due to having an increasingly sedentary lifestyle, not exercising, and eating whatever I wanted. Back then I was about the same height, but I remembered weighing 185 pounds or so. So, I was pretty nervous to say the least.

I hopped on the scale and to my surprise, I was a whopping 289 pounds! Now, I'm 6'3" tall, but still, I was very overweight. Over the course of six years, I had gained 104 pounds! Seeing the number on the scale was such a wake-up call and I remember deciding that day that I had to do something about my weight. I was no longer willing to put up with being overweight. I didn't want to look the way I did any longer. I didn't want to die at an early age of a heart attack or get diabetes. I was faced with the number I saw and I said, "Enough is enough." I told myself, "I'm going to do something about this. I'm going to begin getting healthier and losing weight now."

Over the course of the following months, I lost quite a bit of weight by eating healthier and exercising. I was happy with the results I was seeing. I felt better and had a lot more energy. I worked hard, and the results kept me going. Three years later, I have continued this lifestyle. There are seasons when I eat too much junk food and I don't exercise, but for the most part, I have kept the weight off and I continue to lose weight. But this has taken a complete lifestyle change and hard Spirit-filled work. It has taken encouragement and help from others, commitment, prayer, and addressing the underlying wounds from my past that I was coping with by eating so much and neglecting my body.

Just like the lifestyle change I had to make to get healthy physically, you will have to make a complete lifestyle change to get healthy emotionally and sexually. It will take trusting the Holy Spirit's direction, yielding to God's desires daily, facing the pain from your past, reaching out to others, and a commitment to not slipping back into isolation or secrecy. We will address how to do this throughout the process in greater depths than you may have ever gone before.

Going through this process will probably be the most difficult thing you will ever do. I don't say that to scare you; I say that because I want you to ask yourself if you are ready. As those struggling with addictions, we have subconsciously organized everything in our lives to revolve around avoiding pain. Why? Because pain is hurtful. It's not comfortable. Everything in us wants

> It's clear throughout Scripture that we do not just let go and let God.

NOTES

to take the easy road and live a comfortable life. But that's not what Christ has called us to and that is not what this process entails. In this process, you will be running toward the pain in your life as opposed to running away from it. You'll find that you have unresolved wounds from your past that you have been avoiding for a long time and coping with them by going to the desires of your flesh. It's time to finally take the hard road. Make the decision to put a stop to acting out sexually and start asking for help, facing the pain that you have been avoiding for years. It is going to be painful, but it is worth it.

This process is about starting a new lifestyle and living life on God's terms, not your own. Coping mechanisms work for a while, but you eventually get stuck and things stop working; you become enslaved to your desires. God has created this world to function a certain way and when we don't follow suit, life starts to get out of control. For example, there are many consequences that come as a result of struggling with sexual sin. Our relationships may start to deteriorate as we hide behaviors and isolate from others. Our view of ourself consistently diminishes as we struggle with the same issue and experience increasing shame. Our view of individuals changes as we objectify them in our minds or by the material we watch. We hurt others by keeping secrets, hiding behaviors, and lying to others. Jesus came to bring us abundant life, which is the most satisfying kind of life we can experience. As we follow Christ and His commandments, we experience this abundant life and satisfaction in Him. When we turn away from Him and turn to our coping mechanisms or behavior that is not in line with His design, we experience guilt, shame, grief, frustration, and dissatisfaction.

Our goal in this process is to start a new lifestyle. Just as one who is overweight and eats junk all the time may start a new lifestyle, waking up early to go to the gym every day and eating healthy, so we are beginning a new lifestyle of recovery. A lot has to change, but by God's grace and the power of the Holy Spirit in your life, it can and it will.

With that said, I want to encourage you to do the hard work throughout this process. I'm not talking about trying harder or behavior modification. I'm talking about trusting the process and the Holy Spirit who is at work within you. Give it your all. You will get out of this process what you put into it. Have you hit rock bottom and said, "Enough is enough"? Are you willing to do whatever it takes to get free from a crippling desire for pornography or masturbation? If your answer is yes, you are in the best place possible. Of course, on our own we are doomed to a life of slavery to sin. But, for those of us in Christ, God lives inside of us. The Holy Spirit lives in us and gives us the power to overcome sin in our lives. As Romans 6:18 (NIV) says, "You have been set free from sin and have become slaves to righteousness." The Holy Spirit gives us the ability to become more and more like Christ. That is great news! He changes our desires to match His. That's probably a main reason why you are reading this right now, because He is at work in your life both to will and to work for His good pleasure. He doesn't just give us new desires to walk in godly ways, He gives us the ability to carry that out, but this is a constant battle and a combined effort between ourselves and the Holy Spirit.

It's clear throughout Scripture that we do not just let go and let God. We don't just idly sit by and expect God to change us. He has given us a very active role in our sanctification (the process of being conformed to the character of Christ). Romans 8:13 (ESV) says, "For if you live according to the flesh you will die, but if by the Spirit you put to death the deeds of the body, you will live." It is clear in this verse that we have a very active role in fighting sin. That means you can do something about the sin in your life. You can say, "Enough is enough. I'm sick of struggling with this sin in my life, and I'm going to get help!" You can take steps to grow and to change. You can work hard and fight the desires of the flesh because the Spirit lives inside of you. It is my prayer that you will surrender control of your life and your desires to God and work as hard as you can in this process, through the power of the Holy Spirit. That doesn't mean you should just put your willpower to the test to fight sin and just try to resist temptation. No, it means you focus on all of the aspects outlined in this healing process. It means you call a group member when you're enduring temptation and process what stress or pain you may be tempted to cope with. It means you get rid of access to the temptation that is luring you in. It means you address the underlying wounds that you are tempted to medicate and allow the gospel to heal your deepest pain. You must work hard at this process.

For the joy set before you, the possibility of freedom, healing, and your future family, make a commitment to work hard in the power of the Holy Spirit and embrace the process ahead of you!

This idea of working hard is biblical in nature. Paul tells us in 1 Corinthians 15:10 (ESV), "I worked harder than any of them, though it was not I, but the grace of God that is with me." Now for some context here, Paul was a former Pharisee. Pharisees were the well-known religious leaders of the time who followed all of the Jewish rules and rituals. They were highly esteemed men of honor, who were looked up to by society. But when Jesus began His public ministry, told people he was God, and gained a lot of followers, the Pharisees hated Him and thought He was an imposter. Years after Jesus' death and resurrection, Christianity had spread like wildfire. Many were surrendering their life to Christ and spreading the gospel all over the middle eastern world. Paul had made it one of his primary goals to stop the spread of Christianity. He worked with others to do whatever it took to get Christians to stop talking about Jesus—whether imprisonment or execution, he had a mission.

So, in the verses prior to verse 10 of chapter 15, Paul talks about how he used to persecute the Church, but that God saved him and he was converted to Christianity. He tells us that God's grace toward him, God saving him, was not in vain. No, God had big plans to use Paul. We know from the rest of the Bible and history that God did use Paul to spread Christianity, plant churches, and write many letters that became part of the Bible. God saving Paul stirred within him a passion to work hard for the sake of the Gospel. Paul did not just sit by passively and go about his life. He worked hard to spread the message of Christ. He labored and toiled for years, he was shipwrecked, he was beaten, and he gave up his reputation. He worked hard. The Holy Spirit gave him the desire to do these things and the ability to carry them out.

We are told in Philippians 2:13 (ESV), "For it is God who is at work in you, both to will and to work for His good pleasure." So when we obey God, when we fight sin in our lives, when we work hard to grow in godliness, it is actually because God is working in us. God is at work in you for His good pleasure. Press into that. God has given all of us the desire to work hard at defeating sin in our lives and the ability to carry that out.

For the joy set before you, the possibility of freedom, healing, and your future family, make a commitment to work hard in the power of the Holy Spirit and embrace the process ahead of you!

NOTES

NOTES

Getting healthy is a choice. It is going to take discipline and a commitment to breaking free in the face of all odds, no matter the cost. You can choose to apply this process and walk in freedom. You can choose to face the pain of your past and allow the gospel to heal your deepest wounds. God has given you everything you need to be set free through the Holy Spirit at work in your life and your Living Free group.

So, my question to you is, "Will you give this process all that you have?" In response to God's scandalous and extravagant love that He lavished on you, will you work harder than ever before? I'm not encouraging you to work hard in an attempt to pay God back for the work He did on the cross to reconcile you to himself, forgive you of your sins, and to adopt you into His family. I'm encouraging you to look at His love for you and all of the things He has done and to allow your love for Him to motivate you. As we look to Christ and understand everything He has done for us more and more, we can't help but become overwhelmed with gratitude, awe, and love. Out of this response, we can't help but become more and more like Him and want what He wants for our lives. God is wild about you and He is so glad you are on His team. He didn't die for trash, He died for those that He loves more than we can understand. As part of that, He wants you to live abundantly, to enjoy Him, to throw off the sin that so easily ties you down and to be set free. He is more committed to your sanctification than you are.

On the days that you want to quit, will you endure the temptation and ask for help from others? Will you endure the difficulty for the joy and freedom set before you? Will you be disciplined by doing your homework, making phone calls to other group members, and taking steps to increase your self-awareness by using the FASTER Scale regularly? Are you going to pursue this recovery process with the same passion that you pursued your addiction in the past? If you cannot answer yes to all of these things, this group may not be for you, or you may not be ready to go through this process.

My prayer is that, by God's grace and the Spirit's work in your life, you would say yes to all of these things and do whatever it takes to get free. The choice is yours. Many have walked this path and experienced victory. Thousands have been set free from their sexual addiction, myself included. Will this be your story? Will you say, "Enough is enough"?

Sometimes we can be faced with such a big challenge that we are tempted to lose hope or to give up completely. In these moments, it's important to remember what God helped us accomplish in the past, so that we can take a step of faith and risk accomplishing something in the future. Think back to times where you accomplished something by working hard in the power of the Holy Spirit and trusting God to come through.

In the chart below, list your decision, time and circumstance, action steps you took, and resulting change you saw in your life, and what you learned. Spend some time filling out the following Accomplishments Chart. Look back to this chart often to remind yourself what God brought you through so that you can trust Him to bring you to healing through this process.

ACCOMPLISHMENTS CHART

DECISION	TIME & CIRCUM-STANCE	STEPS TAKEN	RESULTING CHANGE	WHAT I LEARNED

1.

2.

3.

4.

5.

For one of your assignments this week, you'll be faced with the results of your Sexual Addiction Screening Test (SAST-R). Facing these results may be extremely difficult, but please remember, if you are in Christ, you are not defined by your behavior. You are a loved, forgiven, righteous, son of God who He delights in. Those results will give you the opportunity to see the extensiveness of your current addictive lifestyle and to say, "Enough is enough."

ASSIGNMENTS FOR NEXT TIME

1 Fill out the past accomplishments chart.

2 Take the Sexual Addiction Screening Test (SAST-R) in Appendix III.
- » Although the questions are phrased in present tense, please answer each according to your entire life.
- » Please complete the scoring, filling out the Core Item Scale, the Subscales and the Addictive Dimensions on the page that follows the test.
- » Please notice the cutoff scores in each of the categories at the end of the test and transfer your scores to the following chart. Be prepared to discuss your results with your group.

3 Meditate daily on Philippians 2:13 and Romans 6:18.
- » Write down how these verses apply to you. What do they teach you about God? What do they teach you about your need for Jesus and the gospel? How is God asking you to respond?
- » Be ready to share your observations at your next group meeting.

4 Talk with God daily and ask Him to give you the desire to say, "Enough is enough." Ask Him to motivate you to give your hardest Spirit-filled work in this process.

5 Continue making accountability phone calls and make sure to fill out a Commitment to Change, FASTER Scale, and Check-in before the next group meeting.

LESSON THREE
YOUR FUTURE & CURRENT DIRECTION

During the spring semester of my senior year in college, I applied to work for a large campus ministry. Almost everything looked great on my job application. I had led Bible studies, discipled students, and led our movement in the area of evangelism. I was one of the most involved volunteers and I absolutely loved ministering to younger students. I was well known by the students and staff, and I had great references on my application. But there was one issue: I couldn't seem to kick my ongoing struggle with pornography. I was in the thick of the battle that had lasted almost a decade. Like many guys I knew, I was introduced to pornography in middle school and quickly became hooked. I spent years trying to stop my behavior, but couldn't do it alone. I had learned to hide my struggle and lived in a cycle of isolation, secrets, and shame. In college, I would abstain from pornography for up to six months at a time, but then find myself, once again, at the place I promised myself and God I would never return.

In mid-spring, I received a phone call about my job application. I was told that everything looked great on my application, except for my struggle with pornography. I was told that my application would be revisited in two months and I would be given some time to work on this area of my life. It was in that moment that I realized what was at stake. My dream was to be involved in full-time ministry and to work for this organization, but unless things changed, that couldn't happen. That moment was a wake-up call for me and I realized the direction I was headed. So, like many Christians in this battle with good intentions, I put my willpower to the test, began asking for prayer daily, and went to bed early to prevent temptation. I made it two months without any issues and was then accepted to work for this campus ministry. I quickly realized there was more to the battle than I thought. Three months later, I found myself right back where I started, looking at pornography again. But I thought the struggle was over? How could this happen? I thought I was finally free.

It was at that time, I realized I needed more help. I began going to a Pure Desire sexual addiction recovery group in my area and came to face the reality that I had an addiction, not just an occasional struggle. I learned about the effects that pornography had on my brain and why I couldn't stop my behavior (See Appendix I). For the first time, I began to come to grips with the denial in my life and truly face my addiction.

During those initial months, I realized where I was headed and the external consequences I would face if I continued in that direction. I wouldn't be able to have the job I wanted, the job that I thought God had called me to. I also began to think of my future wife and family. I didn't want to bring this issue into my future marriage. I didn't want to be cheating on my wife by looking at other women lustfully. I didn't want to be hiding activity from my wife and kids and ruining the ability to have a healthy relationship with them. I took a step back and thought about where I would be if my behavior continued, and that motivated me to say, "I need to get help."

YOUR FUTURE & CURRENT DIRECTION

> **I took a step back and thought about where I would be if my behavior continued, and that motivated me to say, "Enough is enough. I need to get help."**

NOTES

I began to dream about what God could do through my story, once I got free from my addiction. I began to think of the hope I would be able to bring other guys. I began to dream of leading other guys through sexual addiction recovery groups and help them find the same freedom that I would find. I began to dream of seeing recovery groups all over the world on college campuses. This vision of what God could do through me and my story is what the Holy Spirit used to motivate me to keep moving forward in healing. One of the reasons you are reading this workbook right now is because God made that vision come to fruition.

So, begin to dream big. Dream about what God could do through your journey to freedom from sexual addiction. Maybe you want to start a thriving ministry on your campus or in your church and see hundreds come to freedom and healing from sexual addiction. Maybe you want to have a thriving relationship with God and to experience deep intimacy with Him, but that keeps getting stifled by your porn use. Maybe it's specific experiences you could have with your future wife or kids as a result of being healed and having a close relationship with them. Maybe you love everything about art history and want to take your future wife to the Sistine Chapel to see the beautiful ceiling that Michelangelo painted. Below, write some dreams you want to see happen as a result of being set free from sexual sin. Please be specific. Take some time and visualize the experiences in your mind once you write your responses. Return to these dreams throughout the coming year.

1. _____
_____
_____
_____
_____
_____

2. _____
_____
_____
_____
_____
_____

3. _____
_____
_____
_____
_____
_____

Maybe you can't see what's at stake in your life right now. Maybe you don't see the many consequences at work when you relapse. But believe me, your current direction determines your destination. Whether you realize it or not, every decision you make on a daily basis sets the course of where you will end up. Are you headed in a healthy direction or a destructive direction? How will this addiction affect your future marriage and family if it continues?

You may have great commitments, hopes, dreams, or even prayers, but you have to address the daily direction you are headed. In this journey of recovery, you will discover just how deadly denial is and can be in your life. You'll have to come to grips with where you will end up if you continue living the way you are living now. Your daily direction in life determines your destination and eventually your destiny. Denial can never change this no matter how sincere or committed to Christ you may be.

You may not see the consequences of your relapses; instead, it may be more like a sickening sense that you're missing out on what God has for you and the feelings of enslavement to what your flesh desires. You know you are capable of so much more spiritually. You hunger to experience more of Christ, but this cycle of masturbation or acting out and promises to stop continue to keep you chained to the ground. Whether you have seen the devastating consequences of your sin or feel stuck in your addiction, this workbook will help you finally get free. I mean really free. Not just six months of sobriety then another repeat of the cycle. I mean really free.

That is not to say it is going to be easy. As mentioned in Lesson Two, it will probably demand more of you emotionally and spiritually than just about anything you have ever done before. As you will discover in this process, your addiction has been a way of coping with buried pain for years, so your pain level will probably increase, not decrease. You will finally face the deep pain within that you have been medicating for years. As with many guys, your addiction may have began at an early age, which means you've been struggling with this issue for quite some time.

It takes a courageous man to face the pain he has been running from for so long. The good news is that you will not be alone in facing the pain. The men in your Living Free group will be standing with you as well as facing their own pain. Don't worry about the source of the pain quite yet, we will get to that later. There is one thing you must focus on right now: it is time to stop denial and face the pain.

Denial has to stop. It is easy to say, but so difficult to do. For starters, most men can't see how much denial has clouded their perception of reality through the years. It is like a slow process of poisoning. Little by little, cover up becomes a way of life. As a man of God, the shame factor is so high that it may seem like the only option you have is to lie, but that is a lie from the enemy.

I wouldn't be writing this today if I hadn't done one simple thing—stop my denial. I had to admit to myself that I couldn't fight this battle alone. I had to wake up and ask for help. This workbook will help you start to see yourself in a whole new light and come to understand the enemy you have been fighting all these years. Please don't waste any time in making this decision; denial stops today.

> Your daily direction in life determines your destination and eventually your destiny. Denial can never change this no matter how sincere or committed to Christ you may be.

NOTES

I struggled to give up my addiction and face the pain that I had been medicating for years. I was comfortable coping with the pain from my past. I was in denial about the fact that I had an addiction, not just a struggle, and the hard Spirit-filled work that I would have to do to get free. When I was told my job application would be revisited, I began to face the truth of my situation.

You may or may not see the consequences of your sexual behavior, but they are there. Your relationship with Christ may be in the tank. Your discouragement in this battle may be through the roof. The first step is breaking through denial. Don't wait another moment. You are not getting any younger and your Heavenly Father has tremendous blessings ahead for you. However, you will never be able to fully receive those blessings unless you break through denial. Today is the day to drive a stake in the ground and declare that you have an addiction and are choosing to get help. By the grace of God you will break through denial.

Remember this truth, breakthrough doesn't come into your life by some sudden massive change. Breakthrough comes because you stay headed in the right direction for a sustained period of time.

So, now that we have discovered that our direction in life will determine our destination, let's look at Proverbs 7. Here we see that the young man described is headed down the highway of denial and being dishonest with himself, which always leads to emotional and moral destruction.

1 My son, keep my words and treasure up my commandments with you;
2 keep my commandments and live; keep my teaching as the apple of your eye;
3 bind them on your fingers; write them on the tablet of your heart.
4 Say to wisdom, "You are my sister," and call insight your intimate friend,
5 to keep you from the forbidden woman, from the adulteress with her smooth words.

6 For at the window of my house I have looked out through my lattice,
7 and I have seen among the simple, I have perceived among the youths, a young man lacking sense,
8 passing along the street near her corner, taking the road to her house
9 in the twilight, in the evening, at the time of night and darkness.

10 And behold, the woman meets him, dressed as a prostitute, wily of heart.
11 She is loud and wayward; her feet do not stay at home;
12 now in the street, now in the market, and at every corner she lies in wait.
13 She seizes him and kisses him, and with bold face she says to him,
14 "I had to offer sacrifices, and today I have paid my vows;
15 so now I have come out to meet you, to seek you eagerly, and I have found you.
16 I have spread my couch with coverings, colored linens from Egyptian linen;
17 I have perfumed my bed with myrrh, aloes, and cinnamon.
18 Come, let us take our fill of love till morning; let us delight ourselves with love.
19 For my husband is not at home; he has gone on a long journey;
20 he took a bag of money with him; at full moon he will come home."

21 With much seductive speech she persuades him; with her smooth talk she compels him.
22 All at once he follows her, as an ox goes to the slaughter, or as a stag is caught fast
23 till an arrow pierces its liver; as a bird rushes into a snare; he does not know that it will cost him his life.

24 And now, O sons, listen to me, and be attentive to the words of my mouth.
25 Let not your heart turn aside to her ways; do not stray into her paths,
26 for many a victim has she laid low, and all her slain are a mighty throng.
27 Her house is the way to Sheol, going down to the chambers of death.
Proverbs 7 (ESV)

The scene in Proverbs 7 is being described by the wisest man of his day. Solomon is looking out the window and sees a young man strutting down the street with testosterone squirting out of both ears. The guy is a moving sexual target. And the woman, porn site, or strip club, are irresistible to him and they know it. He is an easy mark. As Solomon watches, he can clearly see what is coming. In fact, everyone around the young man clearly sees what is coming.

Years ago, best-selling author and psychiatrist, Scott Peck, uttered a classic one-liner that I come back to time after time: "Mental health is a commitment to reality at all costs."[1]

Sexual addictions are all about trying to escape the pain or loneliness of our lives with a sexual high. That is why the most challenging part of the healing process is acknowledging the fact that we have a problem. Our struggles with sexual issues have blinded our ability to acknowledge what is real in life.

Our sexual addiction usually starts because reality is just too much to bear. In life, when we escape reality for the briefest moments it can bring a sense of relief. But the problem is that it can become habitual or a lifestyle. That is when addiction becomes our deadly friend, leading us down the highway of denial.

A severe avoidance of reality usually begins early in life. It frequently starts in our family of origin. That is not to blame our parents for our problems, but if we never understand the defects in the "software" that was downloaded into our brain, we will never have a shot at winning the battle. Over half of sexual addicts come from rigid, disengaged homes.[2] And some of the most rigid, disengaged homes I have ever seen are "Christian" homes that focus on performance and not sinning. Life is always black and white for them. Rules far outnumber any form of relationship. There is only one way of doing things—the right way.

Once the child enters the turbulent times of adolescence there are essentially two options to deal with the pain within: open rebellion and reaction or quiet compliance with a secret life lurking behind the scenes. Either of these paths can become a deadly environment in which sexual bondages can explode in the person's life. The noose of sexual addiction only tightens because he made a commitment to Christ at some point and now finds himself violating the deepest core beliefs of his life. Welcome to insanity of the most painful kind.

There is only one way out. You must be honest with yourself. The direction of your life will determine where you end up in life no matter how much you may want to deny reality. Did you notice the total lack of honesty in Proverbs 7?

Answering the following questions for next week will help you understand where you're headed.

① What observations did you make about Proverbs 7 as you meditated on it this week? How do you relate to the young man in Proverbs 7?

___

1. Peck, M.S., M.D. (1978). *The Road Less Traveled: A New Psychology of Love, Traditional Values and Spiritual Growth.* New York, NY: Simon & Schuster, Inc.
2. CSAT Certification Intensive Training Manual Week One – day one, page 4 of 15

2. When have you been blind to reality in your life like the young man? Share with the group one of your "blind spot" moments in life.

_____
_____
_____
_____
_____
_____
_____

3. What were the lessons you learned the hard way from such moments?

_____
_____
_____
_____
_____
_____
_____
_____

Did you notice the depth of "unreality" found in Proverbs 7, especially in verse 15? The young guy was thinking to himself, *I am so special. I am the man of her dreams. This is amazing; she came out to look for me!*

The Proverbs 7 woman, whether she is in the flesh or on today's XXX porn site, will lead you down the highway of destruction. And you will pay a terrible price. Notice how Solomon tries to break through the young man's denial. The kid is telling himself he is a rock star and this woman can't get enough of him. This is the best thing that has ever happened to him, and Solomon is crying out, "No, no, no—get real! You are a piece of meat headed to the butcher shop. This thing will tear you apart. You are a proud stag caught in a noose and the more you pull the worse it gets. Then you look up and the hunters from hell surround you with arrows aimed at your heart. This is going to wound you deeply. Like a bird caught in a net that realizes flying is over, your dreams are dying."

Now, some who read these words may feel a mounting sense of grief and shame over what has happened in their lives. You may be asking yourself, "How could I have been so stupid?!" Well you are in a room with a bunch of guys who have made similar mistakes. Don't let grief and shame control your life.

Later on, we will deal with those adversaries, but right now your job is to make sure you don't repeat the mistakes of the past. That means you have to break through the denial structures in your brain. To do so, spend time this week identifying where you'll end up if your addiction continues and the external consequences you may face. External consequences are simply the results that your sin may have on yourself or others.

EXTERNAL CONSEQUENCES

Example: If I continue in my addiction, I will destroy my future marriage and my wife may leave me.

1. _____

2. _____

3. _____

4. _____

5. _____

6. _____

7. _____

8. _____

9. _____

10. _____

Lastly, come up with two natural consequences you will implement when you relapse. These will be implemented in addition to what is already provided below. Implementing natural consequences is not a way of experiencing punishment for sin or paying penance. Christ bore all of our sin on the cross and there is no wrath of God or condemnation left for us who have surrendered our lives to Christ.

Natural consequences are simply a way of experiencing and associating our sin with the natural pain that it causes ourselves and others. An example is getting rid of the computer, tablet, or smartphone for three weeks that you used to relapse and not getting it back until you see three weeks of sobriety. Another example could be only having Internet access in public places. If you continue to relapse, consider implementing a consequence of selling or donating the device that you used to access porn. Explain the consequences in detail below. Your leader will need to look at the Implementing Consequences portion of the *Leader's Guide* to explain this in further detail.

NATURAL CONSEQUENCES

1. Within 12 hours of a relapse, fill out a FASTER Scale Exercise, call a group member to process the relapse, and fill out a Relapse Analysis (Appendix II).

2. _____
_____
_____
_____
_____
_____
_____

3. _____
_____
_____
_____
_____
_____
_____

ASSIGNMENTS FOR NEXT TIME

1 Answer the questions on the previous page in regards to what God may want to do in your life once you come to freedom from sexual addiction. Dream big and take time to visualize these experiences.

2 As you meditate on Proverbs 7 this week, answer the three questions on the previous pages about the passage.

3 Complete the External Consequences chart. Be sure to address how it will affect your future marriage and family.

4 Come up with two Natural Consequences for all future relapses and begin implementing all three when relapse occurs.

5 Read The Neurochemistry Of Addiction found in Appendix I.

LESSON FOUR
THE FASTER SCALE

In this lesson, we are diving deeper into a tool that will help take away the mystery surrounding relapse. The tactic used to prevent relapse by most guys is to do some sort of confession and repentance, and then white-knuckle through the temptation. This might work for a little while, but the pressure cooker inside you will inevitably grow too powerful for you to restrain any longer; you'll give in to the very thing you swore you would never return to. Have you discovered that white-knuckling just doesn't work?

Many guys come into a recovery process thinking their relapses are completely random and chaotic. When I ask them why they just relapsed, they will look at me with a little panic in their eyes and admit they have no idea. You need to learn a new way of relating to the temptation that creeps into your life. The FASTER Scale helps you learn this new way by revealing what's going on behind the scenes in your heart and mind.

James 1:14-15 (ESV) describes a progression away from life toward death: "But each person is tempted when he is lured and enticed by his own desire. Then desire, when it has conceived gives birth to sin, and sin when it is fully grown brings forth death."

Temptation leads to sin which becomes death. Think of it this way: our evil desires drag us away from dependence upon God to dependence upon ourselves, giving birth to sin. Live in sin long enough and it will bring about death. This is what the FASTER Scale describes as well. Our sin grows more pregnant as we move down through the categories of the FASTER Scale and gives birth to death when you relapse.

Here's the big problem: when you are living in continual relapse you can't experience intimacy with God or others because you are living in what James describes as death. Just as life and death cannot coexist, neither can intimacy and relapse.

If relapse is relational death, what is life? Life is found in close, intimate relationships with God and others, where you learn to trust them, as well as entrust yourself to them and their care. The English word "catharsis" is defined as "a release of emotional tension, as after an overwhelming experience, that restores or refreshes the spirit." It has its origin in the Greek word "katharos" that is translated as "cleanses" in this verse.

> *But if we walk in the light, as he is in the light, we have fellowship with one another and the blood of Jesus his Son cleanses us from all sin.*
> 1 John 1:7 (ESV)

This is what John was getting after when he wrote that verse. Because Jesus died on the cross for your sin, confession in a safe group of friends is the first step to returning to the light where you begin to feel refreshed. He's not condemning you for your sin and neither are your friends.

> **You will always act according to what you actually believe, not what you think you believe.**

NOTES

Walking in the light is not a one time event. It's a way of life that keeps our heart restored, refreshed, and experiencing life the way God designed it.

You will discover that this battle is not really being waged between your legs, but primarily between your ears and in your heart. The enemy has been feeding you lies your whole life. These lies were reinforced as you experienced hard circumstances and sin from others. As you've increasingly bought into them, those beliefs shaped your behavior, and that has been destroying your life. Changing your behavior really comes down to changing your beliefs so how you live matches what you believe. This is called integrity. You will always act according to what you actually believe, not what you think you believe.

For example, you might claim to believe that God loves you no matter what, yet you continually find yourself trying to earn His approval. While your head says that God's love is abundant and unconditional, your life reflects your true belief, which is that you need to earn His approval. That lie from the enemy was reinforced somewhere in your story.

By the power of the Spirit, you have to hunt down these core lies that push you to violate how you truly want to live. This is where the battle lies. You need to learn what the battle looks like in your life so you can stop getting bushwhacked by the enemy. The FASTER Scale will help you grow increasingly aware of the thoughts and emotions in your life that are generated by your faulty core beliefs.

> *Core beliefs create emotions and thoughts that drive behavior. If you want true change you must go back to the source that is your belief system. If we create a new belief system it will lead to new thoughts and behaviors that then lead to brand new and healthier behaviors. This is how permanent change occurs through the renewing of the mind.*
> Adapted from *The Genesis Process* by Michael Dye[1]

How our emotions, thoughts, and behavior are affected by our core beliefs is kind of like an apple tree. Let me explain. The fruit is what the tree is known for. The quality and taste of the fruit is determined by the health of the leaves and branches. While the fruit represents our behavior, the branches and leaves are like our thoughts and emotions. If you pay attention to the leaves and branches, you will find clues as to the health of the tree and quality of fruit you should expect.

The leaves and branches are fed by the trunk of the tree. The trunk is like the core beliefs you hold, and those core beliefs shape the branches and leaves, and thus the fruit.

The trunk of the tree is fed by the roots of the tree. Those roots represent your life experiences, and generally the stronger memories are associated with strong emotions. If you've ever tried to dig out a tree, you know that the roots are strong, and hard to get at. It takes a lot of work.

---

1. Michael Dye and Patricia Fancher. *The Genesis Process. A Relapse Prevention Workbook for Addictive/Compulsive Behaviors.* (Auburn, CA: Michael Dye, 1998; 3rd Edition 2007). 115.

RESTORATION: Restoration is defined by accepting life on God's terms, with trust, grace, mercy, vulnerability, and gratitude. This depicts "surrender." This is accepting both the good and bad with an attitude of gratefulness for God's love, moving toward others openly and honestly, and facing and resolving problems. It is becoming part of the solution to your problems rather than the problem.

Joe's "Recovery" lifestyle is marked by a humble and dependent attitude where he knows his limits, lives within them, and often asks for help in making progress in life. He still experiences stress and the ups and downs of life, but since he is asking for help and living with no secrets, he faces challenges head-on with the help of God and others.

FORGETTING PRIORITIES: Neglecting the priorities of a restorative way of life are the first steps toward Relapse and can happen weeks before the actual relapse. This comes in the form of denial, flight, or a change in what's important. These "actions" often come in the form of avoiding what you know is the right thing to do. This can be so subtle it's hard to see: a master tactic of the enemy. You can see this most easily by looking at how you spend your time, energy, and thoughts.

Here, you might begin to avoid simple life tasks or recovery commitments. It is so important to become sensitive to when you are beginning to live in this category. According to the verse in James we looked at earlier, this is when you begin to live independently of God. In some small way you are saying to God, "I don't need you or your help. I can handle it. I will take care of myself." This attitude, if not repented of, will ultimately lead to Relapse. Recovery priorities can sometimes feel difficult or painful, and your reaction will be to avoid the pain. When you choose comfort over difficult priorities, anxiety begins to well up.

Joe has committed to his friends that he won't mindlessly surf the Internet and will completely avoid social media. He can get online for specific reasons and has also committed to only being on his phone in public places. He has been doing great for quite a while, but has grown a little complacent staying true to this recovery priority. His heart slowly hardens and he ignores the boundaries he set up. *There's no harm in just checking what movies are playing*, he thinks. He is now headed down the road to Relapse by moving onto the FASTER Scale and "Forgetting Priorities."

ANXIETY: Forgetting Priorities will bring on some Anxiety. It feels like a growing background noise of undefined fear where you are getting energy from emotions. In this category, old messages are played over and over again in your mind. In recovery circles, this is called "blaming people, places, and things for the way you feel." When you choose to worry about things, especially things you can't control, you feel an emotional charge, an anxious adrenaline rush. Faith and worry cannot exist in the same mind at the same time. Unfortunately, your ability to see and resolve today's problems is greatly diminished.

While alone in his room after being on the movie site for a while, Joe is fighting off a little temptation to watch certain movie trailers. He feels a twinge of guilt for doing what he's committed to not doing. *Now I'm going to have to confess this to the guys*, he thinks. He feels a tiny bit of conviction for this and realizes he should probably call a friend to admit what's going on. He's embarrassed and doesn't want to be a bother, so he pushes through the conviction, buying into the lie that he can handle it. Now he feels some underlying anxiety mixed with the boredom and loneliness because he knows he's headed in the wrong direction, but reaching out feels too inconvenient right now.

SPEEDING UP: Living with Anxiety will cause you to speed up. In this category of numbing the pain, feelings of fear, anxiety or depression are subconsciously avoided by Speeding Up. This can look like an inability to relax, working too much without eating regular meals during the day, or bingeing at night. Consuming a lot of caffeine and sugar is another way to speed up. Working long hours, going out every night, staying up late, over- and/or under-eating, and compulsive spending are some ways that you outrun depression and anxiety and deny that you have physical or emotional needs. Unfortunately, Speeding Up is often praised and mislabeled as "hustle" in our culture (even in the Church), at the expense of our mental, emotional, spiritual, and relational health.

Joe bought into the lie that he can handle the temptation when he's alone. *After all, look how well I've been doing*, he says to himself. So, instead of reaching out, he decides to get off the movie site because of the temptation there and heads out the door for class. The next few days go well, but he finds himself alone and bored again and decides to browse a social media site. He blows through the conviction he feels, believing he can handle it and starts checking out his friends' profiles. He starts feeling pangs of comparison and rejection again and for the next week he puts in an extra hour at the gym each day to "get out the extra energy" he's feeling. The core belief that "I have to earn love" gets triggered by the comparison and fuels Joe's isolation and over-exercising.

TICKED OFF:
Living sped up eventually makes you angry because outrunning the anxiety doesn't work. You start to feel threatened because the Spirit is convicting you of your isolation and you increase the energy of pushing Him and others away. When you feel threatened, anger is one of the best ways to isolate from others. You may shame and blame others, pushing them away with an attitude of "I don't need anyone" or "No one understands me." The result is that you are pushing people away when you need them the most. Christians often see anger itself as a sin and conceal it, so be on the lookout for anger's cousins, resentment and passive aggressiveness.

Joe's friends have noticed that something is a little off with him and they've brought it up at their group meetings. He brushed them off a few times, but he's started getting defensive and irritated at their observations. So, this week he decides not to pick up the phone when guys call and complains to himself how irritating it is when guys "constantly" interrupt his day. If he were paying attention, Joe would realize that he's spending more and more time on social media and he's getting sucked back into old patterns of behavior that lead to Relapse.

EXHAUSTED:
Stay angry long enough and you will eventually become Exhausted. Remaining in this category for any length of time will cause you to feel tired, hopeless, and depressed. Moreover, if a crisis occurs at this category, you are unable to cope. The survival part of your brain creates a craving for your addiction.

Joe gets home late one night from hanging out with friends and is tired, but not feeling ready for bed quite yet. He picks up his phone when he's alone in his room and flips through social media to see what he's missed. A picture catches his attention and even though he knows he shouldn't, he decides to click on it anyway out of curiosity. Before long, he's spent an hour clicking links and is cruising some pretty sexually stimulating images. He rationalizes it away by telling himself he's not looking at porn, even though he's feeling aroused.

RELAPSE:
Returning to the place you swore you would never go again. Giving up, giving in, out of control, lost in your addiction. Lying to yourself and others. Feeling you just can't cope without it; at least for now. Relapse first feels exhilarating, but it soon turns to feeling like death.

Let's pause and look at Joe's life right now. He has gone from living in the light with his friends to exhausted and isolated. He's continuing to mindlessly browse the Internet late at night alone in his room when he's feeling lonely. He's started comparing himself to others more and is working out excessively to feel better about himself and outrun the anxiety he's started feeling. The core belief that he has to earn love fuels his resistance to return to the light. On top of that, he's feeling irritated at his accountability partners and is actively avoiding their support.

It took a month, but Joe finally relapses and decides to search out porn. He goes on a three-day binge. Next week he has to decide if he will confess to his friends that he has looked at porn and masturbated, or if he will continue to hide. Hiding the forgotten priorities ultimately lead to a relapse. Wouldn't it have been so much easier to confess the movie site and experience the love and grace of his friends?

All of the categories have one thing in common: procrastination. As you fail to deal with problems, you move down the FASTER Scale. Crisis comes at a time when you are least able to deal with it emotionally. The short version of the FASTER Scale is Speeding Up > Ticked Off > Exhausted > Relapse. Many people don't know what life is like not being sped up. Procrastination only makes problems worse, and isolation eliminates the wise counsel of God, your friends, and family who will help you see the big picture and resolve problems. You must accomplish isolation in order to relapse. Regular, true accountability is the antidote for isolation.

There are two ways to progress down the scale. The first is a slow progression due to procrastination caused by fear. The second is a speedy descent when your emotional wounds get touched by something in life. As you pay attention to where you are on the FASTER Scale, you will learn how you procrastinate out of fear and what your wounds are. This scale paired with lessons in this workbook will bring great clarity to both of these areas. As long as you apply what you are learning, you never have to wonder why you are relapsing. Additionally, as you spend more time living in restoration, it will become much easier for you to detect where you are on the FASTER Scale. Life in Relapse is chaotic, so don't get too frustrated if the scale doesn't make sense at first. It will become more clear as you use it.

Let's talk about some realities of the FASTER Scale that will help you to master this tool and expedite your victory over sexual bondage.

Truth One: We all have weakness, faults, and shortcomings (sin). "It is not the healthy who need a doctor, but the sick. I have not come to call the righteous, but sinners." (Mark 2:17 NIV) Ephesians 4:13 tells us that we are to be raised up to the fullness of Christ. There is not one person who has accomplished that in this life. Remember, your Living Free group is here to grieve with you in your struggles and to celebrate with you in your victories. Your group can't do that if you aren't open to sharing with them. Choose to learn vulnerable transparency within your group and be honest with yourself about your evaluations of how well or poorly you have done. You can easily deceive others and even yourself, but if you truly want healing there is one option: get honest with yourself and with your Living Free group.

Truth Two: You will be battling against the cravings of addiction. We still have the desire and appetite to return to the behaviors of addiction. Michael Dye states in *The Genesis Process* that "the right thing to do is usually the hard thing to do."[2] Resisting the cravings can be hard, but you will be learning the tools by which you can challenge those cravings. The good news is that those cravings are tied to our core beliefs and once we challenge and change those beliefs we will create new and positive cravings for the right behavior. Hold on to this hope and truth.

Truth Three: The FASTER Scale is a downward only scale. It is impossible to climb up the scale. The only way to not end up in Relapse is to get off the scale. You get off the scale by choosing to actively trust God and others with your fears and hurts, and letting them walk with you in whatever you are facing. You can't win this battle intellectually; it must come experientially. In other words, you must take steps of faith and risk trusting God by choosing to live His ways and within His boundaries. This means bringing all of yourself into the light with friends you know care for and are committed to you. You will discover that this is an extremely practical way of walking in step with the Spirit and is truly a Spirit-filled process.

Truth Four: You do not leave one category of the FASTER Scale behind as you progress to the next. Instead, as you go down the scale you add one category of the scale to the previous ones. Think of it like an ocean. Restoration is bobbing around on the surface taking life as it comes. Relapse has no emotional flexibility and is where stress fractures break under the great pressure.

---

2. Dye, Michael. *The Genesis Process: For Change Groups.* Auburn, CA: Genesis Addiction Process and Programs, 2012. Pg 62 Print.

Truth Five: The FASTER Scale is generic until you become more self-aware. As you become more self-aware, you may bring your unique behaviors to the scale. Your healing and self-awareness go hand in hand. This is critical to understand. As you use the scale more, you will want to personalize it by adding what you learn about yourself to the various categories. You might discover that a way you speed up is not listed in the scale, but is something you need to pay attention to each week.

Also, remember from Lesson One, that there are other behaviors you may want to consider as a Relapse besides sexual behaviors as you move forward in your healing. Again, these could be behaviors that you go to when you are at the end of your rope, such as overeating or drinking too much alcohol.

Truth Six: You can't skip a category. You don't go from Forgetting Priorities to Speeding Up (and not have Anxiety). It is the universal pattern of Relapse whether you are aware of it or not. The challenge for you will be to trust the scale and ask God to reveal the areas you aren't able to see quite yet. Truth Five will help you fill in the blanks if you're struggling with certain categories on the scale.

Truth Seven: If you feel like the FASTER Scale is drudgery and it becomes a tool of obligation, its effectiveness will be negated. Almost without exception, men don't want to actually take an inventory using the FASTER Scale as it pertains to the previous seven days of their lives. We take the shortcut of filling out the "same old, same old" and we gain nothing and are missing the point. This occurs because we don't want to take the time, thought, or energy to actually go back and look at the previous seven days. The truth is that we all have general patterns unique to us, that recur every week with sometimes subtle changes to those patterns. Our job is to discover what is driving us and to acknowledge where we are on the scale.

Truth Eight: It does not hurt to look at your scale on a daily basis. Self-awareness is a key ingredient in the healing process God has for you. A daily assessment is a powerful tool and we hope that you will use it.

ASSIGNMENTS FOR NEXT TIME

① Fill out a FASTER Scale Exercise every day this week.

You will see that there are three questions to ask yourself about each category of the scale. Talk with God about the questions and ask Him to begin revealing to you how you are living independently of Him through the behaviors and emotions listed in the scale. A copy of the FASTER Scale for every day this week and every lesson is included in the *Living Free Journal*. If you do not have a *Living Free Journal*, you may consider photocopying the blank FASTER Scale in Appendix II or writing it out on a separate sheet of paper. Be sure to spend at least 15 minutes each day journaling through the questions in the exercise.

② Twenty-four hours before next week's meeting, summarize what you observed about yourself over the week by listing any "ah ha's" or "uh oh's" you've learned about yourself from doing the FASTER Scale.

THE FASTER SCALE[1]

RESTORATION: Accepting life on God's terms, with trust, vulnerability, and gratitude

- ☐ No current secrets
- ☐ Working to resolve problems, identifying fears and feelings
- ☐ Keeping commitments to meetings, prayer, family, church, people, goals, and self
- ☐ Being open and honest, making eye contact
- ☐ Reaching out to others
- ☐ Increasing in relationships with God and others
- ☐ True accountability

FORGETTING PRIORITIES: Starting to believe the present circumstances and move away from trusting God. Denial, flight, a change in what's important, how you spend your time and what you think about

- ☐ Secrets
- ☐ Less time/energy for God, meetings, church
- ☐ Avoiding support and accountability people
- ☐ Superficial conversations
- ☐ Sarcasm
- ☐ Isolating
- ☐ Changes in goals
- ☐ Obsessed with relationships
- ☐ Breaking promises and commitments
- ☐ Neglecting family
- ☐ Preoccupation with material things: TV, computers, other entertainment
- ☐ Procrastination
- ☐ Lying
- ☐ Over-confidence
- ☐ Bored
- ☐ Hiding money

Forgetting Priorities will lead to:

ANXIETY: A growing background noise of undefined fear; getting energy from emotions

- ☐ Worry, using profanity, being fearful
- ☐ Being resentful
- ☐ Replaying old negative thoughts
- ☐ Perfectionism
- ☐ Judging other's motives
- ☐ Making unrealistic goals and to-do lists
- ☐ Mind-reading
- ☐ Fantasy, co-dependent rescuing
- ☐ Sleep problems, trouble concentrating, seeking drama
- ☐ Gossip
- ☐ Using OTC medication for pain, sleep, or weight control
- ☐ Flirting

Anxiety then leads to:

SPEEDING UP: Trying to outrun the anxiety which is usually the first sign of depression

- ☐ Avoiding slowing down
- ☐ Feeling driven
- ☐ Can't turn off thoughts
- ☐ Skipping meals
- ☐ Binge eating (usually at night)
- ☐ Overspending
- ☐ Can't identify own feelings/needs
- ☐ Repetitive negative thoughts
- ☐ Irritable
- ☐ Dramatic mood swings
- ☐ Too much caffeine
- ☐ Over-exercising
- ☐ Nervousness
- ☐ Difficulty being alone or w/ people
- ☐ Difficulty listening to others
- ☐ Making excuses for having to "do it all"
- ☐ Super busy and always in a hurry (finding good reason to justify the busyness), workaholic, can't relax

---

1. Adapted from the *Genesis Process* by Michael Dye www.genesisprocess.org

Speeding Up then leads to:

TICKED OFF: Getting an adrenaline high from anger and aggression

- ☐ Procrastination causing crisis in money, work, relationships
- ☐ Increasing sarcasm
- ☐ Black and white (all or nothing) thinking
- ☐ Feeling alone
- ☐ Nobody understands
- ☐ Overreacting, road rage
- ☐ Constant resentments
- ☐ Pushing others away
- ☐ Increasing isolation
- ☐ Blaming
- ☐ Arguing
- ☐ Irrational thinking
- ☐ Can't take criticism
- ☐ Defensive
- ☐ People avoiding you
- ☐ Needing to be right
- ☐ Digestive problems
- ☐ Headaches
- ☐ Obsessive (stuck) thoughts
- ☐ Can't forgive
- ☐ Feeling superior
- ☐ Using intimidation

Ticked Off then leads to:

EXHAUSTED: Loss of physical and emotional energy; coming off the adrenaline high, onset of depression

- ☐ Depressed
- ☐ Panicked
- ☐ Confused
- ☐ Hopelessness
- ☐ Sleeping too much or too little
- ☐ Can't cope
- ☐ Overwhelmed
- ☐ Crying for "no reason"
- ☐ Can't think
- ☐ Forgetful
- ☐ Pessimistic
- ☐ Helpless
- ☐ Tired
- ☐ Numb
- ☐ Wanting to run
- ☐ Constant cravings for old coping behaviors
- ☐ Thinking of using sex, drugs, or alcohol
- ☐ Seeking old unhealthy people and places
- ☐ Really isolating
- ☐ People angry with you
- ☐ Self abuse
- ☐ Suicidal thoughts
- ☐ Spontaneous crying
- ☐ No goals
- ☐ Survival mode
- ☐ Not returning phone calls
- ☐ Missing work
- ☐ Irritability
- ☐ No appetite

Exhausted then leads to:

RELAPSE: Returning to the place you swore you would never go again

- ☐ Giving up and giving in
- ☐ Out of control
- ☐ Lost in your addiction
- ☐ Lying to yourself and others
- ☐ Feeling you just can't manage without your coping behaviors, at least for now
- ☐ Result is reinforcement of shame, guilt, and condemnation, and feelings of abandonment and being alone

FASTER SCALE EXERCISE

1. **Check all the behaviors on the FASTER Scale that you identify with.**
2. **Circle the most powerful one in each section. Write it in the corresponding heading below.**
3. **Answer these three questions:**
   - **A.** How does it affect me? How do I act and feel?
   - **B.** How does it affect the important people in my life?
   - **C.** Why do I do this? What is the benefit for me?

RESTORATION: _____
A. _____
B. _____
C. _____

FORGETTING PRIORITIES: _____
A. _____
B. _____
C. _____

ANXIETY: _____
A. _____
B. _____
C. _____

SPEEDING UP: _____
A. _____
B. _____
C. _____

TICKED OFF: _____
A. _____
B. _____
C. _____

EXHAUSTED: _____
A. _____
B. _____
C. _____

RELAPSE: _____
A. _____
B. _____
C. _____

LESSON FIVE
TRUE ACCOUNTABILITY—SITUATIONAL AWARENESS

Last week you learned about the FASTER Scale, which helps you observe what is going on inside yourself so you can begin fighting the real battle waging in your soul. Your emotions are not the battle front. They are the check engine light for what is going on inside your mind in your thoughts and belief systems. Our belief systems are formed by life experiences from the family environment we grew up in, the world around us, sermons we have heard, and even Bible studies we have done. One of the biggest challenges in this battle for sexual health is seeing your belief systems for what they are, not what you want them to be.

This week you will be learning what we call True Accountability. It's a way of thinking and acting that helps you walk in the light and solve problems, instead of living in Relapse. Last week, you also learned that what keeps you stuck in Relapse is procrastinating out of fear of making changes to your life. So, if you can learn to face your fears and make changes to your lifestyle, relapse becomes a thing of the past. This is where accountability done right can be a real game changer for you. Accountability should never feel like punishment or condemnation, but should be powerful, positive, and supportive, providing you with foundational support for making tough changes in your life. The four parts of True Accountability are the FASTER Scale, Double Bind, Commitment To Change (CTC), and Help. These four are a tightly integrated unit that, when practiced as a whole, become a very powerful set of life skills that help break isolation and build relationships. These are necessary foundations for living a life that does not routinely involve relapse.

True Accountability teaches you situational awareness that will help you evaluate your battle and construct a battle plan. Situational awareness is simply knowing what's going on inside you and acting on intelligent decisions based on what you observe. It is a simple and necessary skill, yet many guys have no understanding of it and they keep getting taken out by the enemy. Environments that need effective situational awareness will often offer some form of training to build this skill. The military calls it the OODA loop which stands for Observe, Orient, Decide, Act.[1] I've also seen it taught as See it, Own it, Solve it, Do it. Each part is vital and has an important role in bringing about change in your life. For you to have success in your mission of achieving sexual sobriety and living a life of integrity and character, you will need to develop the skill of situational awareness in your own life.

To develop situational awareness you will learn to use the FASTER Scale, Double Bind, CTC, and Help. The FASTER Scale teaches you to observe your battle. The Double Bind teaches you to orient to the battle. The CTC teaches you how to do the hard, but right thing in the battle. Asking for Help is putting this all into action in the power of the Holy Spirit, which is also called True Accountability. Is this a complicated process? No. Can it be a challenge? Yes. Which is why we are going to ask you to practice this each week.

---

1. Hammond, Grant T. *The Mind of War: John Boyd and American Security*. (Smithsonian Books, 2001).

TRUE ACCOUNTABILITY—SITUATIONAL AWARENESS

1 What has accountability looked like for you in the past?

_____
_____
_____
_____
_____
_____

2 In what ways did you find it helpful or a hindrance in your recovery journey?

_____
_____
_____
_____
_____
_____
_____

What you are learning right now in the battle for your sexual sobriety will serve you for the rest of your life. Situational awareness is a lifelong skill you can put into practice long after you've been set free from the bondage of sexual sin. The enemy is always trying to undermine your faith and character.

This is not a battle you can win alone. You will need to have a group around you that fights for you while you fight for them. Look at what God has to say about spiritual warfare and the armor we are to wear in Ephesians. Pay attention to the bolded words in this passage.

> Finally, **be strong** in the Lord and in the strength of his might. **Put on** the whole armor of God, that you may be able to stand against the schemes of the devil. For we do not wrestle against flesh and blood, but against the rulers, against the authorities, against the cosmic powers over this present darkness, against the spiritual forces of evil in the heavenly places. Therefore **take up** the whole armor of God, **that you may be able to withstand** in the evil day, and having done all, to **stand firm**. **Stand therefore**, having fastened on the belt of truth, and having put on the breastplate of righteousness, and, as shoes for your feet, having put on the readiness given by the gospel of peace. In all circumstances **take up the shield of faith**, with which **you can extinguish** all the flaming darts of the evil one; **and take the helmet of salvation**, and the sword of the Spirit, which is the word of God, praying at all times in the Spirit, with all prayer and supplication. To that end, keep alert with all perseverance, making supplication for all the saints, and also for me, that words may be given to me in opening my mouth boldly to proclaim the mystery of the gospel, for which I am an ambassador in chains, that I may declare it boldly, as I ought to speak.
> Ephesians 6:10-20 (ESV)

Paul uses the second person plural verb form (you all) for the verbs in bold. This passage is not only addressing individuals. It is addressing the hearers as a community. It means this battle is not fought alone, it's fought in community through the power of the Holy Spirit. Isolated Christians are defeated Christians.

Here's a typical double bind you might be familiar with. Joe loves God with all his heart and wants to walk closely with Him. He has also struggled with looking at porn and masturbating for most of his life. He is sick of the guilt and shame that comes from looking at porn and masturbating, but nothing he has tried has helped him to stop for more than a few weeks at a time. Joe has identified on the FASTER Scale that he's living in "Ticked Off" and he can't seem to figure out what's driving his irritability. As he describes what's going on for his friend, he says that he's most often irritable when he's feeling bored.

Here's where it pays to talk this stuff through with trusted friends. What Joe's friend observed is that Joe isn't actually bored, he's lonely. Many guys confuse the two. Boredom just means you need some intellectual stimulation. Boredom doesn't usually create the angst that you feel when you are "bored." More likely, you are craving intimacy and relational depth. Joe is lonely and needs connection with some good friends, but he's also fearful that he will experience rejection if he reveals his true needs, something he experienced while growing up.

The only cure for loneliness is connection, which is a huge double bind for many of us. We need the very thing we fear. Many of us are carrying wounds from our most intimate relationships, our family members. For too many of us, we have come to believe that comfort is not found in intimate relationships, so don't bother looking for it there. This is Joe's faulty core belief that's driving his double bind. It's keeping him from asking for help when he's "bored" and feeling tempted to look at porn.

Joe might phrase his double bind and faulty core belief this way: "Telling someone that I'm tempted to look at porn when I'm feeling lonely and irritable feels vulnerable and scary so I won't call someone out of fear that I'll be rejected and a "bother." But, if I don't make a call, then I will probably end up acting out to medicate my loneliness." It feels like a loss to him to ask for help when he's lonely because he believes it won't be helpful. It's also a loss to not ask for help because he'll end up staying in isolation and giving in to the temptation to look at porn, which will soothe the pain of his loneliness, but increase his shame and guilt. He's stuck between a rock and hard place.

Does this sound at all familiar to you?

THE HARD THING TO DO IS THE RIGHT THING TO DO— PLAN OUT YOUR COMMITMENT TO CHANGE.

Joe has learned that he acts out when he feels lonely because he believes he's a "bother," so he needs to make a plan that helps him confront this battle every day. His plan might be to make one phone call per day to connect with a good friend for 10 minutes. The intention of the call is to share what's going on in his heart and to limit time talking about "surface" topics that don't require vulnerability. His plan could also include a commit to join a Living Free group to build deeper relationships or inviting guys to lunch, so he doesn't eat alone.

The point is that he is learning to be intentional to connect with God and others at a deeper level despite the risk of rejection because he knows if he doesn't, he will end up relapsing to medicate his loneliness. This isn't something you do of your own willpower. If it were easy, you would have done it already. You need the help of the Holy Spirit to face the fears that keep you stuck. Over time, as he follows through with this plan by faith, Joe will discover that his core belief about himself is not true. The Holy Spirit will begin to replace Joe's broken picture of himself with God's picture of him.

ASKING FOR HELP TO ACCOMPLISH YOUR PLAN

The only way out of the hole we have dug for ourselves is to break our isolation and ask for help from other men who know how to fight this battle. We need to ask for help while we are still facing our fears and not after acting out. This is the really scary part for most guys. Asking for help while facing our fear is more difficult than confessing the sin after it's happened. Many guys act out and then wait to confess until after the shame of acting out has passed. Don't fall into that trap.

I just want to say you are awesome for facing your fears and pain and learning to stand strong in this battle. You'll find a surprising amount of healing on that phone when you, by faith, choose to call another guy and let him into your life when you're struggling, rather than calling him after you've already acted out. The men that reach out in the midst of their fear are generally the men who go on to win this battle. By taking these steps of faith in the power of the Holy Spirit you, too, can win this battle. Here's a truth you can rely on: reach out or act out!

We use a few simple questions to help figure this all out. Here's what it looks like for Joe:

FASTER SCALE	DOUBLE BIND		CTC	HELP
Observe the Battle	Count the Cost	Orient to the Battlefront	Decide on a Plan	Act on the Plan with Help
What aspect of the FASTER Scale do I need to change this week? Breaking isolation and connecting with significant people in my life Keeping secrets	What is the cost if I do change? Risk feeling like a bother to others Risk being rejected by others Potentially experience connection and comfort	What is the cost if I don't change? Reinforce my belief that I'm a bother to others Continue to feel isolated and lonely I'll most certainly act out to soothe my pain	What broken belief is keeping me stuck? What is a summary of my two options? That I'm a bother to others and they don't want to hear what I need. Telling someone that I'm tempted to look at porn when I'm feeling lonely and irritable feels vulnerable and scary so I won't call someone out of fear that I'll be rejected and a "bother." But, if I don't make a call, then I will probably end up acting out to medicate my loneliness.	What is my plan to do the hard thing, but the right thing? Try to reduce times that I am alone and commit to asking for help when I'm feeling lonely rather than isolate Make one phone call per day to connect with a good friend for 10 minutes Join a Living Free group Don't eat meals alone. Invite someone to eat with me.	How will I ask for help accomplishing this? Set up calls with the guys in my Living Free group so we have a set time to connect. Invite others to eat meals with me. Ask the guys in the group to make sure I've followed through on these actions steps before the end of the week.

COMING CLEAN WITH YOUR SECRETS

Let's make this practical and talk about one of the biggest double binds every guy faces: secrets. Secrets are the concealment of sin. It's walking in darkness, wearing a mask. It's hiding. The thing about wearing a mask is that as people come to think they know you, they can only know, and love, the mask. We become imprisoned by our secrets, feeling unknown and unloved.

You can see why secrets become one of the most deadly forces hell uses against you. At some point, you come to believe the stories you have told others. Reality becomes distorted and you begin to live the lie. You can find this progression in 1 John 1:6,8,10.

There can't be any secrets in your soul if you are going to live life fully free. Yet, you're terrified to reveal your secrets. Freedom demands the highest levels of honesty and openness. For real intimacy to take place in your life with God, your friends, or girlfriend or wife, there can't be secrets. But getting there is a delicate task. The first steps have to take place in your Living Free group. It is time to take the courageous step of sharing your secrets.

Courage is not a natural trait but is learned, developed, and disciplined into your soul.

> *Few men are born brave;*
> *many become so through training and force of discipline.*
> Flavius Vegetius Renatus, Military Institutions of the Roman Empire, AD 378

God says it this way:

> *For the moment all discipline seems painful rather than pleasant, but later it yields the peaceful fruit of righteousness to those who have been trained by it.*
> Hebrews 12:11 (ESV)

Because God loves you so much, He will give you multiple opportunities to bring your secrets into the light. Work through the following accountability worksheet to help you examine why you harbor secrets, instead of bringing them into the light. After filling out the accountability worksheet, fill out the secrets grid. You will practice accountability like this each week as you continue to face the areas you are stuck in your life.

FASTER SCALE	DOUBLE BIND		Orient to the Battlefront	CTC	HELP
Observe the Battle	Count the Cost		Orient to the Battlefront	Decide on a Plan	Act on the Plan with Help
What aspect of the FASTER Scale do I need to change this week?	What is the cost if I do change?	What is the cost if I don't change?	What broken belief is keeping me stuck? What is a summary of my two options?	What is my plan to do the hard thing, but the right thing?	How will I ask for help accomplishing this?

1. List the secrets in your life using the chart that follows. Some may not be sexual, but they can fuel your sexual behavior. Secrets can be cleverly disguised through omissions—what you chose to omit from the story. It is time to begin developing the courage of real honesty. As you go through this process, you may remember more secrets that you were not aware of or forgot about during this lesson. Please be intentional to share them with the group.
    A. *Note: If you need to share any illegal sexual activity, please revisit the Memo of Understanding at the beginning of this workbook. Facing the consequences of your past actions may be the most important aspect of your healing journey and we are here to support you.*
2. Describe the problems those secrets are creating: lack of intimacy with your friends, lack of moral courage, and fear of exposure.
3. Identify the people you have kept these secrets from in your life.
4. Bring your completed chart to your next meeting and be ready to share the results with one or more members of the group. This is a huge step of faith and takes a lot of courage. As each member shares, encourage one another and remind each other of Jesus' love and approval of them, despite how great their shame may be.

| THE SECRET | THE PROBLEM THAT THE SECRET CREATES | THE PERSON(S) I AM KEEPING IT FROM |
| --- | --- | --- |//
| 1. | | |
| 2. | | |

56 ∴ TRUE ACCOUNTABILITY—SITUATIONAL AWARENESS

THE SECRET	THE PROBLEM THAT THE SECRET CREATES	THE PERSON(S) I AM KEEPING IT FROM

3.

4.

5.

⎍ ASSIGNMENTS FOR NEXT TIME ⎍

① **Complete the charts on the previous pages and be prepared to discuss your responses.**

② **Meditate on Luke 15:11-32 and think about the Father's heart in the story and how that models God's heart toward you.**

LESSON SIX
PERSONAL PROMISES

For though we walk in the flesh, we are not waging war according to the flesh. For the weapons of our warfare are not of the flesh but have divine power to destroy strongholds. We destroy arguments and every lofty opinion raised against the knowledge of God, and take every thought captive to obey Christ.
2 Corinthians 10:3-5 (ESV)

When I was in college, I constantly dealt with procrastination. I had an immense amount of trouble not waiting until the last moment to complete assignments, study for tests and exams, and complete projects. I thought I was the kind of guy who worked more efficiently under pressure and with a strict deadline. In hindsight, I realize now that I really wasn't better at working under pressure, but used that as an excuse to procrastinate. As I've continued to learn more about myself, I have realized just how much I was afraid of failure. In college, if I put off work, and did it last minute with minimal effort, I could blame the bad grade on poor effort. If I put a lot of work into an assignment, trying my best, but received a bad grade still, I knew I would feel like a failure, and think my best was never good enough.

No matter how many times I tried to plan out studying or school work, the crippling thought of starting work would lead me to seek out distractions. The only way I was able to get to work was if I reminded myself that I may fail the class if I did not get the work or studying done in time. Procrastination was a way of life for me. The problem was, the more I procrastinated, the harder life became. Stress and anxiety would pile up leaving me feeling worse than had I not procrastinated. If I only knew, in college, the double binds I was constantly facing, then maybe I could have prevented the majority of the stress I endured.

As we learned last week, a double bind is when you have two difficult decisions ahead of you. One is normally more difficult and is the right choice to make. It sounds simple, doesn't it? But we often need help believing, not just knowing, which is the right choice to make. For example, when I was in college, if I had an exam the following week, I knew the right thing to do was to pace myself, study well, and to try my best. I knew in my head that I didn't need to fear failure; that no matter what I did, I wouldn't be a loser because I am defined by who Christ says I am. But my actions showed that in my heart I was actually believing that I was defined by my actions and the score of my test. I needed help believing, not just knowing, the truth of my identity. I needed to get the truth of who Christ says I am from my mind to my heart. But back then, I had no idea any of this was going on. It was all operating at a subconscious level.

Looking back, I needed to renew my mind as Paul urges us to in Romans 12:2 (ESV) which says, "Do not be conformed to this world, but be transformed by the renewal of your mind, that by testing you may discern what is the will of God, what is good and acceptable and perfect." I needed to stop allowing my thoughts about myself to be conformed to what the world had said

> The good news is that we can renew our minds and change the way we think about ourselves and others.

NOTES

about me and to renew my mind and develop new thoughts about myself in light of what God says about me.

Now, procrastination may not be your biggest struggle, but since you're part of this group you most likely have some negative core beliefs about yourself, that don't line up with God's view of you. At the root, these core beliefs drive your actions, sinful choices, and struggles on a daily basis. Deep down, you may believe that you are worthless, or that no matter how hard you try, you will never measure up in life. You may believe that you are truly alone, or that people only pretend to like you. You may believe you are unlovable because of the things you've done in life.

These lies we believe often come from painful experiences from our past. We live in a fallen world, with imperfect people, so we are often hurt most by those we spend the most time with. It could have been the hurtful words or actions from family members or friends. Or maybe the lack of affirmation and loving words from those you needed to hear it from. Those are valid experiences that can reinforce the lies the enemy wants us to believe. The good news is that we can renew our minds and change the way we think about ourselves and others.

Before we get into the practicals, it's important to have a better understanding of the brain. You may recall learning about the prefrontal cortex and the limbic system in The Neurochemistry of Addiction, found in Appendix I. As a refresher, the limbic system is where our emotional memory is located; it's where our trauma or pain from the past and core beliefs are stored. It's the "fight or flight" part of your brain that influences your decision to react to pain and run to coping mechanisms. It's what the Bible refers to as the heart and it is primarily associated with the right side of the brain.

The prefrontal cortex is primarily associated with the left side of your brain. It is the area of your working memory and concentration. This is where executive planning, social awareness, and impulse control take place. The prefrontal cortex allows you to delay gratification. It is the part of your mind that is primarily engaged when you quote Scripture to yourself, hear a sermon, or remind yourself of the gospel.

We often find ourselves wanting to obey God, but struggling to do so. Paul speaks so clearly of this struggle between his prefrontal cortex and limbic system, or his mind and his heart, when he says in Romans 7:15 (ESV), "For I do not understand my own actions. For I do not do what I want, but I do the very thing I hate."

Let's go back to my experience in college. At the time, I would have said that I knew my identity was in Christ, not in my test grade, but my actions showed that I didn't always believe that. The truth of my identity in Christ hadn't sunk into my limbic system and transformed my core beliefs. I could preach the gospel to myself all day, but at the time, I had many experiences in life that were telling me I was worthless, and only a few experiences communicating God's love and approval for me. There was a big disconnect between my mind, or prefrontal cortex, and my heart, or limbic system.

When it comes to fighting lies and trying to believe the truth, the solution is not to beat yourself up and try harder to believe your identity in Christ. The solution is to get the truth of who you are and how God sees you into your limbic system, so it changes your heart. In Christ, we are loved (1 John 3:1), we are chosen (1 Peter 2:9), we are free from condemnation (Romans 8:1), and the list goes on and on.

In Judges 6, we learn of a man who had lost sight of his God-given identity just like we have. His name was Gideon. The story begins in Judges 6:11 with Gideon's unusual entrance. The angel of the Lord showed up to speak to Gideon who is beating wheat in a winepress because he's hiding from the Midians who had overrun Israel. The angel said, "The Lord is with you, oh valiant warrior." Here Gideon began to complain: Where is God? How come we haven't seen miracles? If God is with us, why are we suffering? Finally he said something to the effect of, "You can't choose me. I am the youngest in my family; in addition, our tribe and community aren't capable of beating the Midianites."

We can't forget that Gideon resisted God because he saw himself as weak. He didn't think that he and his community could handle the enemy whom he perceived to be invincible. God had to train him in who he really was, and Gideon had to realize that God can do anything. Through God's leading, Gideon and his army of 300 finally defeated the Midianites and Israel wanted him to become their ruler. Gideon's life changed when he began to believe and live out his God-given identity as a valiant warrior. Gideon went from hopelessly asking where God was in all this mess to walking with God and seeing God do miracles through him.

Our spiritual warfare is on a similar front. Who we are in Christ has to sink down into our hearts and our core beliefs. Right now we are fighting the wrong battles; because of our fears we, like Gideon, are fighting the fight of survival. To survive is not to win. Winning is all about conquering.[1]

At the end of this lesson you will find a list of Scripture outlining truths about you as a follower of Christ. You can use these truths to help you in the process of renewing your mind. Practically, think of a moment when you have experienced some of these truths. Then, when the enemy attacks with the desire to find your identity or worth elsewhere, remember that moment, as vividly as you can—smell, sight, touch—and that passage of Scripture. Essentially you are preaching the gospel to yourself. With time, and by the power of the Holy Spirit, this will renew your mind and restore your heart.

Let's start by first identifying three faulty core beliefs that have led us to agree with the enemy's lies about who we are. Again, these core beliefs are heart knowledge, not head knowledge. In my experience, the majority of guys struggling with sexual addiction have a deep sense of worthlessness that drives their addiction. Take some time to really think about what the driving core belief is behind many of your struggles in life.

> The solution is to get the truth of who you are and how God sees you into your limbic system, so it changes your heart.

NOTES

---

1. Flanagan, Harry. *Seven Pillars of Freedom Workbook*. 4th ed. Gresham, OR: Pure Desire, 2015. 74.

FAULTY CORE BELIEFS

Example: I am worthless.

1. _____

2. _____

3. _____

For each core belief you've written, identify a verse in Scripture that combats the lie and a time you experienced that truth. Combined, this will create a Personal Promise. It's a promise from God about who you are that you can rest in during tough times. In my own life, 1 John 3:1 (ESV) has been a huge source of encouragement when combating feelings of worthlessness. It says, "See what kind of love the Father has given to us, that we should be called children of God; and so we are…" So when I feel rejected, worthless, or like a failure, I quote that verse to myself as I dwell on a time I experienced God's fatherly love.

My experience happened the first time I went to a campus ministry worship gathering my freshmen year of college. I had been running away from the Lord and was filled with bitterness and anger toward God for things that had happened in my life. Let me describe the memory to you. I walked into the meeting, which was held in a dining hall. The room was dimly lit, and because it was an all-worship meeting there was music playing and different stations set up around the room with different ways to respond to God.

I found my way to a table in the back of the room and sat down by myself. Within minutes, I broke down and wept. So much frustration and bitterness toward God was released and I experienced the love and presence of God in a mighty way. I felt so loved and valued by God, which contradicted my experiences in the past of feeling worthless. Despite my rebellion, anger, and resentment toward God that had built up over the years, I experienced the undeserved love and forgiveness of God and turned my life over to Him. I continued to weep for a couple of hours, even after the meeting had ended. I was comforted by friends who came up to me and just showed me love. That night I experienced 1 John 3:1 in a tangible way.

So how about you? Go ahead and identify a verse that combats each of the core lies that you listed above. Next, write a sentence or phrase that summarizes the time you experienced the truth from that verse.

PERSONAL PROMISES

DEFINING PASSAGE	EXPERIENCE
Example: 1 John 3:1	When I experienced that I'm a loved child of God.

1.

2.

3.

Now that you have three Personal Promises, your next challenge is to meditate on these regularly. Post them on your wall, in your car, in your bathroom, or wherever you'll see them on a daily basis. Make it a point to spend a few minutes reminding yourself of these promises every morning and evening. It's amazing how your day can be different when you start out by thinking God's thoughts about you rather than believing lies about yourself. This allows you to truly live out who God created you to be.

This may sound strange, but when you meditate on your Personal Promises, it's helpful to do deep diaphragmatic breathing. To do this, get comfortable in a seated position and place your feet flat on the floor. Inhale and exhale slowly through your nose. When you inhale, push your stomach out as far as possible. Doing this triggers a physiological relaxation response causing the gut to release serotonin in your bloodstream. On the other hand, shallow breathing involves little stomach movement and reinforces the body's fight or flight response rather than relaxation.[2]

When you sense your limbic system is firing up and trying to take over your prefrontal cortex or higher reasoning, you now have the ability to engage deep diaphragmatic breathing. This may take some practice to get down, but if you make it your go-to response instead of believing lies about yourself, you will be creating new neurological pathways in your mind.[3]

Another tactic I'd recommend is visualization. Whenever you become mindful of yourself starting to agree with the lies you've believed, mentally visualize yourself back in the experience and invite Jesus to speak into it through the Scripture you have memorized. Sometimes it may take a while for your beliefs to change in the moment. In those cases, it's important to keep fighting those lies with the truth and visualizing the past experiences that back up the truth. This exercise is renewing your mind.

---

2. Wolf, O.T. (2009, October 13). "Stress and memory in humans: Twelve years of progress?" Brain Research. 1293: 142-54.
3. Roberts, Dr. Ted. *Seven Pillars of Freedom Workbook*. 4th ed. Gresham, OR: Pure Desire, 2015. 194.

You will find in this process that many of the things you react to in life trigger your negative core beliefs about yourself. Maybe you get angry when someone does something that makes you feel rejected or worthless; you fear that happening again since it happened to you a lot growing up. Maybe you fear not being in control because you want to feel safe and protect yourself since you were hurt by others in the past. Maybe you are depressed or often feel sad because you don't feel like you ever measure up. Maybe you get anxious, stressed, or worry about the future because you don't think you have what it takes to handle it.

You may have heard it said that we are our own worst critics. I believe that's true, especially when it comes to the thoughts we have about ourselves. We can often go throughout our day constantly beating ourselves up or telling ourselves the lies that we believe as a result of the pain from our past. But by implementing these Personal Promises into your life, God's truth of who you are will penetrate the depths of your soul so you can stop reacting to pain from your past. You'll learn how to truly take your thoughts captive to obey Christ and renew your mind.

ASSIGNMENTS FOR NEXT TIME

1. **List out your three Faulty Core Beliefs.**

2. **Write down your Personal Promises (the memory and the defining Scripture) and meditate on them daily. Be prepared to share them with your group.**

3. **Read through the Who I Am In Christ list.**

WHO I AM IN CHRIST

THE WORD OF GOD SAYS:

1. I am God's child for I am born again of the incorruptible seed of the Word of God that lives and abides forever. (1 Peter 1:23)
2. I am forgiven of all my sins and washed in the blood. (Ephesians 1:7; Hebrews 9:14; Colossians 1:14; 1 John 2:12; 1 John 1:9)
3. I am a new creation. (2 Corinthians 5:17)
4. I am a temple where the Holy Spirit lives. (1 Corinthians 6:19)
5. I am delivered from the power of darkness; Christ brings me into God's kingdom. (Colossians 1:13)
6. I am redeemed from the curse of the law. (1 Peter 1:18-19)
7. I am holy and without blame before God. (Ephesians 1:4)
8. I am established to the end. (1 Corinthians 1:8)
9. I have been brought closer to God through the blood of Christ. (Ephesians 2:13)
10. I am victorious. (Revelation 21:7)
11. I am set free. (John 8:31-32)
12. I am strong in the Lord. (Ephesians 6:10)
13. I am dead to sin. (Romans 6:2,11; 1 Peter 2:24)
14. I am more than a conqueror. (Romans 8:37)

15. I am a co-heir with Christ. (Romans 8: 16-17)
16. I am sealed with the Holy Spirit of promise. (Ephesians 1:13)
17. I am in Christ Jesus by his doing. (1 Corinthians 1:30)
18. I am accepted in Jesus Christ. (Ephesians 1:5-6)
19. I am complete in Him. (Colossians 2:10)
20. I am crucified with Christ. (Galatians 2:20)
21. I am alive with Christ. (Ephesians 2:4-5)
22. I am free from condemnation. (Romans 8:1)
23. I am reconciled to God. (2 Corinthians 5:18)
24. I am qualified to share in his inheritance. (Colossians 1:12)
25. I am firmly rooted, established in my faith, and overflowing with gratefulness and thankfulness. (Colossians 2:7)
26. I am called of God. (2 Timothy 1:9)
27. I am chosen. (1 Thessalonians 1:4; Ephesians 1:4; 1 Peter 2:9)
28. I am an ambassador of Christ. (2 Corinthians 5:20)
29. I am God's workmanship created in Christ Jesus for good works. (Ephesians 2:10)
30. I am the apple of my Father's eye. (Deuteronomy 32:10; Psalm 17:8)
31. I am healed by the stripes of Jesus. (1 Peter 2:24; Isaiah 53:6)
32. I am being changed into his image. (2 Corinthians 3:18; Philippians 1:6)
33. I am raised up with Christ and am seated in heavenly places. (Ephesians 2:6)
34. I am beloved of God. (Colossians 3:12; Romans 1:7; 1 Thessalonians 1:4)
35. I have the mind of Christ. (Philippians 2:5; 1 Corinthians 2:16)
36. I have obtained an inheritance. (Ephesians 1:11)
37. I have access by one Spirit to the Father. (Ephesians 2:18)
38. I have overcome the world. (1 John 5:4)
39. I have everlasting life and will not be condemned. (John 5:24; John 6:47)
40. I have the peace of God that transcends all understanding. (Philippians 4:7)
41. I have received power—the power of the Holy Spirit; power to lay hands on the sick and see them recover; power to cast out demons; power over all the power of the enemy; nothing shall by any means hurt me. (Mark 16:17-18; Luke 10:17-19)
42. I live by and in the law of the Spirit of Life in Christ Jesus. (Romans 8:2)
43. I walk in Christ Jesus. (Colossians 2:6)
44. I can do all things (everything) in and through Christ Jesus. (Philippians 4:13)
45. We shall do even greater things than Jesus did. (John 14:12)
46. I possess the Great One in me because greater is He who is in me than he who is in the world. (1 John 4:4)
47. I press toward the mark for the prize of the high calling of God. (Philippians 3:14)
48. I always triumph in Christ. (2 Corinthians 2:14)
49. My life shows forth his praise. (1 Peter 2:9)
50. My life is hidden with Christ in God. (Colossians 3:3)

LESSON SEVEN
MATRIX OF ADDICTION

I remember sitting in traffic headed north, while waiting for the light to change. Everyone around me was getting impatient because of the congestion. Out of the corner of my eye I noticed a brand new Camaro at the corner service station. The gleaming burgundy of the custom paint job still sticks in my mind. It was a classic. The driver was trying to cut across two lanes of jammed traffic and then across a turn lane and head south. Once he pulled in front of me, he was totally blocked by the cars ahead of him from seeing the oncoming traffic he was trying to merge into. I looked up and noticed this truck just ripping down the hill, headed our way. Instinctively, I cried out to the driver of the Camaro to stop. He didn't stop, but pulled directly in the path of the speeding truck. The sound of my fading cry was soon drowned out by the sounds of shattering fiberglass, screeching metal, and exploding glass. The Camaro was totaled!

The guy driving the Camaro was so blinded by the immediate he couldn't see or sense the obvious. We have all been there. It seems to be part of being a guy. Testosterone can do that to you. But God's desire for us is to live life on His terms, which involves using wisdom. By the power of the Holy Spirit, and asking God for wisdom, we can gain insight into our situations and struggles.

The Camaro driver found it intolerable that he was going to have to wait. He was desperate to escape the reality he faced. Just as he wanted to escape the confines of the traffic congestion, we can try to escape the pain or loneliness of our lives with our sexual behavior. We may react in one of two ways to deal with the pain within: open rebellion or quiet compliance with a secret life lurking behind the scenes. Either of these paths are ways of trusting ourselves and our coping mechanisms, rather than turning to Christ. But what Jesus promises is so much better.

In Matthew 11:28-30 (ESV), Jesus says, "Come to me, all who labor and are heavy laden, and I will give you rest. Take my yoke upon you, and learn from me, for I am gentle and lowly in heart, and you will find rest for your souls. For my yoke is easy, and my burden is light."

When we are heavy laden, full of pain, or weary, Jesus offers us peace and rest as we surrender to living life on His terms. But when we choose to cope with our pain on our own, a crash becomes inevitable.

Now, here is where I am headed with this story. Like the Camaro driver, you have probably crashed your life sexually. Otherwise you wouldn't be interested in this workbook. You can tell yourself things like:

» *Well, my problem is not as bad as that guy's!*
» *Since I haven't acted out in six months, I must be healed.*
» *I can handle the problem.*
» *I have prayed and promised God, my girlfriend/wife, myself, and others that I will never do it again.*

But if you don't understand what set up the crash in the first place, you are destined to repeat it. And repeat it. And repeat it. You get the picture. You need to clearly understand the matrix of the addictive process in your life. The damage will only deepen until you do.

Your shame and embarrassment will try to keep you from looking carefully at the sequence of the crash. But if you don't, it's only a matter of time before you will act out again. At the bare minimum you will be living a double life. Denying what caused the crash in the past will make you deceitful in the present. You will not be able to understand how your spiritual adversary is leveraging your weaknesses against you. You will be a stranger to certain parts of your soul.

In 1983, Dr. Patrick Carnes described in his book, *Out of the Shadows*, a cycle of addiction that included four stages: Fantasy, Ritual, Acting Out, Despair. As the understanding of addiction has grown over the years, people have added more stages to the original four. I like these six stages to describe the matrix of addiction, which you have found yourself in over and over again. They are: Catalyst, Fantasy, Ritual, Acting Out, Denial, and Despair.[1] Until you can see your own cycle of how you end up doing the very things you swore you would never do again, you will never be able to walk in freedom.

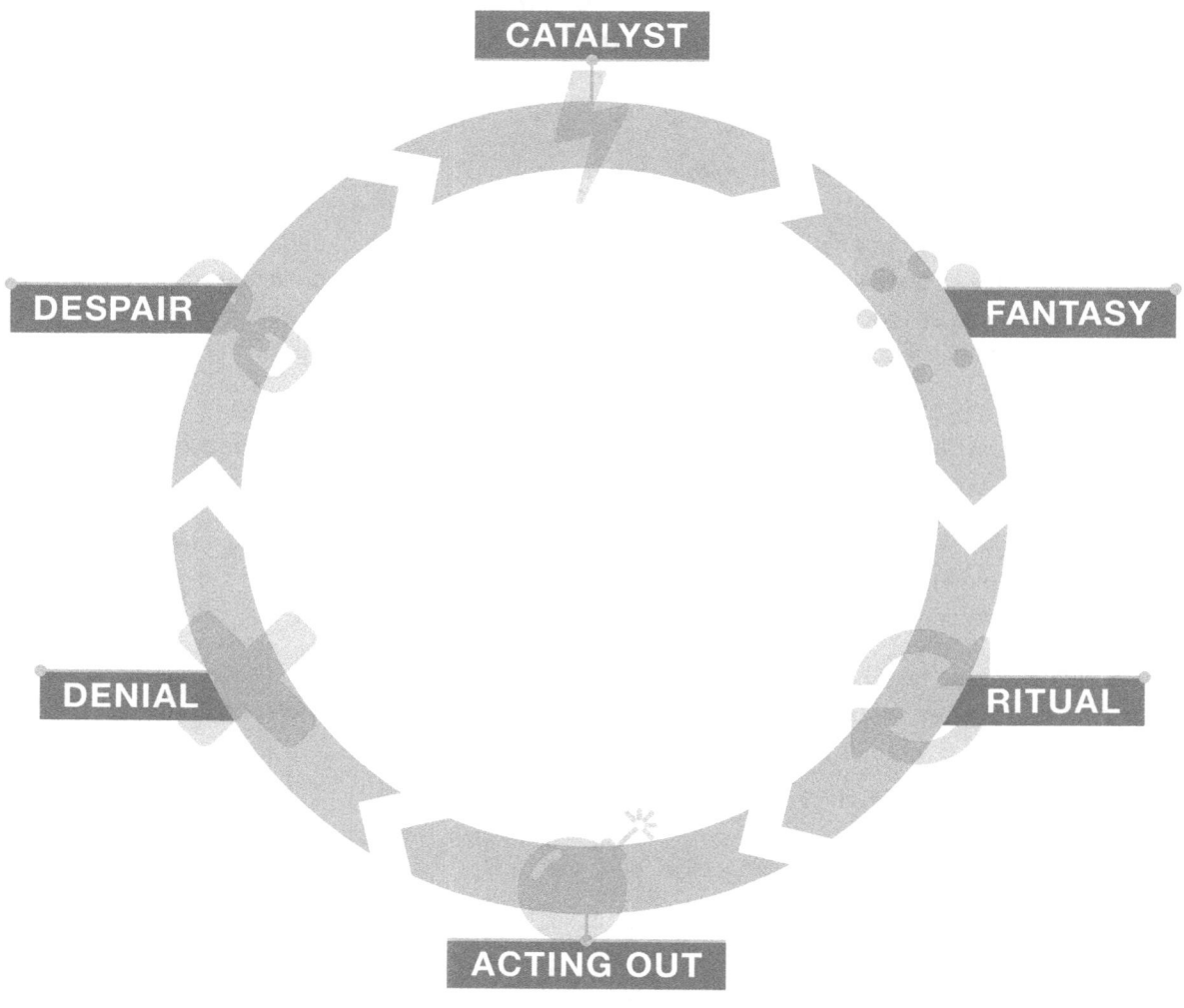

---

1. Carnes, Patrick, PhD. *Out of the Shadows: Understanding Sexual Addiction* (3rd Edition). (Center City, MN: Hazelden, 2001) 26.

STAGE ONE — CATALYST
A catalyst is anything that causes an over-reaction to a situation. Often, it is something that causes you to feel shame, blame, or guilt and is pain related. Both successes and failures can be a catalyst and cause you to want to act out because of how the catalyst makes you feel. So, if you flunk a test you might feel tempted to act out. And yet, if you ace the test you might still want to act out. The catalyst isn't to blame, it's how you've wired your brain to cope with the stress.

STAGE TWO — FANTASY
After becoming triggered by a catalyst, you'll notice your fantasy life increasing. Your brain is looking for a way to cope and fantasy is the first step toward acting out. These may or may not be sexual in nature, but you're starting to move away from reality and toward the fantasy. You might realize how to circumvent your filter software during this stage. Or you might plan for a time to act out in the future. Confessing your fantasy life quickly is key to avoiding a relapse.

STAGE THREE — RITUAL
This is where your fantasies start to become reality. You might start cruising your favorite social media sites or just jump to your favorite porn site. You might start texting that girl you found attractive or who you know will flirt back with you. This is the stage where you can spend hours in the trance of looking at porn, ever looking for a greater "high" that will increase excitement, intensity, and arousal. This is the stage that addicts try to prolong in an effort to avoid the pain triggered by the catalyst. You might end up spending hours, and even days moving through your ritual before acting out.

STAGE FOUR — ACTING OUT
Many guys try to put this stage off for as long as possible. This is the actual sex or orgasm that brings the ritual to completion. After acting out, you find yourself right back where you started only now you have increased the shame, blame, and guilt that were triggered before. What you are hopefully learning is that you act out in order to escape emotional discomfort (stages two and three), not for the actual orgasm. Orgasm is what brings you face to face with reality again.

STAGE FIVE — DENIAL
How did I end up doing this again? Ever thought something like that after acting out? You're in the middle of the shame; realizing what you've just done again, you'll want to escape it again. If the shame doesn't fuel another ritual, then you'll probably turn to denial and start making promises and justifications for what just happened. *I just have a stronger sex drive than most guys. Nobody needs to know what just happened. I didn't hurt anyone. Connecting with that person online wasn't acting out because we didn't actually touch each other.* Denial is the easiest way to rationalize your behavior and it also protects you from what's coming next.

STAGE SIX — DESPAIR
This stage is where shame, blame, and guilt return in full force. The enemy takes full advantage of you here and does everything he can to reinforce the lies he has convinced you to believe about yourself and God. You're left facing whatever it was that originally started this crazy cycle and are now feeling more powerless than ever.

CHANGING THE MATRIX

The easiest way to get off the crazy cycle is to not get on it to begin with. But this requires that you know what your cycle looks like and how it begins. Once it's started, it's vital you make changes in Stage Two; if you spend much time in fantasy, your limbic system will begin to take over and you won't be able to stop the cycle. The reality is that you are not powerless to stop this cycle. God has given you everything you need to win this battle. Knowing your matrix will be key to that victory.

> *His divine power has granted to us all things that pertain to life and godliness, through the knowledge of him who called us to his own glory and excellence, by which he has granted to us his precious and very great promises, so that through them you may become partakers of the divine nature, having escaped from the corruption that is in the world because of sinful desire.*
> 2 Peter 1:3-4 (ESV)

The following is what your matrix will look like if you make changes in Stage 1. Instead of isolating and coping with your pain, this matrix will move you into the light and into relationship with God and others. The stages of the matrix of restoration are Catalyst, Recognition, Reminder, Reach Out, Freedom, and Rejoice.

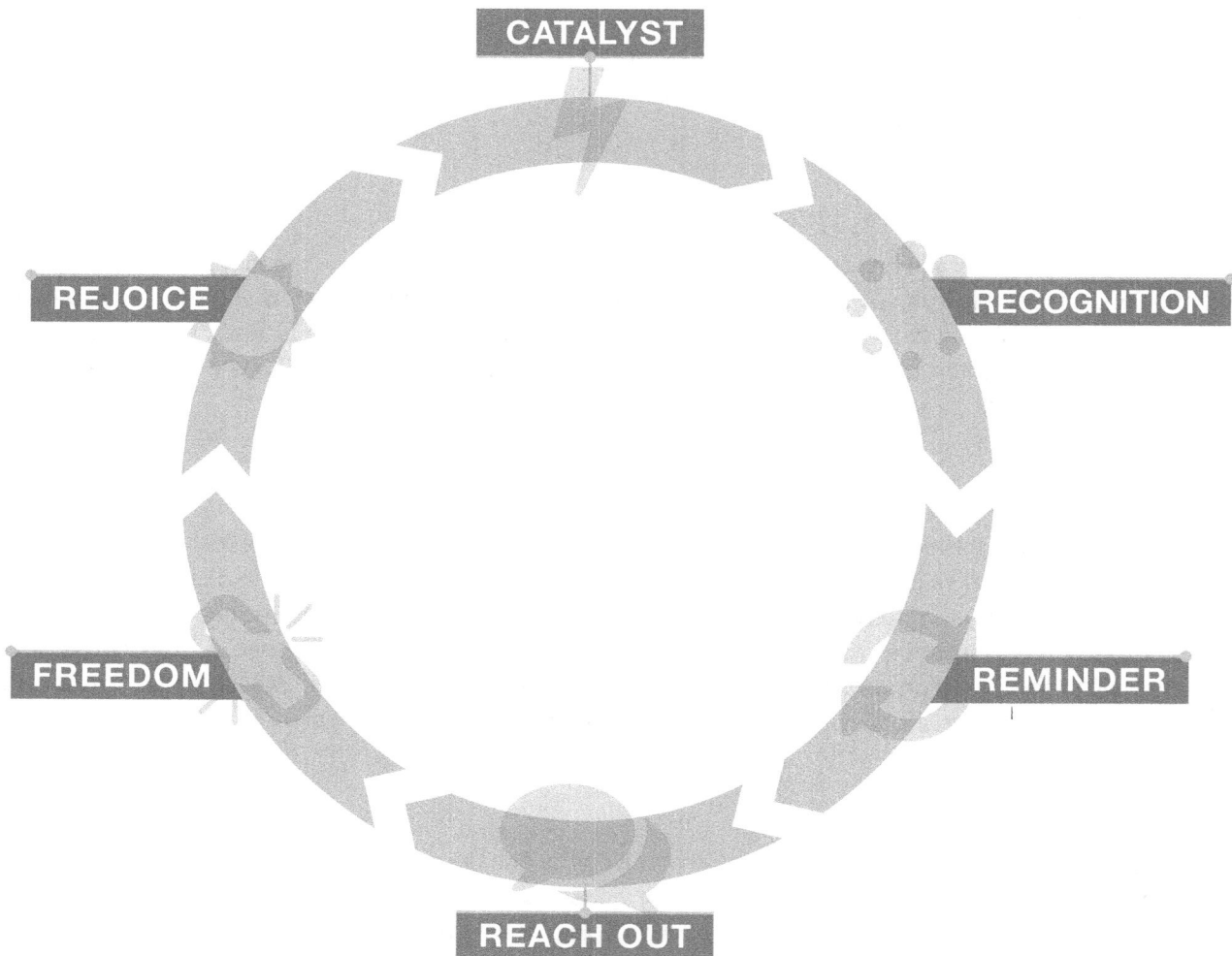

STAGE ONE — CATALYST
This is exactly the same as in the matrix of addiction. Pain doesn't go away, but how we respond to it can change.

STAGE TWO — RECOGNITION
As in most lessons in this workbook, awareness is what will make the difference. Instead of moving into fantasy, recognize what the catalyst might be compelling you to do and make a choice to do something different. You might naturally want to isolate, but now is the time to walk by faith toward God and others.

STAGE THREE — REMINDER
Now that you've moved into the light with your emotional discomfort and are bringing it to God and others, you need a reminder as to why it's worth the effort to move to the next stage of Reaching Out. This is where your Personal Promises have tremendous power. They remind you of who you really are and why it's worth the work of recovery. Post your Personal Promises all over the place so you can have easy access to them. Put Post-it® Notes around your house. Put a picture that represents a promise as the background on your phone. Keep a list of them in your wallet for easy access.

STAGE FOUR — REACH OUT
This is the doozy. You have to actually reach out and call someone. No excuses here. Just do it. Reach out or act out. If you don't follow through in this stage, you can actually short circuit the matrix of recovery and retreat back into isolation. It's in reaching out to God and others that you find the comfort and companionship that your hurting soul needs.

STAGE FIVE — FREEDOM
When you reach this stage it doesn't mean the pain will be gone. In fact, the pain might be worse because you won't be medicating it. You'll be processing the pain and moving through it. However, you'll also be discovering freedom, instead of the death trap of relapse.

STAGE SIX — REJOICE
This is the fun part! Rejoice in seeing God show up in your life in ways you never thought possible. You get to magnify Him privately by praising Him in your worship and publicly with others, sharing how you've seen Him provide for you as you are learning to walk in step with His Spirit. Woohoo!

PERSONALIZING THE MATRIX OF ADDICTION

Most of the addictive thoughts that lead to your crash occur at the limbic level. Your prefrontal cortex or higher reasoning power is not primarily involved. If it were involved, you would have stopped your behavior long ago because of your commitment to Christ. Instead, you are reacting at an instinctive level. As you work on this, if you draw a blank, ask the Holy Spirit to reveal the sequence to you.

Remember, relapse doesn't just happen in your life; a relapse is always preceded by certain types of thoughts and actions. I have not depicted relapse as a steady downward progress for the simple reason that it doesn't feel that way. If it did, you wouldn't go there. It starts out feeling like something you can handle and then, suddenly, gets out of control. You act out once you get to the point of "no return." This is a limbic decision, so you are frequently unaware that a transition has taken place. This is precisely why it is so important you draw out a picture of several of your addiction sequences, so you can understand your thought process prior to the crash. Understanding the sequence will enable you to catch yourself in the future and hopefully bail out or prevent the crash.

Let's look at an exercise that will help you stop setting yourself up for a crash. Through this process of becoming self-aware, you'll be able to go to Jesus to experience rest and healing for your soul, rather than avoiding your pain through coping strategies. I have depicted a typical matrix of addiction compiled from what I have heard from many men. The critical factor in doing this exercise is for men to hear what they say to themselves along the way. These are excuses that we use, the rationalizations we tell ourselves to feed the addiction. Once we have acted out, the lies we have told ourselves along the way seem ridiculous, but then it is too late. We have to learn to pick up on the excuses during the process and refute them.

TYPICAL MATRIX OF SEXUAL ADDICTION
A=ACTION | E=EXCUSE

CATALYST
A: Saw on Facebook that I wasn't invited to a party.
E: I didn't want to go anyway (denial of the pain of rejection).

FANTASY
A: Went to Facebook to browse photos of that cute girl from class that I would love to date.
E: I wasn't actively looking for porn.

RITUAL
A: Spent extended time looking at porn sites and masturbating.
E: I need this to feel better.

ACTING OUT
A: Actual orgasm through masturbation or sex
E: I've come this far, I might as well masturbate.

DENIAL
A: Justification of behavior
E: "I'm not hurting anyone," or "I deserve this."

DESPAIR
A: Deep shame and frustration
E: I feel powerless to change and not worth being invited to a party. I hate myself.

MY MATRIX OF ADDICTION
A=ACTION | E=EXCUSE

In the space below, describe your "matrix of addiction" or trajectory of relapse. What are your excuses that precede your crash? If you have never taken the time to do this type of exercise, it can really challenge you.

CATALYST
A:
E:

FANTASY
A:
E:

RITUAL
A:
E:

ACTING OUT
A:
E:

DENIAL
A:
E:

DESPAIR
A:
E:

Now, let's take it deeper. Think through your last several relapses. What were the preconditions? Identify your moods or things that had or had not occurred in your life prior to your relapse. These may have happened up to a week or more before you hit the trigger that sent you into your matrix of addiction.

1. _____
2. _____
3. _____
4. _____

If you do this exercise thoughtfully, you will probably discover there are some very common preconditions to your relapses. Your addiction is primarily a process whereby you medicate your pain within. It could be that something in the present reminds you of the pain of something from your past. It could be boredom, loneliness, fear, or a haunting sense of worthlessness, despite all your achievements.

The sequence is almost always triggered by some inner emotional discomfort. Once you have relapsed enough times, your brain changes the way it actually functions. You end up operating on "autopilot" and it's slowly killing you over and over again. This difficult exercise helps you to finally identify the destructive autopilot switch, so you can begin to turn it off. You have begun to identify your addictive lifestyle.

IDENTIFY THE FOLLOWING IN YOUR LIFE:

1 Are there any common elements that are part of the preconditions?
i.e. fighting with my girlfriend, stress around final exams

2 What is common in your rituals that set you up for relapse?
i.e. cruising social media for cute people, mindlessly surfing the web, flirting in class

3 Your attempts of trying to "keep the lid on" include:
i.e. confessing more and pleading with God, working out more, working harder at school

4 Stop and look back over what you have written. What are your observations concerning the battle that you have been fighting?

A. _____
B. _____
C. _____
D. _____

MATRIX OF RESTORATION

Now, I also want you to think back over your most recent victory. See if you can outline how it happened by filling in the matrix of restoration.

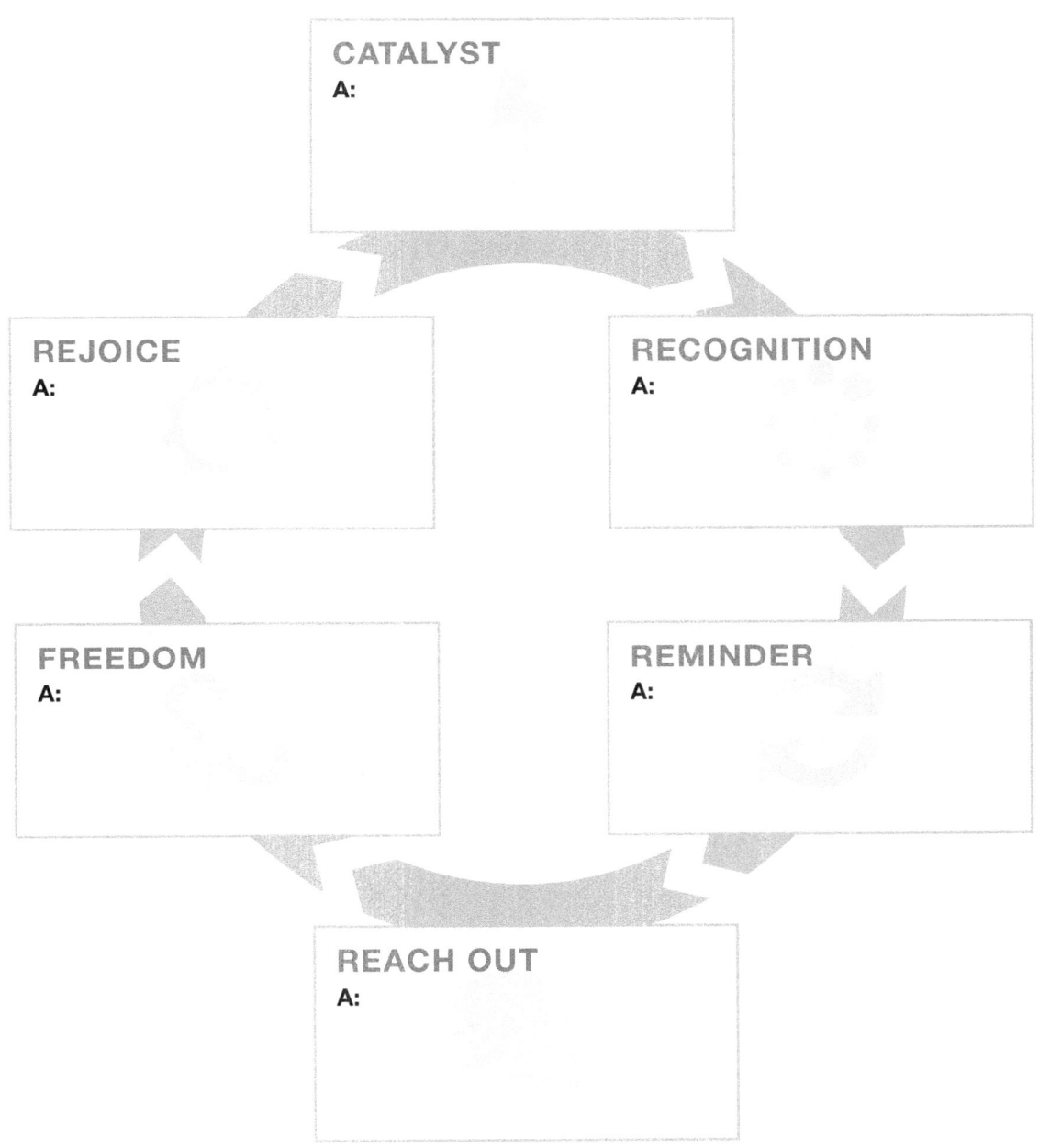

─╱╲─ ASSIGNMENTS FOR NEXT TIME ─╱╲╱╲─

① **Meditate on 2 Samuel 9:1-13.** Read the passage through at least five times and find yourself in the story.

② **Answer all of the questions on the previous pages** and be prepared to share with your group all that you have discovered about your Matrix of Addiction and Restoration.

LESSON EIGHT
BATTLE PLAN

Then Jesus told his disciples, "If anyone would come after me, let him deny himself and take up his cross and follow me. For whoever would save his life will lose it, but whoever loses his life for my sake will find it.
Matthew 16:24-25 (ESV)

Before reading any further, take some time to meditate on this passage. This is a very important exercise because it gives you significant insight into Jesus' battle plan for your life. Jesus is helping us to understand that the moment you deny yourself, you have removed yourself from the realm of the enemy's control. Therefore, the enemy can't hold you hostage anymore; instead, you become free to follow Jesus.

Please notice the fact that Jesus didn't say, "Take up my cross," but, "take up your cross." His cross was to die for the sins of the world; that is obviously not your cross. When Jesus faced the cross it meant death; when we face our cross it means life and abundance. Granted, it doesn't initially feel that way because your cross is found where your will runs counter to God's will in your life. But Jesus is saying to you right now, "That part of your life that is not working, that part of your life where we are at odds—I have a gift for you if you will surrender it to Me. I can touch that point of shame and pain and give you freedom."

You will never be able to hear those words until you understand that every interaction with God is encased in grace. This is the essence of God's battle plan for your life. The enemy takes you hostage through shame. Jesus sets you free through grace. Learning to trust this gift of grace will allow you to go on to victory, which is precisely why He gets so excited over what lies ahead for you.

Let's consider one of the most famous battle plans of the Bible. God's people have been wandering around the desert for forty years after their escape from slavery in Egypt. Moses has died and Joshua has taken leadership. The Hebrews are camped on the banks of the Jordan River about to enter the Promised Land. After living in the hot, dry, sandy desert, they can almost feel and taste the lush beauty of the land. But as they prepared to cross over into the land God had given them, they knew that it was not empty. People of other tribes and nations lived there, standing in the way.

This story is history, but it's also an analogy of your own life. There is a better life waiting for those who will follow Jesus' battle plan instead of their own. You are on the threshold of moving into this better life, but first you must learn to fight the enemy of your soul. Let's see what this first battle in the Promised Land can teach us.

> Here is the bottom line: the enemy has no way to predict what you will do if you aren't being driven by your own self-interests.

NOTES

> *Now Jericho was shut up inside and outside because of the people of Israel. None went out, and none came in. And the Lord said to Joshua, "See, I have given Jericho into your hand, with its king and mighty men of valor. You shall march around the city, all the men of war going around the city once. Thus shall you do for six days. Seven priests shall bear seven trumpets of rams' horns before the ark. On the seventh day you shall march around the city seven times, and the priests shall blow the trumpets. And when they make a long blast with the ram's horn, when you hear the sound of the trumpet, then all the people shall shout with a great shout, and the wall of the city will fall down flat, and the people shall go up, everyone straight before him."*
> Joshua 6:1-5 (ESV)

What kind of battle plan is that? God is asking all the men of war and the pastors to march around the city, tooting their horns and yelling at the top of their lungs. Really? The walls are then supposed to fall down flat? Seems crazy to me. Here's the point: trying harder doesn't work! God's people didn't have the necessary weapons to take a walled city. They needed to learn that this was going to be God's battle on God's terms. Their best efforts just wouldn't be enough. They needed a completely different battle plan.

> *For though we walk in the flesh, we are not waging war according to the flesh. For the weapons of our warfare are not of the flesh but have divine power to destroy strongholds.*
> 2 Corinthians 10:3-4 (ESV)

Just as Joshua needed to learn to fight using God's battle plan, so do you. You might have heard insanity defined as doing the same thing over and over again and expecting a different result. That is the "try harder" approach. You need to try something totally different and possibly foreign to you. Remember, Jesus is actually for you. He's on your side whether it feels like it or not.

Conversely, the enemy has nothing but contempt for you. Look at what he had to say about Job and all of mankind in the Old Testament.

> *Satan answered, "A human would do anything to save his life. But what do you think would happen if you reached down and took away his health? He'd curse you to your face, that's what."*
> Job 2:4-5 (MSG)

Satan is totally convinced that when push comes to shove, self-preservation will always rule in the hearts of men. He sees us as creatures completely run by fear, solely directed by our limbic system. Here is the bottom line: the enemy has no way to predict what you will do if you aren't being driven by your own self-interests. Satan can only forecast selfishness. He is helpless against a man who is living for a cause greater than himself. Here is a picture of what "trying harder" doesn't look like:

- When you decide that the Word of God settles it for you, no matter what you are feeling
- When you obey God despite the difficulties you are going through
- When you do what is right despite the costs
- When you face your addiction and choose to accept God's grace, not controlled by shame and fear
- When you risk rejection and ask God and others for help rather than trying to do it by yourself
- When you make a stand for your life by living honestly in a group of other safe men and let them speak into your life

The way you begin to see victory in this battle for sexual wholeness is by constructing a winning Battle Plan. Your ability to accept God's grace and face your addiction is directly connected to you having a battle hardened relapse prevention plan. In the previous lesson, we went through the difficult and challenging process of constructing your matrix of addiction. Now, we want to take the lessons and observations from that lesson and construct the Battle Plan.

Having a clear target in life is crucial. It is a life or death matter in winning your battle with sexual bondage. The lessons in this workbook will help you learn to identify the places where you are uniquely vulnerable. Unless you have a very clear picture of your unique wounds and the beliefs in your life that cripple you, there is no way you can win the battle.

The only relapse that can become fatal is the one you are not willing to learn from. Instead of turning against yourself and spiraling into a deeper shame cycle, you must ruthlessly and graciously face your part in the process. Relapses never just happen; they are always preceded by a clear sequence of choices that we make. This is what the Matrix of Addiction taught you. The problem is we are usually not even aware that we are making these choices. They are taking place beneath the radar of our conscious mind, at the unconscious level. Therefore, and this is huge, we must chart out a clear path of how we move from Restoration to Relapse based on the insights we have gained or we will just continue the insanity. This is precisely why "trying harder," doing more and more of the same thing we've always done, is a losing strategy.

The Three Circles graphic in this lesson is designed to give you a very clear and convenient method of displaying all you have discovered so far. It will be an invaluable aid in understanding your battle. Think of this like shooting a gun or throwing darts. It doesn't take much effort to hit at least some part of the target. But it will take discipline, practice, and help to consistently hit a bullseye. Living in Relapse is like spraying bullets all over the target. Living in Restoration is doing what it takes to hit the bullseye with the help of God and others.

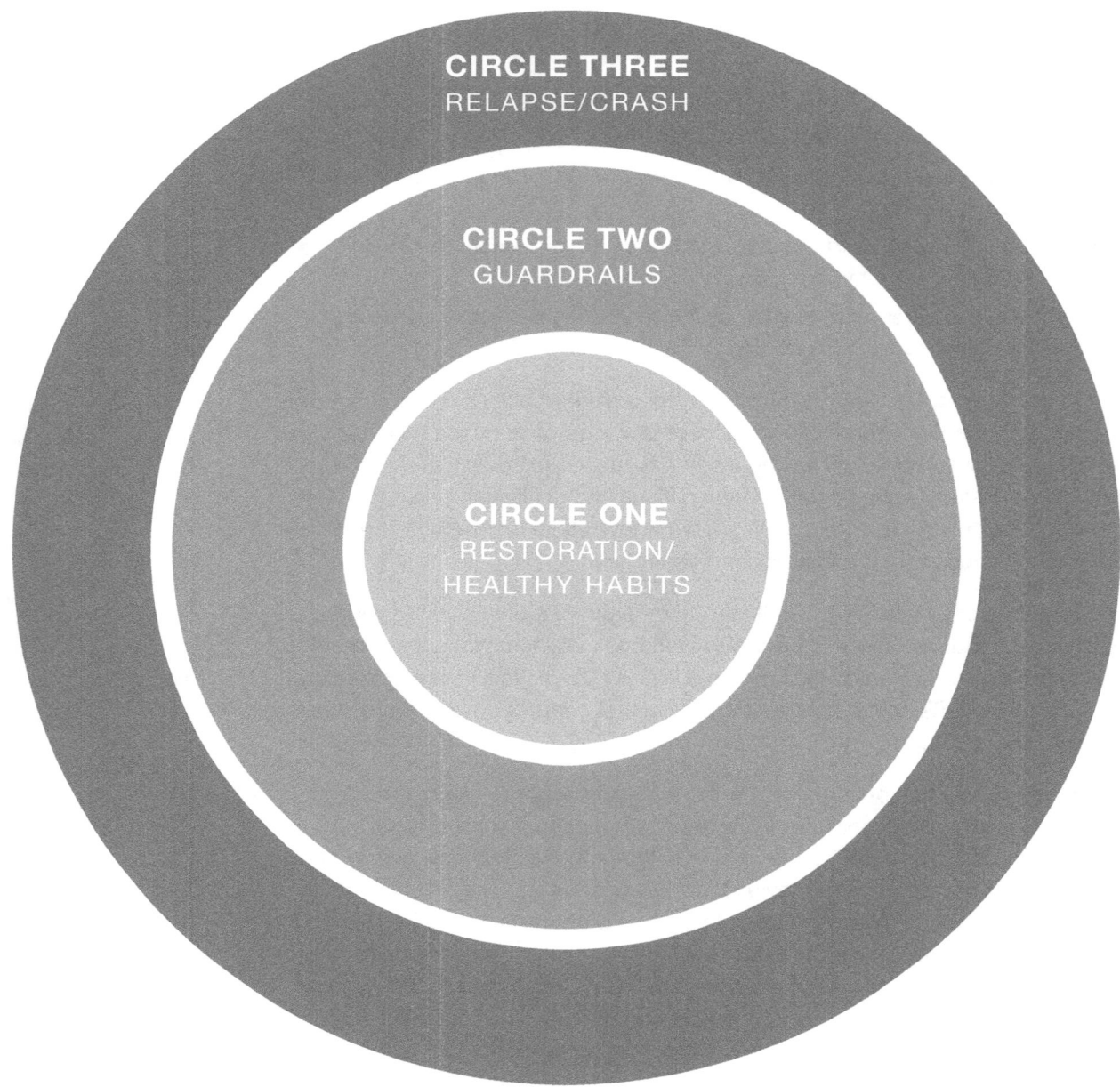

Circle One is the bullseye, your target. These are healthy habits that support your healing and also describe what healthy sexuality looks like for you. The question of healthy sexuality can be a real puzzle for someone who has been struggling with sexual bondage for years. When I ask a guy to describe what healthy sexuality is for him, I get this blank stare. But it is vitally important you think that through because if your only goal is to stop your destructive behavior, you are defeated before you start. You must have a vivid picture of who God has created you to be, as well as what your dreams and hopes are for your marriage or future marriage. Otherwise you will lack the passion to win the war.

CIRCLE ONE ACTIVITIES MIGHT INCLUDE:

» Faithfully doing my homework and recovery disciplines for my Living Free group.
» Developing a lifestyle of confession to Jesus and others when I mess up.

- Playing a sport for the fun of it, instead of having to win.
- Using self-control and delayed gratification when I'm sexually tempted.
- Gaining insight and understanding about why I feel sexually tempted.
- Exploring new healthy hobbies and interests in my life.
- Developing a great ability to listen to and affirm my girlfriend/wife.
- Being totally honest in all of my dealings and admit when I am wrong.
- Developing some deep friendships.
- Developing a meaningful and deep devotional life.
- Learning to pace myself and not take an "all or nothing" approach to life.
- Developing healthy eating habits and a workout routine.
- Learning how to really relax when I need to instead of just vegging out.
- Being physically and emotionally present and encouraging my friends and family.

Next is Circle Two. These are those behaviors that fall between the devastating behaviors that totally demoralize you and the healthy sexuality you truly cry for in Christ. When these signs show up in your life they tell you that you are no longer living in your target zone and that you have begun to move away from a life dependent on Jesus and others. These are the "dashboard lights" that tell you you're heading toward the cliff. Just like the dashboard light that comes on in your car telling you that you need to change the oil soon; ignore this light at your own peril. These Circle Two behaviors don't mean immediate destruction, but they are your "wake up call" that you need to make a change in your life. A crash is looming if you ignore circle two.

These Circle Two behaviors are a slippery slope that will eventually lead you back into Circle Three if you don't develop strong boundaries and stay in touch with the fact that you are powerless over your compulsions. In Circle Two list people, places, situations, and things you must avoid because you feel your temptation increase around them. List mental "slippery slopes" such as rationalizing, justifying, blaming, patterns of anger, or isolating. List activities that can set you up, such as cruising social media, surfing the web, flirting at work or class, lying or choosing to omit certain facts, watching certain R-rated movies, driving by the strip club or ex-girlfriend's house. Look at what you have been circling on the FASTER Scale in any of the F-A-S-T-E categories. Forgetting Priorities is the beginning of the slippery slope and leads you down toward Relapse. Exhausted behaviors may almost look like Relapse because a relapse is imminent. You are just waiting for the circumstances to be right to facilitate a relapse.

Circle Two can also be seen from a positive perspective. It is where we construct the critical guardrails of our life. Guardrails are placed in areas where it is less safe to drive, intended to keep us from driving into areas that are potentially deadly. Guardrails are "truth speakers" in our lives and aren't meant to feel cushy. They are designed to inflict a little bit of pain to keep us from experiencing devastatingly painful consequences. Guardrails are not naturally and easily built in our life and can feel like they keep us from something we want.

- I don't want to save money. I want to buy that car, power tool, or big boy toy, now.
- I know I am in a relationship, but I want to flirt with that cute girl in class. I am not hurting anyone.
- I know I shouldn't eat that dessert, but I have been good all week. I will be better tomorrow.
- I know I shouldn't surf the Internet alone, but I am bored.

The big problem with guardrails, as so many guys have told me, is they get in their way. It gets between them and what they crave. They have thoughts like, "They restrict me. I am not experiencing as much fun as I possibly could. They are limiting my life!" Don't fight the guardrails, be thankful for them. Banging your head against the guardrails will only give you a headache and a flat forehead. Remember, healthy sexuality is not about getting as close to sin as you possibly can without sinning. It's about living in freedom and honoring God with a heart of integrity and honesty, even in the dead of night.

Circle Three describes the place where you need to die to selfish impulses; otherwise, the enemy will eventually kill you. These are the places, once you are there, you will always act out. Circle Three behaviors need to be clearly defined so you know with certainty when you are engaging in them. No gray areas here. I used to like to give myself what I now call, "greasy grace." I'd find some way to spin and rationalize my behavior to not have to call them relapses, looking for a way out of the consequences of my choices. It took brave and compassionate men in my life to routinely call me out on my craziness and show me what honesty really looks like. Clearly defining your Circle Three behaviors, so there is no fuzziness, will allow you to avoid the death trap of "greasy grace" and be honest about parts of your life where you might be tempted to be the least honest.

Inside Circle Three write down the compulsive, self-defeating behaviors from which you must abstain if you have any hope of being free. This is not about being legalistic; it's about knowing your limits and being honest with yourself.

YOUR CIRCLE THREE LIST MIGHT INCLUDE COMMENTS LIKE:

- » No sex of any kind outside of marriage
- » No viewing of porn and masturbation
- » No strip clubs or massage parlors
- » No surfing of TV or Internet alone
- » No gambling, drinking or drugs

I also call Circle Three the "crash." We are not planning on relapsing; but if we do, we must honestly look at Circle Three and ask three questions. Think back to your last relapse and answer the following questions.

① How did I end up back in Relapse again?

② What were the steps that lead me to this crash?

③ How do I need to revise my Matrix of Addiction in light of what I am learning from this relapse? What did I miss?

BIG TRUTH NUMBER ONE

Whether or not you have guardrails in your life, the pressure of temptation will exist. Here is what I mean. The place you decide to put a guardrail in your life is where the temptation begins. Let's say you finally decide to install a filter of some sort on your phone and computer. At some point, you might be tempted to search for porn to check and see that the filter is actually working. The guardrail can actually fuel the crazy thinking. If you decide to not place any guardrails in your life, the tension doesn't go away. You just zoom closer to the cliff of horrendous consequences. However, the further back you construct the guardrails in your life, the easier it is to resist the magnetic pull of temptation and avoid plunging off the cliff. The cravings feel less strong in Forgetting Priorities than they do in Exhausted. Compromise doesn't ease the tension; it only moves us closer to the cliff of losing sight of who we really are in Christ.

But we can so easily tell ourselves, "Oh, if I just give in to the temptation then I will not have this tension any more. The temptation will be gone." The truth is if you lie to yourself once, it becomes much easier the next time. Eventually, it will become such a lifestyle that you no longer know the truth or know who you really are in Christ.

> *But Daniel made up his mind that he would not defile himself with the king's choice food or with the wine which he drank; so he sought permission from the commander of the officials that he might not defile himself. Now God granted Daniel favor and compassion in the sight of the commander of the officials.*
> Daniel 1:8-9 (NASB)

Daniel made an insane choice. King Nebuchadnezzar has just offered him the gift of a lifetime. A free graduate education at one of the finest universities in the world at the time. If that is not enough, he gets food right off the king's table. The vast majority of his countrymen, those who were still alive after Babylon destroyed Jerusalem, were wondering where their next meal was coming from. But Daniel made an incredibly wise choice; he knew where all this was headed. Nebuchadnezzar was a diabolically brilliant man. He ordered the best and brightest of the nations he conquered to be brought to and trained in Babylon. Slowly, their culture and belief structures would be stripped away until they would become superb ambassadors for Nebuchadnezzar, his gods, and his way of life.

Daniel saw where all this "great stuff" was headed. He would eventually lose everything he held near and dear. "But Daniel made up his mind." He resolved that this is as far as it goes. He made up his mind even before he knew what the outcome would be. He had never read the book of Daniel, he was writing it. He was a teenager surrounded by the most powerful people in the world. They could have crushed him in an instant. He made the decision because he could predict the end of the story if he just went with the flow of events. He knew where this was leading, and yet, he had no guarantees what would happen if he said, "No!" to the king's offer.

BIG TRUTH NUMBER TWO

I absolutely love the beginning of verse 9, "Now God." Here is the part we tend to forget in the stress of the moment. **God will not only use our guardrails to protect us. He will use them to direct us as well.** The Lord used this pivotal moment of decision to guide the rest of Daniel's life. Daniel saw the potential temptation in what was being offered to him and allowed it to lead him a different way. Let your temptations do the same. Instead of giving in to the temptations and allowing them to lead you to destruction, anticipate them. Bounce off of them back toward the light instead of ignoring them and moving deeper into the darkness.

A friend of mine once found her car scraping along the guardrail on a bridge and her panicked over-reaction almost cost her the loss of her life. She didn't see the guardrail coming and jerked the wheel to get off the guardrail, but that put her car out of control and she nearly went off the bridge! It's vital that you know where your guardrails are so you can trust them. When you hit one, you don't plunge off the cliff by doing nothing or panic by overreacting.

You have to make up your mind before you know the end of your story. Yet you can easily predict the end if you keep sliding toward the Circle Three of destruction. You will never know who you can be in God until you establish some solid guardrails in your life. You have to make up your mind. The only thing that goes away without guardrails in your life is your God-given future.

FILL OUT THE THREE CIRCLES IN THE CHART BELOW WHICH MAKE UP YOUR BATTLE PLAN:

As you experience healing, you will see something interesting happening with these circles. When you begin to walk in greater health and freedom you see two things take place:

1. The majority of the energy you put toward recovery will move from staying away from Circle Three toward staying away from Circle Two. You will begin to realize the things that set you up to fall back into Circle Three are the things listed in Circle Two. Therefore, your Circle Two begins to be combined with Circle Three. They become part of your Abstinence List. You never want to go slamming into a guardrail again in your life because you realize what that means…you're about to head off the cliff.

2. Real health begins to settle deep into your soul when you finally stop focusing on what you don't want to do. Instead, your thoughts and focus is on what you really want to do in your life (Circle One). Your focus has now dramatically shifted from the addiction to health.

Once you complete the Battle Plan it will become a document in progress. At least once every three to six months you should revisit this exercise and adjust your responses to your current level of healing and understanding. You will find that this is an excellent indicator of the progress you are making and an invaluable tool in your fight for freedom.

ASSIGNMENTS FOR NEXT TIME

This is a very challenging lesson. Take your time and provide yourself opportunity for thoughtful responses. The battle plan you are constructing will, in many ways, determine whether or not you truly break free.

① Complete the Battle Plan. Be prepared to share and receive feedback on your work next week.

LESSON NINE
SURVIVAL

I remember when I first began sharing the gospel with others in college. I was terrified. The idea of asking a friend or approaching a stranger and asking them to have a spiritual conversation sounded like the quickest way to be identified as a religious fanatic, yelled at, or lose friends. Plus, I hadn't talked to others about Jesus much before. Sure I had recently been trained in how to share the gospel and how to ask good questions, but it was completely new to me. I wondered why anyone would even give me the time of day to have a spiritual conversation.

But as I took steps of faith, I began to experience many good spiritual conversations. I was always scared to death before initiating those conversations and asked God to give me the words to say and to use me. I witnessed people hear the gospel for the first time and give their lives to Christ. God used me to do His work despite my lack of experience, fear, and inability to answer people's tough questions.

In those incidents, I experienced how God does great work in the midst of our weaknesses. But it takes that willingness to surrender to God in our weaknesses and dependence on the Holy Spirit to experience His great work. It took my willingness to allow God to use me where I was at, rather than pretending I had it all figured out, to see God work as I initiated spiritual conversations with others.

Your weaknesses—when not recognized and yielded to the Lord—can result in something more tragic than missing out on a great spiritual conversation or the opportunity to see someone come to Christ. You can end up living a life that flies in the face of your commitment to Christ, a life where hypocrisy hides beneath the surface. That's exactly where sexual bondage leads you. You become a fake who says one thing and does something else—with tragic lifelong consequences.

The Apostle Paul was a powerful man known for his self-discipline, but this was not the core of his strength. The Lord spoke to Paul as he struggled with a profound weakness in 2 Corinthians 12:9 (ESV). God revealed the source of a strength that will always defeat the forces of the enemy in our lives: "'My grace is sufficient for you, for my power is made perfect in weakness.' Therefore I will boast all the more gladly of my weaknesses, so that the power of Christ may rest upon me."

GOD CAN MAKE US STRONG IN OUR WEAKNESSES WHEN WE YIELD THEM TO HIM.

Paul learned to rejoice over what we might call his stress fracture. We don't know its exact nature. I think the Bible doesn't tell us so we'll have the opportunity to catch the principle and not get hung up on the specific problem. It seems clear: God can make us strong in our weaknesses when we yield them to him. But admitting our weaknesses can be extremely difficult, especially as men. Our tendency can be to live in denial of weaknesses due to fear of feeling inadequate or worthless. We need to see these weaknesses as opportunities to see God work in our lives rather than opportunities to fail.

So how does this apply to your battles with sexual purity? Well, read the words of Dr. Ted Roberts about how your sexual addiction is an opportunity to see God work in your life.

> *I'd grown to love the young man. When he first walked into my office, though, he was in total denial. "I'm not a sex addict," he declared. After I gave him the Sexual Addiction Screening Test you took a few weeks ago, he could no longer deny reality. He scored 8+.*
>
> *I leaned over, speaking gently, "The test clearly indicates you're a sexual addict. Now listen carefully: You're not evil, you're wounded."*
>
> *Tears flooded his eyes. He could no longer hide the truth from himself. He'd also found a safe place where he could get help. Over the next twelve months, we walked through the painful but joyous process of the Holy Spirit bringing in-depth healing to his life.*
>
> *On the other side of the journey, he asked me, "Am I going to be a sex addict for the rest of my life? Am I going to be like an Alcoholics Anonymous member—always introducing myself, 'Hi, I'm Joe the sex addict?'"*
>
> *I pointed out that Alcoholics Anonymous has done plenty of good in our hurting world. But Christ didn't die on a sin-stained cross so I could spend the rest of my life being identified by my addiction.*
>
> *At the other extreme, when I became a Christian I wasn't automatically set free from all previous bondage. Paul's biblical assertion in Romans 6 says, "I have died to sin." This doesn't mean sin is instantaneously extinguished in my life. Death speaks of separation, not extinction.[1] And Paul's declaration is one of potential, not automatic possession. The biblical truth lies between the two extremes of religious denial and endless recovery groups.*
>
> *I told my young friend the normal sequence of recovery from sexual bondage is a two- to five-year journey with a miracle needed every step of the way.[2] It doesn't go on forever, but it's important to understand that the process will reveal the stress fractures in your soul.*
>
> *Years ago, I competed in intense triathlons. After one very exhausting race, I discovered I'd sustained a stress fracture in my right foot. According to the doctor, my prognosis was clear. I had to get a different type of running shoe, change my running style, and get some additional support in the arch area of my left foot. In others words, I had to change my lifestyle.*

---

1. Kenneth S. Wuest, *Word Studies in the Greek New Testament: Volume Three* (Grand Rapids, Michigan: Eerdmans Publishing Company, 1966), 78.
2. Patrick Carnes, *Recovery Process: Volume 1* (Carefree, Arizona: Gentle Path Press, 2009), 7.

> *The young man's score of 8+ on the SAST indicated he'd sustained a stress fracture in his soul. I could definitely help him move into health, but if he didn't change the way he ran during the rough times—if he didn't change the way he processed pain—he would soon be back fighting the same battle in another form.*
>
> *I never introduce myself as an alcoholic or sex addict, but I was once characterized by both these destructive addictions. In fact, I drank so severely as a fighter pilot, I managed to scar my liver. I'm no longer an alcoholic, yet I know deep within my soul exists a wounded place God has healed. If I don't protect that place, hell can strike it and cripple me again.*
>
> *In this battle, you must remember your stress fractures—the wounds of your past. If you refuse to allow the enemy of your soul to attach a sense of shame to them, then you can declare with Paul, "Therefore I will boast all the more gladly of my weaknesses, so that the power of Christ may rest upon me." (2 Corinthians 12:9b ESV). If you scored more than 6 on the SAST a few weeks ago, then somewhere in your soul lies a stress fracture, too.*

Dr. Ted's insights are so crucial in understanding this battle. As God heals your wounds from the past, you have the unique opportunity to help other men who struggle with the similar wounds. God can use your greatest weaknesses by changing them into your greatest strengths. When our stress fractures are triggered and we struggle to believe the truth or that we can't survive without acting out to medicate the pain in our lives, we need the most help. It's in these moments of weakness where we can see God do His greatest work and meet our needs as we surrender to Him.

You may recall this quote from best-selling author and psychiatrist, Scott Peck, that was used in Lesson Three. He once stated, "Mental health is a commitment to reality at all costs."[3] In the blurry haze of temptation, it can be hard to see reality. Sometimes cravings for old coping behaviors will rise up with extreme and seemingly overwhelming force. It's in these moments that Scott Peck's words carry the most weight. It's in these moments that we need to remember who God has called us to be and where we are headed in life. It's in these moments that we need the most help and to hear the truth spoken to us from our brothers. In this battle, we need to constantly dedicate ourselves to reality. The following assignments in this lesson will provide you with a helpful solution for those moments as you continue on in this process.

In this battle, we need to constantly dedicate ourselves to reality.

NOTES

---

3. Peck, M.S., M.D. (1978). *The Road Less Traveled: A New Psychology of Love, Traditional Values and Spiritual Growth.* New York, NY: Simon & Schuster, Inc.

1. LETTER TO YOURSELF

Writing a letter to yourself is one of the most powerful instruments you can place in your arsenal to keep from going back into the old addictive cycle. You'll read it when old cravings for coping mechanisms come up. The enemy will hammer hard at the stress fracture in your soul, the place of your former weakness. Yes, God is healing you, but your history gives you a unique vulnerability. What could you tell yourself in that situation to help you return to sanity and reality?

Write out the letter in detail. At your next Living Free meeting, have your group members write supportive comments in the margins. When the heat is on and your head is going sideways—back to the old addictive craziness—you'll have their support as well. Carry the letter with you at all times. If it's too long, write a summary on a three-by-five card. Your letter should address the following:

- What are the probable situations that would lead you to read the letter? In other words, where's your stress fracture? ("When I feel lonely, rejected, abandoned, worthless…")
- What will happen if you ignore this letter?
- What must you do in order to avoid relapse?
- What is the God-given dream you have in your soul?
- What is ultimately at stake?
- What truth do you need to hear at this moment?

HERE'S AN EXAMPLE OF ONE YOUNG MAN'S LETTER:

Dear Joe,

You're obviously in a tough place right now because you're reading this letter. But just because you're struggling doesn't mean you have to give in. Of course it feels overwhelming right now, because you're probably alone and want to feel better fast.

Please remember you've traveled this path many times before. You always end up in the same place—deep regret. There, you'll feel loaded down with shame and even farther from God than you do now. Also, remember:

- *You'll want to hide what you did from others and lie about it.*
- *You'll never truly enjoy it; it will always make you feel more empty and lonely.*
- *You'll despair over your broken commitments to God and others.*
- *You'll let the other men in your group down.*
- *Your God-given dream will become tainted and seem impossible.*
- *You'll have to face the external and natural consequences of your decision.*
- *Although you know it's not true, you'll struggle afterward with the feeling that any problem you face is God's punishment for your behavior.*

Joe, the enemy and your flesh is whispering false promises into your soul, promises that never work. So identify where the pain is and what you need.

- » *Are you lonely or bored?*
- » *Are you feeling worthless?*
- » *Are you angry or overwhelmed?*
- » *Are you hungry or tired?*

Ask God for help. Call some of your group members immediately. Get what you need and refuse to do the one thing that will only make things worse and crush your heart for God.

If anyone would see what you're about to do—your friends, your parents, your group members—would you still do it? You're called of God and set apart for His purposes. He designed your life to make a difference. What you're thinking of doing will be a major setback. Remember the consequences this will have in your future marriage.

You matter to Christ. He'll meet your needs in a way that respects your value.

Please, Joe, listen to what you've written here. You know in your heart that what you're considering will never fulfill your soul. Don't lie to yourself—respect yourself. Care enough to let this temptation go. Let it pass, it won't last forever. Call a group member and fight this battle together.

Love ya, Joe

2. SURVIVAL KIT

You'll need a survival kit to withstand the onslaught of intense temptation. This is a collection of items designed to keep you spiritually alive—things that provide your life with meaning. The contents of your survival kit will be unique to you. Still, these suggestions may help:

- » Reminders of your progress in the healing journey so far: pictures, note cards from a group member or leader, medallions, or any reminders of significant moments in your healing
- » Family pictures that remind you what this battle is really about
- » Pictures of friends you respect and enjoy
- » Letters or note cards that have spoken encouragement into your heart
- » Copies of specific pages of this workbook that helped you
- » Favorite Scripture verses and the promises God has given you concerning your life and future
- » Phone numbers of your group members and friends to call for encouragement
- » A playlist or the lyrics of Christian songs God has used to touch your heart
- » Any other items that remind you of the man Christ says you are and the one you can be in Him
- » Crash contract as explained next in this lesson

Keep your survival kit in a location where you can get to it when you are in the thick of temptation. If you're staring relapse in the face, don't try to tough it out. Act immediately and reach for your survival kit.

3. CRASH CONTRACT

One of the most powerful items you should have in your survival kit is a crash contract. This is a covenant you walk and talk through with your group members. It spells out precisely what you'll do if you relapse or crash in the healing process. It includes the natural consequences that you developed in Lesson Three. If you have continued to relapse since then, update the natural consequences that you have in place.

This is not a performance agreement—I want to emphasize that. This isn't a commitment to try harder next time. Instead, it's a commitment to not keep your relapse a secret. When you keep your failures to yourself, your sense of shame will rise. And shame lies at the core of all addictive behaviors.

Consider this contract a resolution to no longer live a secret life. You'll live in community and honesty. You'll use the process to reach the core of your woundedness. More importantly, you'll allow Christ to heal you.

Keep a copy of your contract in your survival kit. Your group members or leader should have a copy as well. Below is an example of a crash contract.

I, _____, (your name) hereby commit that if I have a relapse in my sexual purity:

» I won't conceal what I've done from my group or group leader.
» I will call a group member or leader as soon as possible and let him know exactly what I've done.
» I will fill out a FASTER Scale Exercise and Relapse Analysis to identify what led to the relapse.
» I will also do the following (whatever your group or group leader thinks should be the first steps):

_____
_____
_____
_____
_____
_____

» I commit myself to analyzing the crash with the help of others to understand the triggers and reasons it occurred. I do this not only to construct some future barrier, but to understand the woundedness within. After doing so, I will implement the necessary steps or boundaries into my life to prevent going down the same path again.

Agreed to on this date: _____

Signature _____

Learning to walk in the health and purity you long for doesn't happen by accident. As you know by now, it doesn't happen by trying harder, either. Recent discoveries in neuroscience help us to understand how individuals overcome chronic limitations and soar to new heights. Freedom like this involves three critical issues:[4]

» **A Clear Vision:** Know what's at stake and your God-given purpose.

» **Practice:** There's no magic moment where things will automatically improve. True healing involves work—the kind you're doing throughout this workbook. If you didn't finish all the assignments, please go back and do so.

» **Resilience:** Have some ready reserves. The crash contract is an example of this. Don't think of it as a plan to relapse; instead, it's a way of choosing to face your fear of failure and develop a clear plan. Remember, a winner is often the person who gets up off the floor one more time.

ASSIGNMENTS FOR NEXT TIME

1. **Complete the Letter To Yourself.**

2. **Complete the Survival Kit.**

3. **Complete the Crash Contract.**

4. **Be prepared to share all of the above items with your group next week.**

LESSON TEN
LIMBIC HOLIDAY

1 Then Jesus was led up by the Spirit into the wilderness to be tempted by the devil. 2 And after fasting forty days and forty nights, he was hungry. 3 And the tempter came and said to him, "If you are the Son of God, command these stones to become loaves of bread." 4 But he answered, "It is written,

'Man shall not live by bread alone, but by every word that comes from the mouth of God.'

5 Then the devil took him to the holy city and set him on the pinnacle of the temple 6 and said to him, "If you are the Son of God, throw yourself down, for it is written,

"'He will command his angels concerning you,' and "'On their hands they will bear you up, lest you strike your foot against a stone.'"

7 Jesus said to him, "Again it is written, 'You shall not put the Lord your God to the test.'" 8 Again, the devil took him to a very high mountain and showed him all the kingdoms of the world and their glory. 9 And he said to him, "All these I will give you, if you will fall down and worship me." 10 Then Jesus said to him, "Be gone, Satan! For it is written,

"'You shall worship the Lord your God and him only shall you serve.'"

11 Then the devil left him, and behold, angels came and were ministering to him.
Matthew 4:1-11 (ESV)

In this passage, Jesus is led by the Spirit into the desert to fast for 40 days and 40 nights and to be tempted by Satan. By fasting, Jesus was intentionally abstaining from food, spending constant time in prayer and communion with His Father, and turning to God to fully satisfy his needs.

During those 40 days, Jesus was tempted to sin when He was at His weakest. We need to remember that Jesus was fully human and fully God. He experienced the same physical symptoms we would if we fasted for 40 days. If you've ever fasted, you'll know that it is not uncommon for your body to become weak and to have little energy, to get headaches, to feel dizzy or lightheaded, and to feel sick to your stomach. Because Jesus was fully human, He was most likely experiencing some, if not all of these things and more. So, He was most likely starving in the desert, His stomach was aching and His body was weak. Satan himself was present with Him and was tempting Him.

In verses 3 and 4, Satan attacks Jesus in two ways. First, by questioning his authority and saying, "If you are the Son of God," and second, by encouraging Him to satisfy His desire for food. Satan attacks Him in His core identity. Sounds pretty familiar, right? As you have learned so far in this process, the enemy never fights fair and he loves to attack us in our core identity. Behind most of our temptation and pain is the core faulty belief and lie that we aren't worth much. But we know that the opposite is true as children of God. We are of infinite worth and are loved children of God as 1 John 3:1 tells us.

> The beauty of the gospel is that Jesus now lives in us and enables us to fight hard and not give in to sin!

NOTES

Jesus could have easily cast Satan away, or turned the stones into bread to satisfy His hunger, but He didn't. Jesus endured the temptation and fought by stating the truth of Scripture. Satan made false promises of instant gratification, but Jesus knew the truth and stood behind it.

In verse 6, Satan again attacks Jesus' core identity. Satan actually quotes Scripture, but out of context and misuses it, to try to get Jesus to give in and show His power. Could Jesus have thrown himself off of the temple and had the angels catch him? Absolutely. But this was not God's plan for Jesus revealing His public ministry. God had a better plan. Jesus always submitted to the Father's will. Jesus responded once again to Satan by stating the truth of Scripture.

Lastly, in verses 8-9, Satan tempts Jesus once again and makes a false promise of giving Him reign over all the kingdoms of the world in exchange for worshiping him. This was a false promise and a shortcut to the authority that Jesus would later gain after He endured the cross and rose from the grave as we see in Matthew 28:18. Again, Satan tempts Jesus to take the easy way out and to settle for instant gratification. But Jesus once again responds with the truth of Scripture and casts Satan away. He doesn't give in and He knows that true satisfaction lies in obedience to the Father. He has a right view of the entire situation and states the truth to combat the temptation and lies of the enemy.

There are many things we can learn from the temptation of Jesus, but there are a few specifics things I want to draw to your attention:

» Jesus was led by the Spirit.
» Jesus fought temptation and didn't give in to sin.
» Jesus had God's view on the situation.

First, Jesus was led by the Spirit as we see in verse 1. Jesus was not acting on His own accord, doing whatever He wanted. He submitted to the Father's will in all He did and He was empowered by the Holy Spirit. As you may recall from Lesson Two, this process involves your hardest Spirit-filled work. We do not just let go and let God. We have an active role to play in making choices to surrender to God and live life on His terms on a daily basis. Being empowered by the Holy Spirit and led by Him involves turning from our sin and our will for our lives, asking for forgiveness, and surrendering to His will for our lives moment by moment.

Second, Jesus fought the temptation and combated the lies being spoken to Him. Because Jesus is fully God and fully man, He experienced temptation to sin, but He never gave in. I love how Hebrews 4:15 (ESV) puts it, "For we do not have a high priest who is unable to sympathize with our weaknesses, but one who in every respect has been tempted as we are, yet without sin." Jesus knows what it's like to be tempted. He knows what it's like to be presented with the easier way out. I love that our God walked among us and can empathize with our hardships and temptation. He is not a distant God who doesn't understand our struggles. He is a God who walks with us, dwells in us, and understands us.

Jesus knew the truth and He believed it. He didn't let the false promises and lies of the enemy get to Him despite being extremely vulnerable and physically at His weakest. He didn't just throw in the towel because things were tough. No, He kept fighting despite the enemy continually tempting Him.

The beauty of the gospel is that Jesus now lives in us and enables us to fight hard and not give in to sin! Romans 8:11 (ESV) says, "If the Spirit of him who raised Jesus from the dead dwells in you, he who raised Christ Jesus from the dead will also give life to your mortal bodies through his Spirit who dwells in you." This is such a powerful truth. The same power, the same God who raised Jesus from the dead, lives in you! This means that we have the ability to resist temptation just like Jesus did. We have the ability to fight hard in the power of the Holy Spirit and have a choice to not give in to sin when we are tempted.

Third, Jesus had God's view on the situation. He wasn't consumed by His need for food and didn't take the shortcut that the temptation offered Him. No, He understood His mission on earth to live the perfect life, that only He could live, and die on the cross to pay the penalty of sin for all who would repent and believe in Him. He didn't get sidetracked in a moment of weakness. He had a greater vision of what was going on and where He was going in life.

This is a crucial element of withstanding temptation and hardship that we must grasp. Viktor Frankl, an Austrian neurologist and psychiatrist, and Holocaust survivor, is a great example of what it means to make it through hardship as a result of having a greater vision. In his book, *Man's Search for Meaning*, he shares how he was able to keep his mind and hope alive by rehearsing talks he imagined he would give after he was released from imprisonment. In the traumatic environment of a Nazi death camp, he discovered that purpose and meaning were central to his mental strength and health. Or, as he expressed it, "Those who have a 'why' to live, can bear with almost any 'how'."[1] In other words, once you have a clear understanding of where you are headed in life, you can effectively deal with deeply traumatizing situations.

In his book, Frankl tells of one freezing winter day. While being forced to march outside the concentration camp, Frankl developed a terrible cough. He fell to the ground, coughing uncontrollably. A prison guard, irritated by Frankl delaying the group's progress, began beating him. He collapsed on all fours in the snow, convinced he could not get up or move another step. The guard threatened to kill him on the spot. Without conscious effort, he did something he had done endless times in his mind. Frankl found that he was no longer in the field on his hands and knees, but transported in his mind to the future. He explicitly pictured himself giving a lecture in Vienna on "The Psychology of Death Camps and the Psychology of Meaning." As the imagery swept over his mind and body, he no longer felt pain and weakness. He got to his feet as he saw himself telling of his experiences to his audience. He pictured this talk all the way to the work detail and all the way back to the concentration camp. He ended the imaginary talk to an standing ovation![2]

While Frankl's hardship was not necessarily temptation like ours, it was hardship and he could have very easily given up his will to survive in the Nazi death camp. In his difficulty, Frankl had a greater vision of where he was going in life and what would be accomplished if he made it through. His perceived future influenced his brutal present reality.

As followers of Christ, the future He has planned for us enters into us to transform us, long before it happens. "Everything can be taken from us but one thing: the last of human freedoms—to choose one's attitude in any given set of circumstances. We always have the freedom to trust God and choose His future for us no matter what may have happened to us or is presently happening."[3] Viktor Frankl walked through some of the worst

---

1. Viktor Frankl, *Man's Search for Meaning* (New York: Pocket Books, 1997) 123.
2. Roberts, Dr. Ted. *Seven Pillars of Freedom Workbook*. 4th ed. Gresham, OR: Pure Desire, 2015. 184.
3. Viktor Frankl, *Man's Search for Meaning* (New York: Pocket Books, 1997) 123.

pain a human could experience by looking forward to a speech he was going to give some day. Similarly, we can resist any temptation and endure any hardship in this life as we come to understand what God has prepared for us and how He sees us.

In the previous lesson, you completed several things that will equip you when you're tempted to give in. You wrote a letter to yourself, created a survival kit, and drafted a crash contract. These will all be extremely helpful in weeks ahead as you face temptation and the desire to revert back to old ways of thinking.

So why all of this talk about fighting temptation and withstanding the tactics of the enemy? Well, if you began going through *Living Free* in the fall, you'll be reading this lesson at the perfect time—the winter holiday season. Maybe you've been away at college and will be returning home with your family for several weeks. Maybe you only have a couple days or weeks off for the holiday season. Or maybe you won't be going anywhere, but you'll be seeing many old friends, and extended family. Whatever your situation, it's important to be prepared for the approaching battle ahead.

For me, college breaks were often a huge time of isolation, secrets, and relapse. Throughout the school year, I was involved in accountability relationships, Bible studies, and lived with other Christian guys who were regularly confessing sin and reaching out for help from others when they were tempted to return to sexual sin. But when winter or summer breaks came around, I wasn't involved in that same type of community. Often, I had more time on my hands and fewer friends around me. I would return to the home I grew up in for several weeks at a time. There, I was surrounded by family, old friends, and locations where I had acted out sexually countless times before. Being around my family triggered feelings of worthlessness and failure. Seeing old friends brought up feelings of struggling to fit in and prove myself. Pain from my past was often triggered, influencing my desire to return to porn and masturbation in an attempt to medicate the pain.

I've witnessed countless guys see extended sobriety, only to return home for the holiday season or summer break and revert back to their old ways like I did. I've seen this trend over and over again. Isolation and procrastination lead to masturbation. We know from this process so far that living a life of no secrets, having regular structure, and reaching out for help is the foundation for a healthy recovery. The reason why so many seem to fall back into sin over a school break is because these strategies are not in place.

So, learn from my mistakes and the mistakes of so many others. Set yourself up well for the holiday season and take preventative measures. In this lesson, you'll prepare a plan to help you survive the holidays without going completely limbic. You'll set yourself up well to respond to pain from the past that gets triggered or situations that bring back old memories.

As you may recall from Lesson Six, your limbic system, or emotional brain, is what the Bible refers to as your heart and where your experiences in life are stored. This is the part of the brain that is active when pain from the past or past experiences are triggered. This lesson has been titled "Limbic Holiday" because the holidays can so easily cause us to go limbic. Old feelings, experiences, and pain can be triggered at the drop of a hat by being back around family, friends, and old places.

First, you'll want to talk with your group about how you will continue to meet during the months ahead. Most likely, you'll have several weeks off before the next school semester starts. There are no *Living Free* lessons to go through over the break, so we recommend meeting for an hour a week rather than two hours. Spend the first 40 minutes of the meeting walking through the Check-in and the last 20 minutes walking through the Commitment To Change. I'd encourage you to keep meeting weekly if possible. If everyone will not be in the same location, you may want to consider meeting through video chat, or group phone call. As the holiday season can be a bit busy, it's okay if you take one or two weeks off, but try to continue meeting weekly as much as possible. Come up with a plan for continuing to meet together.

Second, let's create a specific Limbic Holiday Escape Plan for the season ahead.

> *No temptation has overtaken you that is not common to man.*
> *God is faithful, and he will not let you be tempted beyond your ability, but with the temptation*
> *he will also provide the way of escape, that you may be able to endure it.*
> 1 Corinthians 10:13 (ESV)

God has given you everything you need to respond well to the temptation and pain you may face this holiday season. You have the Holy Spirit residing in you, your Personal Promises, your weekly recovery disciplines like the Commitment To Change, and your Living Free group!

Create a specific plan to set yourself up well for the season ahead. Don't walk into the battle ahead blind, come up with a good escape plan.

The Escape Plan has three vital elements:
1. A clear understanding of the alarms in your life.
2. Concrete steps that you must take to back away from the guardrails or triggers in the simplest way possible.
3. A realistic and routine way to practice your Limbic Holiday Escape Plan.

DIAGRAMMING YOUR LIMBIC HOLIDAY ESCAPE PLAN

» Using the following chart, think about the main things that will trigger you. Is it seeing certain people? Is it being home alone? Is it the potential of arguments with parents, relatives, or friends? Begin with the clear signs of trouble, the alarms. What are the feelings, emotions, thoughts, and triggers that tell you the enemy is picking up his sword and that you are getting set up for a relapse?

» What actions do you usually find yourself being drawn into as the first steps in Relapse?

» What steps can you take to fight instead? How can you stop this insanity in its tracks?

» How can you practice these steps on a frequent basis when you are not struggling with possible relapse? What would be a great escape plan for you to practice?[4]

» *Note: If being around your family or friends for the holidays triggers so much pain, don't be afraid to include leaving as a last resort to prevent relapse and stay clear headed. Include staying at a friends house in your escape plan.*

LIMBIC HOLIDAY ESCAPE PLAN

ALARM—SIGNS OF TROUBLE	ACTIONS THAT MOVE ME TOWARD RELAPSE	IMMEDIATE ACTIONS TO PREVENT RELAPSE	HOW TO PRACTICE THESE STEPS ROUTINELY
Example: Argument with parents	Getting really angry, feeling disrespected, and numbing out. Increasing desire to cope with the feelings.	Get out of the house and call a group member. Take deep breaths and meditate on my Personal Promises. Call a group member to break isolation and relationally connect. If things get so bad, I will leave and stay at Joe's house.	Call group members even when I'm doing well to make picking up the phone feel normal.

ASSIGNMENTS FOR NEXT TIME

1 **Complete a Limbic Holiday Escape Plan.**

2 **At minimum, continue the following weekly: making three phone calls, completing a FASTER Scale Exercise, Check-in, and Commitment To Change.**

3 **Be sure your group has come up with a plan for meeting over the break.**

SEMESTER I COMMITMENT

The goal in this journey of restoration is not simply to walk through a book, but for the gospel to transform you at a deeper level. Therefore, it is of utmost importance that you actually incorporate into your life this information you have studied.

At the end of the two semesters of *Living Free*, you will be challenged to sign off on the fact that you have not only faithfully completed the exercises, but that you are also making a commitment to integrate these into your life.

And since we live our lives in community, two individuals will need to sign off on the fact that this process is actually taking place in your life. We were wounded in the context of relationships, and we are healed in the context of relationships.

Denial is impossible to remove from our lives without the help of others. The two witnesses who sign this commitment are affirming the fact of your progress toward health and integrity.

I have, to the best of my ability, completed all the exercises found in Semester I. By God's grace, in the power of the Holy Spirit, I will do everything I can to live these truths out in my life on a daily basis. Denial has stopped in my life!

My Name _____ **Date** _____

Signature _____

AFFIRMING WITNESSES

1 *I affirm the fact that* _____ *has grown in integrity and honesty in his life by the grace of God. Denial is no longer part of his life.*

My Name _____ **Date** _____

Signature _____

2 *I affirm the fact that* _____ *has grown in integrity and honesty in his life by the grace of God. Denial is no longer part of his life.*

My Name _____ **Date** _____

Signature _____

LESSON ELEVEN
COMMITTING TO YOUR TEAM

You then, my child, be strengthened by the grace that is in Christ Jesus, and what you have heard from me in the presence of many witnesses entrust to faithful men, who will be able to teach others also. Share in suffering as a good soldier of Christ Jesus. No soldier gets entangled in civilian pursuits, since his aim is to please the one who enlisted him. An athlete is not crowned unless he competes according to the rules. It is the hard-working farmer who ought to have the first share of the crops. Think over what I say, for the Lord will give you understanding in everything.
2 Timothy 2:1-7 (ESV)

Welcome back from the break. Hopefully, you were able to set yourself up as you continued meeting with your group, kept up with recovery tools the past few weeks, and didn't revert back to the old binge-purge cycle of addiction, feeling like you got the shaft. Hopefully you were able to flourish, despite the difficulties and pain that may have arose over the holiday season, and were able to thrive, not just survive, over the holidays.

Now that you're halfway through this process, we'll be revisiting some crucial aspects that will allow your Living Free group to flourish. As a refresher, you may want to re-read Lesson One. But first, let's look at 2 Timothy 2. These are some of the last words that the Apostle Paul ever wrote. Here, Paul writes to Timothy from prison, shortly before his death.

We don't know what Timothy is feeling at this point. Maybe he's discouraged, maybe he's weary from all the work he has done for the gospel, or maybe he's going strong and is excited about what the Lord is doing. Regardless, Paul encourages him to keep going. In these verses, Paul tells him to be strengthened in the grace that is in Christ, to be strengthened in the truths of the gospel. He tells Timothy to take what he has learned and to pass it on to many others who are trustworthy and able to teach others. That's a big task. That's a lot of things to teach and to model to others. He tells Timothy to stay strong in the ministry God has called him to and endure difficulties, while keeping his eyes on Christ.

In verses 3-6, Paul tells Timothy to work hard and to keep his focus on pleasing God. He makes a comparison to an athlete competing in a sports events, while following the guidelines and rules that have been set out before him. In doing so, he reminds Timothy that living life on God's terms through obedience is where true satisfaction and blessing is found. Throughout these verses, it's clear that Paul is not encouraging Timothy in any easy tasks. He is encouraging Timothy in the most worthwhile tasks of working hard as he minister to others with the gospel, obeying Christ, and enduring hardship. He is calling Timothy to be disciplined and to focus on the truths of the gospel, despite how he may feel.

Maybe you had a tough break. Maybe it was a time full of painful triggers and reverting back to old ways. Maybe you're growing weary in keeping up with your weekly homework and phone

> I want to encourage you to be strengthened in the grace that is in Christ Jesus. Remember all of what Christ has done in your life so far through this process.

NOTES

calls. Maybe you're thinking this process isn't working for you and that you'll never see the freedom you want to see. I'd encourage you to take a moment to look back at Lesson Three and remind yourself of what God may want to do in your life through your journey. You are now halfway through this process, so I want to encourage you to be strengthened in the grace that is in Christ Jesus. Remember all of what Christ has done in your life through this process. Remember how Christ saved you and took the wrath of God for your sin. Remember that the Holy Spirit dwells inside of you and is constantly healing you as you take steps of faith throughout each week. Don't give up. Be strengthened in the gospel.

I want to encourage you to commit once again to fight this battle well with the team of guys in your group. You can't win this battle alone. You need the help of the guys in your group and the Holy Spirit at work within you. Don't forget, we are wounded in the context of relationships and we must be healed in the context of relationships. God created us to live with other people in our lives who will walk alongside us and be in the fight for healthy sexuality with us at all times. Despite how you may feel, commit to working hard in the power of the Holy Spirit alongside the team of guys in your group. It's time to take this up a notch.

CHECK-IN

How has the Check-in been going? Has your group been staying on time and allowing everyone to share? Keeping track of time and giving everyone the same amount of time to share will help with the Check-in. Sometimes you may have to cut someone off during their Check-in if they go too long; suggest that they share the rest with a group member later.

Let's revisit the Check-in. The Check-in is a set of questions that review each person's behavior and emotional state from the previous week. As mentioned previously, going over the Check-in takes up the first 40 minutes of each group meeting. The purpose of the review is to help you become more aware of the addictive and healing processes that are at work in your life. The Check-in also includes using the FASTER Scale and CTC, which all can be found in the Appendix II. Have you been filling out a FASTER Scale Exercise before filling out the Check-in questions each week? Have you been filling out a Relapse Analysis (Appendix II) after every relapse? These questions should be filled out within 24 hours before the weekly group meeting starts. Below, you will find good examples of answers to each question. Blank copies are also provided in Appendix II and the *Living Free Journal*.

1 What is the lowest level you reached on the FASTER Scale this week? (If there was a relapse be sure to fill out a Relapse Analysis, found in Appendix II.)
The lowest level I reached this past week was Ticked Off. I was supposed to meet a friend for lunch, and drove 15 minutes to meet him but he canceled right when I got there, so I saw it as a huge waste of time.

2 What level did you find yourself predominantly living in?
I lived in Anxiety this week. I've constantly been worrying about a big test I have next week because I may fail the class if I don't get an A on the test. I've been living in fear and having trouble concentrating on other important things in life.

3 What was the double bind you were dealing with in question one? In question two? How could you have practically implemented the harder choice?
Being Ticked Off at my friend: I got angry due to my fear of feeling disrespected and rejected. I especially fear feeling rejected because I experienced that so much from my Dad and friends growing up. The harder choice in this double bind was to ask God for forgiveness for my anger; call a group member to process my emotions and remind myself of the truth; and deal with my feelings of rejection by reminding myself that God loves me, is proud of me, and accepts me because I am His son. I could have also reminded myself that my friend most likely wasn't trying to reject me or disrespect me, something important just had come up last minute.

Living in Anxiety: I worried so much this past week about my upcoming test because it will cost a lot of money and disappoint my parents if I fail this class. Rather than constantly worrying, the harder choice would have been to call a group member to break isolation, address my fears of being a failure, tell myself how God views me and my true identity, and take steps to study and get out of Anxiety.

4 Where are you on your Commitment to Change from our last meeting?
It was to study for my upcoming test every day for 30 minutes. Each day, I reminded myself that God has gifted me with intelligence and a good memory. I followed through on studying although it was difficult. I also texted with Joe and Jake at 9 am each day when I began studying like I committed to doing.

5 Have you lied to anyone this week either directly or indirectly? Why?
Yes, someone asked me how I was really doing and rather than talking about my fears of the upcoming test, I lied and said I was doing great. I wanted to isolate and avoid my feelings.

6 What positive things have you done to move toward sexual and relational health in your life this week?
I spent time with the Lord every day to grow with Him. I took a girl out on a date, encouraged her, and asked her questions about herself.

COMMITMENT TO CHANGE

Have you been using the Commitment to Change (CTC) to truly set yourself up well to respond to challenges each week? Or has it just become another task that you check off the list? Are you using the CTC as an opportunity to move toward trusting God rather than your coping mechanisms throughout the week? Think through these questions and the adjustments you may need to make.

Now let's revisit the CTC. The CTC is simply a commitment that is developed through answering a set of questions each week that helps you move toward health. As mentioned previously, going over your CTC each week takes up the last 20 minutes of the group meeting. A CTC puts laser focus toward responding to a challenge in the coming week. This challenge could center around a stressful situation that needs to be resolved or that you will be facing. It could be steps that need to be implemented to get off the FASTER Scale (Appendix II and Lesson Four), or it could be implementing a certain healthy activity into daily life, such as going to the gym to exercise several days a week. These questions should be filled out within 24 hours of the weekly group meeting.

How has holding each other accountable to following through on each other's CTC throughout the week been going? Don't forget, you need the help of the group to follow through on your commitments of living in reality and restoration. The battle of renewing the mind must be fought and won on a daily basis, and can't be won alone. Without a battle plan of healthy behaviors, you will default to old unhealthy coping behaviors. Below are the questions to create your CTC. An example of good responses is given. A blank copy is also provided in Appendix II.

① What area do you need to change or what challenge are you facing next week?
I need to stop procrastinating on studying for a test I have next week. I really need to get an A on the test or I may fail the class, so I have been really worried.

② What will it cost you emotionally if you do change?
I will have to face my fears of failure if I work hard and get a bad grade on the test. I will have to be disciplined and ask for help from others.

③ What fear do you feel with what you have chosen to change?
I fear getting a bad grade on the test and feeling worthless. I fear not having what it takes to get a good grade even if I work hard.

④ What will it cost you if you don't change?
I will probably get stressed out and angry the night before the test due to studying like crazy, which will lead me down the FASTER Scale to Relapse. I won't do the best I can do and see that I probably am smart enough to get a good grade if I work hard. I will also probably fail the class if I don't study hard.

⑤ What is your plan to maintain your restoration regarding these changes?
I will study for 30 minutes each day at 9 am until the day of the test. Before studying, I will remind myself that God has gifted me with intelligence and a good memory.

⑥ Who will keep you accountable to this commitment? What are the details of your accountability for this week? What questions should they ask you?
Joe and Jake from my Living Free group will text me at 9 am each day when I begin studying for the test and encourage me. If I don't hear from them, I will text them to let them know I began studying. They can ask me if I have been studying each day at 9 am for 30 minutes and what fears I've been processing that may be driving the desire to procrastinate.

ACCOUNTABILITY PHONE CALLS

Let's revisit accountability phone calls. How are those going?

At the beginning of this process, you committed to initiating at least three phone calls, not text messages, with other people in your group on different days throughout the week. The purpose is to break isolation and check in about your current status on the FASTER Scale (Appendix II, Lesson Four, and the *Living Free Journal*), double binds (Lesson Four), and fulfilling your Commitment to Change. Since sexual sin happens in secrecy, these calls help you develop a lifestyle of constant vulnerability throughout the week. Phone calls are a great opportunity to process what's going on in life and ask for help in living a life of restoration.

If you call another member and they don't pick up, leave a voicemail sharing what is going on. Take the opportunity to begin to process and break isolation, but don't count this as one of your three calls for the week.

Your phone calls should last anywhere from five minutes to thirty minutes, depending on the available time and what is going on in each others' lives. If you're limited by time, be sure to tell the other person how much time you have to talk. If your conversation is cut short and you need to process more that is going on in life, call another group member. Here are the following five questions to check in with one another.

1. Where are you on the FASTER Scale?

2. What double bind are you facing? How can you practically make the harder choice?
(Remember, there is always an easier choice and a harder choice. Moving toward health usually involves the harder choice.)

3. Where are you on your Commitment to Change you made at the end of our last meeting?

4. What challenges are you facing this week? Who will you allow to help you face them?

5. What is your plan to maintain your restoration regarding these challenges? Is the plan you chose at group still applicable? If not, what do you need to pay attention to right now?

NATURAL CONSEQUENCES

Have you been sticking to the natural consequences you have in place after each relapse? Implementing natural consequences is not a way of experiencing punishment for sin or paying penance. We know Christ bore all of our sin on the cross and there is no wrath of God or condemnation left for us who have surrendered our lives to Christ. Natural consequences are simply a way of experiencing and associating our sin with the natural pain that it causes others and ourselves.

So far, you may have implemented getting rid of your computer or smartphone, or only being allowed to access the Internet in public places as a natural consequence. Your leader can refer to the Implementing Consequences portion of the *Leader's Guide* to explain this in further detail. Make any adjustments needed to the first two consequences from Lesson Three and come up with two more below. It's time to take things up a notch and implement something you don't want to do. One idea is giving an additional $20 to a charity every time you relapse.

1. _____

2. _____

3. _____

4. _____

GROUP GUIDELINES[1]

Remember these from Lesson One? Read through them and think about how your group is doing. Guidelines are essential to create a safe environment for open and honest conversations during group time. Read through the guidelines together at your next group meeting. Briefly discuss what each means, and get verbal buy-in from everyone once again. The guidelines should also be reviewed when anyone new joins the group. Some groups will read the guidelines out loud quarterly, some once a month, some weekly. If you haven't done so, you may want to also print them and display them during group meetings as a reminder of how the group operates. These guidelines are straightforward and give you the basics that allow you and the other men to have a great group experience.

LIVING FREE GROUP GUIDELINES

CONFIDENTIALITY IS ESSENTIAL!
What's said in the group is not shared outside the group.

SELF-FOCUS
Speak only for yourself. Avoid giving advice unless given permission.

BE PRESENT
Refrain from texting, being on your phone, or using your computer for things unrelated to the group meeting.

LIMIT SHARING
We want everyone to have a chance to share.

RESPECT OTHERS
Let everyone find his own answers.

REGULAR ATTENDANCE
Meetings should only be missed in the event of an emergency. Let your leader or co-leader know if you can't attend a meeting.

COMMITMENT TO ACCOUNTABILITY
Make a minimum of three phone call contacts a week; if you have relapsed in the last week, then a daily contact is recommended.

LISTEN RESPECTFULLY
No side conversations.

TAKE OWNERSHIP AND BE RESPONSIBLE
If you feel uncomfortable with anything, talk with your leader or co-leader, or your group.

STAY ON THE SUBJECT/QUESTIONS
Avoid off-topic conversations and comments.

HOMEWORK COMPLETION
Allow 30 minutes per day to complete homework. If you don't do your homework, you won't see healing, and you won't be able to participate while the group is processing their homework.

> LET GOD WORK! HE WILL NOT REST UNTIL THE WORK
> HE HAS STARTED IN YOU IS COMPLETED.

---

1. Roberts, Dr. Ted. *Seven Pillars of Freedom Workbook*. 4th ed., Gresham, OR, Pure Desire, 2015. 22.

We have reviewed several of the tools you've been using in this process. Lastly, flip back to Lesson One and look at the Checklist For A Healthy Group at the end of the lesson. Were you able to answer yes to every question on the Checklist? If not, share why. Write out your response below and be sure to discuss it at your next group meeting.

_____
_____
_____
_____
_____
_____
_____
_____
_____
_____
_____
_____
_____
_____
_____
_____

ASSIGNMENTS FOR NEXT TIME

① **Look back to Lesson Three and the three things God may want to do as a result of your journey. Take several minutes to visualize those experiences.**

② **Read through the sections on the previous pages about the Phone Calls, Commitment to Change, and the Check-in. Think about the questions asked and how your group is utilizing these tools. Think about what you or your group may be able to do better to get the most out of these tools. Be sure to talk about this at your next group meeting.**

③ **Make any adjustments needed to the Natural Consequences you have in place and come up with two more. List all four in the space provided.**

④ **Read through the Group Guidelines together at your next group meeting. Briefly discuss what each means, and get verbal buy-in from everyone once again.**

⑤ **Write out your response about the Checklist For A Healthy Group in the space above. Be sure to discuss your response at next week's meeting.**

LESSON TWELVE
IDENTIFYING THE PAIN

This critical lesson will require you to look at the pain in your life that is driving your addictive behavior. This cannot and should not be done alone. We won't sugar coat it; pain hurts. But misunderstanding the purpose and role of pain and God's intention for it hurts more.

The healing that you desire will come as you participate in your Living Free group. It is here that you will process and face your pain, and put the skills you are learning into practice. The Apostle Paul got it right. We alone are responsible for our own conduct, but we help carry each other's struggles in a healing community.

> *Share each other's burdens, and in this way obey the law of Christ.*
> *…For we are each responsible for our own conduct.*
> Galatians 6:2,5b (NLT)

Paul, in Romans 12:15, tells us to cry with those who are crying and to celebrate with those who are celebrating. In the healing process you will be in both camps before you are finished.

Typically, when we think of pain, we tend to think of physical pain. But pain has many forms. Pain can also be relational, emotional, and spiritual. Circle any of the following behaviors or emotions that you consider painful:

- Lonely
- Ache
- Empty
- Humiliation
- Worried
- Uncomfortable
- Annoyed
- Bored
- Stress
- Disappointed
- Agony
- Anxious
- Guilty
- Jealous
- Insignificant
- Relationships
- Hurt
- Irritation
- Anger
- Tired of it
- Troubled
- Discomfort
- Sadness
- Embarrassment
- Concerned
- Ashamed
- Distressed
- Futility

All of these words and phrases represent some form of pain. Did you know that pain is actually a gift God has given you? It blew my mind the first time I heard that pain is a gift. Let me show you what I mean. Adam and Eve have just eaten of the forbidden fruit and are experiencing fear and shame for the first time. Look at their response:

> *But the Lord God called to the man and said to him, "Where are you?"*
> *And he said, "I heard the sound of you in the garden, and I was afraid,*
> *because I was naked, and I hid myself."*
> Genesis 3:9-10 (ESV)

> Just like the check engine light on your car telling you that your car is low on oil, your pain is an indicator that something needs attention.

NOTES

This mystery gift from God is telling them that something is drastically wrong. They had the profound experience of the first therapy session with God as their counselor. God certainly didn't ask His question because He didn't know the answer. He asked it for their benefit. Pain in the form of fear and shame was communicating to Adam and Eve that something was not right and needed to be addressed. It was telling them they needed to move back into relationship with God and each other. Because that is the purpose of pain, it is crucial you learn to see pain from God's perspective. Pain is meant to drive you into the arms of your Heavenly Father who longs to comfort you while you tell Him all about what hurts.

Every one of the words listed on the previous page tells you that something is out of order between you and God or you and others. That is how pain is a gift. Just like the check engine light on your car telling you that your car is low on oil, your pain is an indicator that something needs attention. Hopefully, you've learned to respect and respond to that check engine light. You will need to respect and respond to what your pain is telling you too.

There are people and circumstances that we can't control and sometimes life just happens to us. Grief is a great example. You can try to stuff it, run from it, or bitterly embrace it. But it is beyond our control. We have no say about when loved ones die, when a natural disaster strikes, or a whole host of other tragic life events.

In the spring of 1996, Jerry Sittser and his family were traveling home from a mission trip when their car was hit head-on by a drunken driver. The crash changed Jerry's life. He lost his wife, mother, and daughter. He was severely injured and still had the responsibility for his three other children.

After he came home from the hospital, he did not do well, even though he knew there was life before the trauma and there would be life after the trauma. Please hear his words: "If normal, natural, reversible loss is like a broken limb, then catastrophic loss is like an amputation. The results are permanent, the impact incalculable, the consequences cumulative. Each new day forces one to face some devastating dimension of the loss. It creates a whole new context for one's life."[1]

Jerry began to have a recurring nightmare. In this nightmare, he would be on an endless beach with the sun low in the early evening sky. Darkness seemed to be gathering in the eastern sky and he feared being swallowed up in the darkness. Jerry began to run as hard as he could toward the setting sun hoping that he would be able to stay in the daylight. His nightmare ended in stark terror just as the sun set below the horizon and he was immersed in the darkness. After these nightmares, Jerry would be exhausted and drenched in perspiration because he had actually thrashed in bed as he "ran" toward the setting sun.

He had this horrible dream every night for several weeks. This nightmare was consuming him in almost every way whether he was awake or asleep. After several weeks, Jerry made a great choice. He called his sister and told her of the dream.

---

1. Jerry L. Sittser, *A Grace Disguised: How the Soul Grows Through Loss* (Grand Rapids: Zondervan, 2004) 32.

She responded with an incredibly insightful comment. She told her brother that nobody could catch the setting sun; she told him to turn, face the darkness, even run into the darkness, for in doing so he would catch the rising sun.

Jerry would not have broken the stranglehold of this nightmare if he hadn't shared with his sister. Her words apply to all of us. We must turn and face whatever we fear the most and run into the darkness knowing that there, Christ will meet us and heal our pain.

Note: I highly recommend that you read Jerry Sittser's monumental book, "A Grace Disguised."

Healing from emotional pain comes from allowing it to work through you. The key is to neither embrace nor deny the pain; rather, it is about allowing the pain to wash over you as you process it with God and community.

Think of pain as the ocean tide. You can't control its comings or goings; it is what it is and each wave that washes up on the beach is unique. Likewise, emotional pain will be unique to every one of us. Pain can come with any kind of loss. It can be death such as Jerry Sittser experienced because of a tragic auto accident. It can be the loss of relationship, loss of a job, loss of freedom or mobility, or even loss of self-respect.

Remember, the only way to stay stuck in painful emotion is to stuff it down and avoid it. As you begin to process your pain you need to understand that you can't undo what has been done and you can't stay where you've been. You must go forward into the unknown. God is speaking to you out of that unknown place and you must listen for His voice and follow His guidance. He will lead you through your pain as you process it with Him and others. As you process your pain you may experience a bunch of different emotions. You'll feel anger. You'll want to deny that something actually happened. You might feel numb or depressed. You might feel several of these at once. There is no set pattern to moving through pain, but at some point it won't have the hold on you it once had because you won't fear it so much. You'll also discover that wherever there is pain in your life God is there in the midst to comfort you. Paul once again says it best:

> *For our present troubles are small and won't last very long. Yet they produce for us a glory that vastly outweighs them and will last forever! So we don't look at the troubles we can see now; rather, we fix our gaze on things that cannot be seen. For the things we see now will soon be gone, but the things we cannot see will last forever.*
> 2 Corinthians 4:17-18 (NLT)

Your situation may not seem so light, but Paul is letting us know that if we stay the course, we will end up in a place we cannot imagine. Hang in there. There is true hope for you as you work through the pain and allow Christ to heal you.

Here is a four step cycle I use for processing my pain rather than getting stuck in it. I call it, "Coming Up for Air." When I feel like I'm drowning this helps me emotionally breathe again.

We must turn and face whatever we fear the most and run into the darkness knowing that there, Christ will meet us and heal our pain.

NOTES

AWARENESS

Reactive and/or Painful Emotions → Become aware: stop and reflect.

IDENTIFY

Break isolation. → Ask, "Why am I feeling these emotions?" → Identify your fears, false beliefs, and perceptions.

REFLECT AND SORT

Pray and sort it out with God and others. → Commit to changing direction and make a plan that will help you move toward the light.

RESPOND

Meditate and reflect on truth. + Follow through on your plan. = Stay in the light and walk in step with the Spirit.

AWARENESS

① The first step is awareness. Stop and reflect. Learn to catch your reactive/painful emotions or temptations before you act on them. Become a more reflective person in light of your emotions instead of reactive.

② Develop the ability to stand apart from your negative moods and painful emotions. Be aware of your emotional state. Remember you are not your negative moods and painful emotions. Make a distinction between what you feel and who you are. This is a practice called differentiation.

③ Reflect and evaluate the importance and worth of those around you. Do not take your pain out on a person God greatly values and loves.

IDENTIFY

Determine what thoughts and/or false beliefs are producing your painful/reactive emotions or temptations. Remember, emotions are simply responses to something you are thinking and believing. This will be difficult at first, but as you become more reflective and get in touch with what you are feeling, this process will become easier.

REFLECT AND SORT WITH GOD AND MEMBERS OF HIS FAMILY

1. Meditate and reflect on what's true about you in light of the gospel. Allow God and others to help you process your emotions. Relationships are critical to helping sort out your negative moods and temptations.

2. Talk to God about what you are feeling and why. He is concerned about your inner life. Think through your circumstances in light of what is true of God, you, and others. Ask God to help you identify false beliefs that you may be responding to emotionally.

3. Allow God and His truth to pervade your thinking. This is especially important if you grew up in an unhealthy home. Start building a treasury of positive images, experiences, and thoughts in your heart. Use your imagination to fill your heart with positive emotions by replacing painful images with pleasant ones.

4. Sort things out with God through prayer until your heart is filled with peace.

5. Make a practical plan that will help you move out of the darkness and into the light. This plan will help you to resolve conflicts and problems. Ask for help from others to follow through on this plan.

6. Experience the power and beauty of sorting out what is going on in your inner life with a community of trusted brothers and sisters who know God's heart and perspectives.

RESPOND

1. Be a responder to what the Spirit has shown you. This means you need to take action.

2. Meditate and reflect on what you have discovered about yourself and your responses/reactions.

3. Follow through on the plan you have made to help you live in the light.

4. The combination of reflecting on truth and taking action on your growing self-awareness will help you to live in the light and walk in step with the Spirit.

5. Practice these steps until they become your automatic response and approach to confronting your negative moods and painful/reactive emotions.

It's time to do some soul searching with the help of the Holy Spirit. All of us carry wounds within us that we pick up in life. These wounds need to be processed with the help of God and others so you can move through them and experience the healing that you long for. As you work through this lesson, continually ask God to bring you His comfort as you walk with him into these painful memories.

Look back over your life and identify painful experiences, especially from childhood. These events are like rocks being thrown into a calm lake where they left a splash mark on your soul. You need to identify what part of that painful moment you are responsible for and what part of it you need to let go. Take some time to think through the effects of that rock on the important people in your life. The last question is about how that rock affects your life today. This is the ripple effect from the rock that was thrown so many years ago. Unless you process the pain of these wounds the ripples will continue to surface within you for the rest of your life. Some ripple effects never go away, but with the help of God and others they will no longer control you.

THE 10 MOST PAINFUL EXPERIENCES IN MY LIFE

After you have completed listing each event, rank these moments from #1 most painful to #10 least painful. Examples of painful experiences could be the emotional absence of your dad or your parents' divorce. *Note: these events may have been recurring or happened once.*

___ (RANK) PAINFUL EXPERIENCE _____

1. What part of the pain am I responsible for, and what part of the pain do I need to let go? Who do I need to forgive?

2. How did this event affect the important people in my life?

3. How has this event affected life for me today?

___ (RANK) PAINFUL EXPERIENCE _____

1. What part of the pain am I responsible for, and what part of the pain do I need to let go? Who do I need to forgive?

2. How did this event affect the important people in my life?

3. How has this event affected life for me today?

___ (RANK) PAINFUL EXPERIENCE _____

1. What part of the pain am I responsible for, and what part of the pain do I need to let go? Who do I need to forgive?

2. How did this event affect the important people in my life?

3. How has this event affected life for me today?

___ (RANK) PAINFUL EXPERIENCE _____

1 What part of the pain am I responsible for, and what part of the pain do I need to let go? Who do I need to forgive?

2 How did this event affect the important people in my life?

3 How has this event affected life for me today?

___ (RANK) PAINFUL EXPERIENCE _____

1 What part of the pain am I responsible for, and what part of the pain do I need to let go? Who do I need to forgive?

2 How did this event affect the important people in my life?

3 How has this event affected life for me today?

___ (RANK) PAINFUL EXPERIENCE _____

1 What part of the pain am I responsible for, and what part of the pain do I need to let go? Who do I need to forgive?

2 How did this event affect the important people in my life?

3 How has this event affected life for me today?

___ (RANK) PAINFUL EXPERIENCE _____

1 What part of the pain am I responsible for, and what part of the pain do I need to let go? Who do I need to forgive?

2 How did this event affect the important people in my life?

3 How has this event affected life for me today?

___ (RANK) PAINFUL EXPERIENCE _____

1 What part of the pain am I responsible for, and what part of the pain do I need to let go? Who do I need to forgive?

2 How did this event affect the important people in my life?

3 How has this event affected life for me today?

___ (RANK) PAINFUL EXPERIENCE _____

1 What part of the pain am I responsible for, and what part of the pain do I need to let go? Who do I need to forgive?

2 How did this event affect the important people in my life?

3 How has this event affected life for me today?

___ (RANK) PAINFUL EXPERIENCE _____

1 What part of the pain am I responsible for, and what part of the pain do I need to let go? Who do I need to forgive?

2 How did this event affect the important people in my life?

3 How has this event affected life for me today?

Now let's put the pieces together and look for any themes in your story. Look at what you have written about painful experiences and answer the following questions. Don't worry if you struggle with this. As you share this lesson with your Living Free group, they will help you identify themes in your story.

❓ What themes are in your story and what are the core (limbic) messages that you have come to believe as a result of these themes?

Example: a theme of rejection runs through my story. I've made sense of that by believing the lie that no one cares for me so it doesn't matter how I treat myself.

1. _____

2. _____

3. _____

4. _____

5. _____

❓ As a result of these beliefs, what life issues do you struggle with today? Anger? Trusting authority figures? Sense of worthlessness at times? Or _____?

Example: I am overweight and can't stop looking at porn. No one else cares for me, so why should I?

1. _____

2. _____

3. _____

4. _____

5. _____

You may have discovered, or already known, that you are struggling to forgive people who have hurt you in the past. A huge step of faith will be to release those people into the Lord's hands, so you can become free to move forward into healing. Write down the names of people from your list that you are struggling to forgive or any other names that come to mind. When you are in a safe place, pray the following prayer for each person that you are ready to forgive. You may not yet be ready to forgive someone for what they did to you and that is okay. But you will need to forgive that person before healing can take place. Forgiveness is not the same as trust. By forgiving, you are releasing that person to Jesus and releasing the right to be judge and jury over them. But that does not mean you need to trust them. They need to be a trustworthy person for you to trust them. Be honest with Jesus and the guys in your group about where you're at with those people and let Him move you toward forgiveness in His timing.

> *Lord Jesus, I want to confess that I have not loved, but have resented certain people and have unforgiveness in my heart. Lord, I call upon You to help me forgive. Now I choose to forgive and release all judgments against (read the names of the people you wrote down). I forgive and accept myself, in the name of Jesus. Amen.*

What may God be saying to you through these exercises and the struggles of your life? This is not about tying a pretty bow on your story and pretending everything is okay when it isn't. It's about seeing your story through God's eyes. God never wastes our pain if we allow Him to heal us and use it. As I looked closely at my core beliefs and the life issues that I struggle with, it became apparent that I was ultimately battling with a huge father wound.

As I finally came to grips with that fact in my life, the Lord began to help me see myself from His perspective. I was stunned with what He showed me. The Heavenly Father spoke to my soul and declared, "You are My son and I long to celebrate life and adventure with you. I have created you as a mighty warrior with a tender heart! I have called you to nurture men and lead them into life!"

Take some time and listen to what God would say to you about your deep pain and struggles. Where do you see Him in your story? What would Jesus say to you about what you experienced? What would He say to you about who you are from His perspective in light of these events? How might God want to heal you and use your pain for good?

Spend at least 15 minutes asking God to bring some answers to these questions. Write down and draw what words or images your Heavenly Father speaks over you in the space on the next page.

ASSIGNMENTS FOR NEXT TIME

① Complete the 10 Most Painful Experiences in My Life exercise and be prepared to share your results next week with your group.

Be sure to respond with compassion and encouragement as each member shares his pain. *Note: It will take two to three weeks for each member to share and work through their painful experiences in group. Please allow time to do this before you move on to Lesson Thirteen.*

② As you work through this lesson, take 15 minutes each day to sit quietly and ask the Lord what He would say to you about what you are processing. Be sure to utilize the four step process mentioned in this lesson as you work through your pain.

③ Continue to process these painful experiences throughout the year. Keep working through each moment by processing with God and your group, journaling, and moving toward the forgiveness of those who have wronged you.

LESSON THIRTEEN
SELF-CARE

Healing from addiction requires more than stopping bad or difficult behaviors. Rather, it requires embracing a whole new way of living and redefining who we really are. One of the casualties of investing in our addiction has been our ability to love well. As a result, intimacy with God and others is negatively impacted. We have grown to focus on ourselves more than others. This is not a good thing. This means we tend to place ourselves and our desires over everything and everyone else. I have yet to meet a person in bondage or addiction who started the healing process with a clear sense of loving well.

> *And he said to him, "You shall love the Lord your God with all your heart and with all your soul and with all your mind. This is the great and first commandment. And a second is like it: You shall love your neighbor as yourself. On these two commandments depend all the Law and the Prophets."*
> Matthew 22:37-40 (ESV)

It's fascinating how Jesus stresses the need to love ourselves. It's a key to being able to love others well. If you don't know how to love yourself in a healthy way, you won't know how to love others in a healthy way either. This means your ministry toward others will only be as effective as your ministry toward yourself.

God has called us His temple. The word temple has two choices in the Greek. The first is about a building used for religious functions. The second is the place where God's presence dwells. It is the second definition that Paul intended in his words to the Christians at Corinth.

> *Do you not know that you are a temple of God and that the Spirit of God dwells in you? If any man destroys the temple of God, God will destroy him, for the temple of God is holy, and that is what you are.*
> 1 Corinthians 3:16-17 (NASB)

This verse is both comforting and convicting. It's comforting because God is saying that you and I are so valuable that, "if anyone harms you, I will destroy them." It reveals not only that we have value to Him, but also that He desires to protect us. For people who have lived in isolation it is awkward and even uncomfortable to have God be so loving and intimate with us. Yet, in our heart of hearts this is what we have longed for.

This passage is also very convicting. Paul uses the phrase "if any man" destroys the temple (us) then He will destroy that person. When I look back on my life, or even evaluate it now, I am the one person who has done the most damage and neglect to the temple that is my body. In God's great love for us He actually lets us reap what we sow.

> Your Heavenly Father looks at you and sees you as being worth the life of His Son, and His Son agrees.

NOTES

Do not be deceived: God is not mocked, for whatever one sows, that will he also reap. For the one who sows to his own flesh will from the flesh reap corruption, but the one who sows to the Spirit will from the Spirit reap eternal life. And let us not grow weary of doing good, for in due season we will reap, if we do not give up.
Galatians 6:7-9 (ESV)

Oops, now I have done it; God wants to love and protect me and I mess it up. Even now, I can hear the enemy using Scripture to accuse me, just as he used Scripture to accuse Jesus. Yes, I can almost hear an audible voice saying, "Anyone who isn't with me opposes me." (Matthew 12:30 NLT) The New Living Translation of the verse is even more stark in its comment:

Anyone who isn't with me opposes me, and anyone who isn't working with me is actually working against me.
Matthew 12:30 (NLT)

We need to heed this verse, but our Father is not just waiting for us to fail Him so that He can punish us. He is not the mythical Viking god Thor, with his hammer and lightning bolt ready to take us out because we are His enemies. We are His children who are broken and in need of His grace and power. I am reminded of another verse penned by the Apostle Paul:

Each time he said, "My grace is all you need. My power works best in weakness." So now I am glad to boast about my weaknesses, so that the power of Christ can work through me.
2 Corinthians 12:9a (NLT)

That's clear enough for me. I know that I am weak spiritually and I believe that God's grace is ultimately all I need. His strength will be revealed in the acknowledgment of my weakness and my dependence on Him. Remember that we are moving toward accepting life on His terms. Therefore, we need to risk learning to lean on Him. He won't let us down. We're His kids and He is our perfect Father who is on our side.

The Father and the Son mutually agreed that the Son would give up His life on your behalf. Do you realize that this makes you worth the life of the Son to our Heavenly Father? Your Heavenly Father looks at you and sees you as being worth the life of His Son, and His Son agrees. Together they are saying to you, "We love you so much! You are so precious to us that we'll even sacrifice ourselves for you." Wow! When I came to that realization, I was so humbled and in awe of them both.

Do you value yourself like the Father and Son value you? If you are truly finding value in yourself, you will become someone who is learning healthy self-care; that is, healthy ways of coping with the stress and strains of life. As we move toward self-care, and better stewardship of the life God has given us, we will have greater intimacy with Christ and a more satisfying life.

What are the healthy ways you cope and nurture (love) yourself?

_____
_____
_____
_____

One of the great battles in learning to value and care for yourself is over self-judgments. How do you justify being critical, having contempt for yourself, or even self-hatred? Please list below those judgments you have held against yourself and your rationale for believing them.

_____
_____
_____
_____
_____

NURTURING OURSELVES SPIRITUALLY

Paul tells us in 2 Corinthians 5 that to be absent from the body is to be present with Christ. Think about that; my body is only a vessel that allows me to move around this world. My body is a part of my being, but it is not the totality of who I am. In fact, my eternity is tied to my spirituality, not how much I know or how much I do. It is the state of being in relationship with Him. We are not human doings, we are human beings.

In Revelation 2, Jesus is giving a status report on various churches. When He gets to the church in Ephesus, He can't find fault with their behaviors. Now that is incredible. The King of Kings couldn't find fault with any of their behaviors. What a marvelous church! But Jesus does expose their area of need. He tells the church at Ephesus that they have abandoned their first love. Unless they repent (turn around) and do the things that they did at first, this church would lose its authority and influence within the Christian community. Paraphrased, Jesus was telling them, "You have been so focused on doing things right, that you have lost sight of the point. Spend more time with me instead of worrying about doing things right." They had a serious battle with perfectionism and self-righteousness.

Now, that gets my attention. I know that I am often guilty of perfectionism and self-righteousness. How about you? I am guessing that many of you, like me, get caught up being more of a "Martha" than a "Mary" in life. Martha complained that Mary wasn't helping, and Jesus praised Mary for wanting to spend time in His presence.

> *Now as they went on their way, Jesus entered a village. And a woman named Martha welcomed him into her house. And she had a sister called Mary, who sat at the Lord's feet and listened to his teaching. But Martha was distracted with much serving. And she went up to him and said, "Lord, do you not care that my sister has left me to serve alone? Tell her then to help me." But the Lord answered her, "Martha, Martha, you are anxious and troubled about many things, but one thing is necessary. Mary has chosen the good portion, which will not be taken away from her."*
> Luke 10:38-42 (ESV)

The good portion is spending time in the presence of God. How are you doing with that?

TWO SIMPLE STEPS WILL MOVE YOU TOWARD INTIMACY WITH GOD.
First, purposely choose to dedicate 15 minutes to an hour, not to devotions in the classical sense, but to be quiet in His presence. Only read as the Holy Spirit leads you; keep paper and pen close by so that you can write down the promptings that come from being in His presence.

The second step is to journal. I know, I know. It's hard to embrace journaling. But please give me a chance to state my case. In this fast-paced world we need some regulators, something to slow us down. That is the role of journaling. It slows us down, allows us to think and gives us a chance to become more self-aware. Journaling charts our progress over time and will allow you to create a wonderful map of your recovery journey. I'd encourage you to look at the FASTER Scale as a way to journal out what you're feeling. This will help you to use this tool at a deeper level and avoid the trap of doing it out of obligation.

SWORD DEVOTIONAL: LEARN TO JOURNAL IN RESPONSE TO THE WORD OF GOD[1]
Practicing the SWORD Devotional will help you tie to Scripture the truths you discover. In other words, you will be touched but unchanged if journaling God's Word is not part of your experience. This process involves some of the most significant renewing of your mind you have ever experienced, which only happens when you encounter the supernatural power of God's Word in your heart and not just in your head.

The term SWORD (Scripture. Wait. Observe. Request. Dedicate.) can be helpful in the journaling process. It reminds us that this is about spiritual warfare. This isn't just about sinning less; this is war. We must approach each day of the rest of our lives with the weapon of the Word of God in our hearts and on our tongues. The steps for doing this devotional are at the end of this lesson.

NURTURING OURSELVES MENTALLY

How do you think outside your box? Scientists tell us that the quality of our life and the strength of your brain is partially tied to keeping your brain stimulated with new mental experiences.

Mentally, are you in a rut? Do you study or have interest in only one or two areas, or do you have some variety? Even when it comes to reading my Bible, I love to switch to other translations regularly because the new phraseology allows me a fresh look at familiar passages.

I love to read. I read many books and try to always have a book on hand. Some are just brain candy and others make me really think. Books are a great alternative to becoming zoned out on your phone.

Mental self-care isn't just about books; it's also about hobbies. I've discovered it myself and heard it from other guys as well, "I'm amazed at how much time I get back now that I'm not acting out or lost in fantasy all the time." If you've got time on your hands you'll struggle with being bored. A hobby is a great way to fill that void. You're going to have to replace your current hobby of sexually acting out with something a bit more productive and nurturing.

I decided to teach myself how to wet shave using a double-edged blade and a shaving brush after seeing it on a list of hobbies. Turns out, it's an excellent way to practice self-care principles. I've noticed that if I'm in a rush, not thoughtful about what I'm doing, or I'm distracted, I cut myself. But if I go slowly and am thoughtful and present, enjoy the process, and don't put too much pressure on myself, then I get an amazing shave and feel great as I start my day. I've also learned to settle for an excellent shave instead of a perfect shave. Striving for perfection only left my face feeling raw from too many passes of the blade. This has been a great way for me to remind myself what good self-care looks like.

---

1. Roberts, Ted. *Seven Pillars of Freedom Workbook.* 4th ed. Gresham, OR: Pure Desire, 2015. Print. 95.

Take a look at this list of 50 manly hobbies and circle the ones you have interest in.

- Archery
- Astronomy
- Backpacking
- Ballroom Dancing
- Birdwatching
- Body Building/ Weight Lifting
- Bouldering
- Chess
- Coffee Roasting/ Brewing
- Collectibles
- Cooking
- Darts
- Drawing/Painting
- Fishing
- Fly Fishing
- Flying
- Gardening
- Geocaching
- Golfing
- Grilling
- Hiking
- Hunting
- Improving Your Memory
- Learn To Code
- Learning a Foreign Language
- Leather-working
- Letter Writing
- Magic (Card Tricks)
- Model Building
- Motorcycling
- Mountain Biking
- Musical Instruments
- Off-roading
- Photography
- Playing Pool
- Martial Arts
- Reading
- River Rafting/ Kayaking
- Road Biking
- Rock Climbing
- Running
- Scuba Diving
- Shooting/ Marksmanship
- Skiing/ Snowboarding
- Smoking Meats
- Tomahawk/ Hatchet Throwing
- Vinyl Records
- Wet Shaving
- Whittling
- Woodworking

NURTURING OURSELVES PHYSICALLY

God has given you stewardship over your life. Does the life you live own you or do you own the life that you are living? Breaking out of isolation, passivity, and procrastination will set you free of having circumstances owning your life. Instead, you can begin to take ownership, with the guidance of God, and begin to live life in a way that glorifies Him and blesses you. If you don't take responsibility for yourself, you will always have those people around who are more than happy to run your life for you.

Nurturing ourselves physically is not just about exercise and eating healthy. Though they play a role, there is much more. Do you regularly go to the doctor and dentist for both preventative and restorative checkups? Do you regularly get enough sleep? How do you work through stress in healthy ways? How is your basic hygiene? Do you take your medications regularly?

Stress is behind a vast majority of the obstacles that keep you from living a healthy life. The busyness of life also adds to stress and we need to learn to live free from the tyranny of the urgent. Slowing down and learning to relax in your faith and lifestyle will bring you to a place where you have the opportunity to be renewed.

Four basic ways to physically care for yourself involve nutrition, exercise, water, and sleep. Think of this like reading the daily N.E.W.S. Checking this N.E.W.S. is better for your health than checking the local and national news. That news can give you heartburn and headaches. If you're struggling in any of these areas, the good news is that it is never too late to get started. Write down an evaluation of how you are doing in each of these areas and some ideas of how you can improve. I included a few suggestions in some of the categories.

NUTRITION	EXERCISE	WATER	SLEEP	OTHER
		Drink 1 oz of water per pound of bodyweight per day.	Turn off media 30 minutes before bedtime. Go to bed by midnight or earlier daily. Minimum 7 hours of sleep	Basic hygiene practices. Trim nails, brush teeth twice daily, shower regularly, etc. Regular Dr visits.

NURTURING OURSELVES RELATIONALLY

Then the Lord God said, "It is not good that the man should be alone; I will make him a helper fit for him."
Genesis 2:18 (ESV)

We were made for relationships. God says so. Period. End of story. If we don't give ourselves permission to develop great friendships, we miss out on a sense of belonging and knowing we are truly loved. Life will merely be about existing, which is not what God has called us to.

What is your priority to develop friendships? I know that if it weren't for the friends that God sent my way during my healing, I would not have made it.

Does this sound familiar? You spend hours upon hours on some social media platform, and yet you feel more lonely and disconnected than ever. Despite having thousands of "friends" online and knowing the intimate details of what a classmate from several years ago ate for dinner last night, you find it hard to make time to connect with your closest friends.

My friendships are a priority in my life. I have friends I go to coffee shops with and we simply enjoy hanging out and investing in each other. I have a small group that I attend weekly. These people are not just members of a men's group; they are the core and most important piece of my ongoing recovery. They are wonderful friends who are the hands and feet of Jesus in my life.

FIVE TIPS TO BUILDING GREAT FRIENDSHIPS

1. Take a genuine interest in others.
   A. Practice listening and asking good questions.
   B. Focus on remembering details about people you spend time with, especially their names.
   C. My wife has expressed how much she wants me to "listen with my face." This means I need to put away my phone and make eye contact with her.

2. Offer to help people with no strings attached.
   A. Find out what is important to someone and ask if there is any way you can help them achieve their goal.
   B. Go the extra mile to not just hang out with someone, but try to make them happy, too. Know someone's favorite kind of coffee? Buy them a coffee and bring it to them just to show you care for them.

3. Mix up your routines.
   A. Get out of your comfort zone. How are you supposed to meet anyone new if you don't go somewhere outside of your normal routine?
   B. This will force you to be intentional. If you're the new guy trying to make new friends, you'll have to work to make connections.

4. Reconnect with long-distance friends or old acquaintances.
   A. You already have shared experiences with them, so it will be easier to connect with them than a stranger.
   B. Scan their social media pages and then ask questions about their life, building on your previous connection.

5. Talk to everyone.
   A. Say hello and acknowledge people with a smile. You never know who you might meet in line at the grocery store. Look for opportunities throughout your day to show the love of Jesus to people and initiate spiritual conversations.
   B. One thing I'll do is thank developers for a helpful app they created. I'll share with them how I might use their app more if they made certain tweaks. I've actually become friends with someone on the other side of the country by using this approach.

ASSIGNMENTS FOR NEXT TIME

① Practice the SWORD devotional every morning this week.

There are 31 chapters in the book of Proverbs. Read the chapter related to the day of the month for each day this week. Take 15 minutes each day to work through the devotion. For example, if today is the 15th, then do the SWORD devotion on the 15th chapter of Proverbs.

② Self-care goals: write down at least one goal and one or two action steps for each of the four self-care areas: Spiritual, Mental, Physical, and Relational.

_____
_____
_____
_____
_____
_____
_____
_____
_____
_____
_____
_____
_____
_____
_____
_____
_____
_____
_____
_____

③ Pull out your Battle Plan from Lesson Eight and add these self-care goals to what you have already written for Circle One.

Keep your Battle Plan accessible to frequently remind yourself about your priorities. Focusing on your self-care goals will help give you a huge boost in avoiding Relapse and building a balanced life.

④ Be prepared to share your updated Battle Plan and how you experienced the SWORD drill at the next group.

STEPS FOR DOING THE SWORD DEVOTIONAL

SCRIPTURE
Which verse or group of verses stood out to you in your reading? Write them out in your own words below.

_____
_____
_____
_____
_____

WAIT
Take three deep breaths and wait on the Holy Spirit. Put aside any thoughts and worries of the day. Meditate on the Scripture. Read the verse(s) above out loud, slowly, and attentively. Then pause to let it sink in. Let the Holy Spirit speak to you.

OBSERVE
What did you notice about the passage from above? What words or images is the Holy Spirit bringing to your mind? Was there something the Holy Spirit spoke to you while you waited? What does this passage reveal about your brokenness and your need for Christ? Write your observations below.

_____
_____
_____
_____
_____

REQUEST
Ask God to show you where and how the Scripture and observations apply to your life. Write the application below.

_____
_____
_____
_____
_____

DEDICATE YOURSELF
Looking at how the Scripture applies to you, what is one thing that needs to change? Remember, this is not necessarily about something you need to do (or stop doing). Perhaps, the change is in the way you see God, yourself, or others. Pray and ask the Holy Spirit for help in this area.

LESSON FOURTEEN
HOT BUTTONS

By now, you have begun to identify some of the deep emotional wounds, or trauma, in your life that led you to coping through an addiction. Trauma, put simply, is an overwhelming experience that has a negative impact on an individual's mental and emotional processing ability, from the moment of impact into the future.[1] Trauma can be caused by a painful moment of high intensity or consistent recurring painful moments of lower intensity. We will talk more about trauma in the weeks to come, but the point is to acknowledge that most of us have experienced some kind of trauma in our lives.

A few lessons ago, you identified and shared your Top 10 Most Painful Experiences. Some of these moments probably resulted in trauma in your life. In this lesson, we will look at some of the ways that we respond when trauma from our past is triggered. There are often hot buttons in our lives that are pressed—our triggers—leading us to fight, flight, or freeze as a way of coping with the pain from our past. Trauma can be triggered instantly in our lives. It could happen in an argument, a moment of criticism, being judged, cut off in traffic, failing a test, and the list goes on and on. All of these instances, or hot buttons, can subconsciously trigger similar events from our past, leading us to react, rather than respond.

One of most difficult things about past trauma in our life is the strong defense mechanisms we can build in response to the pain. The things that hurt us so deeply are the things that we can be the most out of touch with at an emotional level. This is because a common defense we use when we are traumatized is to freeze, or to go numb. We mentally check out; therefore, we have little or no feeling in those areas of our disowned pain. We essentially apply emotional Novocain. Thus, we lose access to the feelings that would serve as indicators of the location of the wounds. Somewhere inside of us we hurt, but we don't know just where. This dilemma can drive the addiction ever deeper into our soul when we accidentally bump into that wound.

A particular action or statement from another person presses on the old wound, triggering a response in us that is clearly an overreaction, so we fight. We continue the overreaction by blaming others because this is where we are numb or out of touch. Instead of dealing with our overreaction and finding out why we acted that way, we project our unfelt pain onto the situation. This creates so many more problems on top of the original ones that we get lost and distracted by them. We are caught in a double noose keeping us tied up and blind to the original pain that drives the whole cycle.

Unprocessed trauma or pain, will lead us to develop hot buttons in our lives to protect ourselves. When these hot buttons are pressed by situations or people in our life, we will react in one of three ways, sometimes cycling through all three.

FIGHT: OVERREACTION USUALLY EXPRESSED IN ANGER

"Be angry and do not sin; do not let the sun go down on your anger..."
Ephesians 4:26 (ESV)

Our limbic system, or emotional brain, responds so frequently to major threats, or trauma, with anger because initially, it can feel effective. It drives others away and makes us feel more powerful and less vulnerable. Not all anger is bad. There is righteous anger that gives you the courage to fight for others. The problem is, our anger is almost never about helping others. Instead, it is about the survival brain overpowering higher reasoning and telling us that we have to fight to survive. The main role of reactive anger is to numb out our fears. Therefore, if we refuse to face and feel our fears, they will always control us. The unchallenged trauma programing of our past will end up being the software that directs our actions in the present. Addressing the fear behind our anger is a key way to see healing take place in our lives.

Answer the following questions to identify the ways you react through fight.

1. Who, what, when, or where can your anger hot buttons get pushed?

Example: *Lately, I've gotten angry or gone limbic when I feel like I'm going to be left out of something. It's terrifying and reminds me a lot of high school. It's not so much anger as it is fear.*

___

2. Why is this person, place, or action such a trigger for you?

Example: *I fear not being good enough to be invited into things. It seems like people are avoiding me on purpose or something.*

___

3. What lies beneath that anger? What are the fears that lead you to power up by getting angry?

Example: *I'm afraid I'm not good enough. If people really knew me, they would definitely leave me.*

___

4. Can you remember a time in your past where you first felt this deep response of fear and/or anger?

Example: *The first time I really remember a response of fear and/or anger was in high school when my girlfriend dumped me; I kind of made a vow with myself that I would never trust another woman.*

___

FLIGHT: SHUTTING DOWN, RUNNING AWAY OR WITHDRAWING

In Genesis 3, Eve bought into Satan's lie that God was holding out on her. She fell for the lie that knowing good and evil like God would make her wise. Adam didn't engage or intervene to help Eve, he just stood by passively. Yet, God created Adam to act. He was created in the image of a mighty and loving God who acts and intervenes. The choices of Adam and Eve's decisions passed down a passivity and apathy that affects us today. Adam started the downward spiral of male passivity.

Like Adam, many of us lean toward passivity in one way or another. Many of us can also seek to avoid conflict at all costs because a lot of us never witnessed healthy disagreements between our parents. Whether it was witnessing yelling matches or that lingering awkward silence of unresolved disagreements, their emotional dysfunction can cause a deep avoidance and fear of conflict in our lives at an early age.

Answer the following questions to identify how you react through flight.

1 When you were growing up, how did your parents deal with conflicts between them?
Example: My dad was always pretty quick to get angry. If my mom disagreed with him or did something that upset him, he became pretty reactive. It always seemed like it was his way or the highway. My mom could never win. She tried to avoid conflict at all costs.

_____
_____
_____

2 What issues or situations do you fear most and withdraw from?
Example: Not being good enough, feeling like a loser, facing rejection.

_____
_____
_____

3 What causes you to worry the most in life?
Example: Not measuring up. I worry that I won't graduate with good enough grades and a good resume. I fear that I won't get a job I like after graduation and that I will be trapped in it. I fear people finding out about all of my flaws and rejecting me.

_____
_____
_____

4 Do you remember when you first started worrying about this issue? Is there a particular incident that comes to mind?
Example: In the first grade, I came home with a bad report card and my parents were pretty angry. Throughout my childhood, it seemed my parents were happy with me and treated me better when I got good grades and performed to their standards.

_____
_____
_____

FREEZE: NUMBING OUT OR APPEASING

Why Zebras Don't Get Ulcers is a great book. If you think about it for a moment, you can understand why the author chose that title. A zebra's life is fairly simple. The primary time of stress in their life occurs about once a week when the lions show up to eat one of them. However, if they can outrun the slowest zebra, no problem—they can go back to munching grass. Even if the lion catches one, they still have a backup plan…play dead. This triggers a profoundly altered state of numbing. In this state, the numbed-out animal is less restricted by debilitating pain and is able to escape if the opportunity arises.[2] And, if you saw the zebra narrowly escape the teeth of the lions, you would notice that afterwards, the animal would literally shake; he is actually processing the trauma of the situation.

However, we as human beings face a huge problem in dealing with intense trauma in our lives. We can have the lion attacking us 24 hours a day. Peter expressed it well: "Be sober-minded; be watchful. Your adversary the devil prowls around like a roaring lion, seeking someone to devour." (1 Peter 5:8 ESV)

The term "prowls" carries a sense of continual activity. Through unprocessed traumatic incidents in our life, the feelings of that moment can be frozen within, so that we experience them as facts. For those like me who grew up in an alcoholic home, those feelings can become so ingrained that they seem like undeniable facts. We can let them run us; we can let them define who we are and how we relate to others in life.

I remember the first time I realized how differently I was acting around a strong male authority figure. I wasn't myself; I was withdrawn and anxious. As I instinctively placed my hand on my chin, I felt the scar and it all came back to me. One of my stepfathers threw me against a brick fireplace and cracked open my chin. I now have a large scar at the bottom of my chin.

When something doesn't make sense, usually your emotional brain or limbic system is overpowering your prefrontal cortex, the higher reasoning part of your brain. In other words, past trauma is turning your feelings into false facts. Many of us try to "deal" with our emotions. We mistakenly work at trying to manage them, control them, tolerate, or suppress them. We would be much better off simply noticing them and using the information they bring; acting on them is optional.

---

2. Peter A. Levine, *In an Unspoken Voice: How the body release trauma and restores goodness.* (Berkeley, CA: North Atlantic Books, 2012) 50.

TRUTHS ABOUT THE HEALING OF TRAUMA

Most people think of trauma as a "mental" problem. However, trauma is something that happens in the body. The mental states associated with trauma are important, but the physical states or limbic states are equally important. The instinctive touching of the scar on my chin was part of the healing process. Therefore, it is important that you learn to listen to what your body is telling you, as well as focusing on what is biblically true.

Stay focused on what God says about you while tracking your bodily reactions and feelings, so you can begin to effectively process and release the trauma from your soul. Peter described our enemy as being "like a lion." As we allow ourselves to come out of freezing or appeasing we will discover that there is only one true lion—the Lion of the tribe of Judah and He wars on our behalf. He is for us not against us! This is not an easy process because you must develop the capacity to face uncomfortable physical sensations and feelings without becoming overwhelmed by them. In this process, you may need someone trained to deal with trauma to walk with you. And, remember, the challenge is worth it; trauma is the noose beneath the noose. If you want to walk in freedom and purity you will have to process the trauma in your life.

① What are you most afraid of and why?
Example: Right now, I'm afraid of failing and that people won't like me because I'm a failure.

_____
_____
_____
_____

② When you bring to mind what you are most afraid of in life, what body sensations are triggered? Where do you feel it?
Example: I thought about this a few minutes ago and felt the physical reaction to it. I felt like crying; I really am afraid that I will fail at many things in life. I have been working so hard to show everyone that I'm not an idiot and I can figure things out.

_____
_____
_____
_____

③ What do you think Jesus would say to you when you have those feelings?
Example: I think Jesus would want me to know that it's going to be okay. It's okay if I fail, because Jesus has my back. People still love me regardless of how I perform and He still loves me.

_____
_____
_____
_____

④ **What causes you to freeze or appease in life?**
Example: I freeze when I know I have some self-examining to do in life. If I know I should think through some aspect of my life, I'll just not think about anything and try to numb out.

⑤ **Why do you think that is such a strong reaction for you? When do you remember freezing or appeasing for the first time in your life?**
Example: I definitely shut down a lot growing up. I would appease and do the easy thing when I was with my family and then came alive outside of that. I really was kind of dead with my family.

Lastly, you'll take two tests in Appendix III of this workbook to help you identify trauma in your life. Please remember, because we live in a fallen world, most of us have trauma. Things people say and do can hurt us deeply and leave lasting emotional wounds in our life. The point of taking these tests is to help us come to grips with how we have been wounded, so that we can move toward healing. For more information about trauma, have your group leader refer to the Identifying Abuse And Trauma section of the *Leader's Guide*.

ASSIGNMENTS FOR NEXT TIME

① **Complete the questions on the previous pages for fight, flight, and freeze.**

② **Take the FACES Test and PTSI Test in Appendix III and be prepared to share your results with the group. Pay close attention to the categories of the PTSI in which you have moderate to severe trauma.**

LESSON FIFTEEN
FACING YOUR WOUNDS

After working through Lessons 12 and 14 you may have come to realize you have endured some serious whacks to your soul. This is one of the big reasons you got out of control with your sexual activity. You have used sex to medicate your pain. As you experience healing, you will begin to see a dramatic decrease in your cravings to act out. A first of its kind study was done with Chinese adolescent Internet users.[1] The study discovered a strong correlation between increased Internet addiction and stressors from interpersonal problems, school problems, and anxiety. Pain was fueling their acting out.

You may have never realized how those wounds affected your relationships, your responses on the job when you are under pressure, or in some other area of your life. You can't outrun these wounds, and you can't ignore them either. If you try to ignore the warning signs your body is blasting, it is only a matter of time before things are going to get even more painful. So it is with trauma, or emotional wounds. Just trying to ignore them or blaming others for your problems will only make matters worse.

You must learn to face the enemy head-on. Your wounds aren't your enemy, but the enemy will take advantage of your wounds. This is your only option to deal effectively with this threat. It is critical that you execute your response with wisdom. Reacting to your past pain too violently will only make you more reactive. Being passive about the pain of your past with statements such as, "It is no big deal. Forget the past and let's move on in life" are simply denial by another name.

> EMOTIONAL WOUNDS HAVE THE ABILITY TO MAKE YOU SO
> ANXIOUS, ANGRY, DISSOCIATED, OR SPACED OUT
> THAT NOTHING YOU READ OR DO WILL HELP.

So, what do we do? There is no single solution we can apply to the problem. We cannot patch up the impact of emotional wounds with a pill or with surgery. Yet, if left untreated, it grows and morphs into a destructive beast that erodes the very fabric of your soul. Emotional wounds have the ability to make you so anxious, angry, dissociated, or spaced out that nothing you read or do will help. This is because your processing center or prefrontal cortex is "shorted out" and shut down when your wounds get inflamed.

THE "GIVENS"

I have discovered several "givens" in dealing with emotional wounds. First, there is no one-size-fits-all approach to how people traverse the terrain of their wounds to health. There is no single prayer, spiritual exercise, or clinical protocol that will make it all go away. Because emotional wounds involve the wounding of multiple dimensions of our being, there is no "one solution"—be it spiritual, emotional, behavioral, or intellectual.

Second, the healing process is not linear. It can feel like a confusing mess. It is like a spiral moving forward and up rather than forward movement in a straight line. When we feel like we are going backwards, God is having us circle around and pick up some of the hidden aspects of our story at a deeper level. This is why you may feel out of control: you are moving in emotional spirals. But remember, the spiral circles around, eventually moving you forward and up again.[2]

Third, every person on the planet has been or will be wounded because we live in a fallen world full of broken people. We vow to not be wounded or made vulnerable again. Whenever this vow is threatened, we begin to control people and circumstances to ensure the vow stays intact.

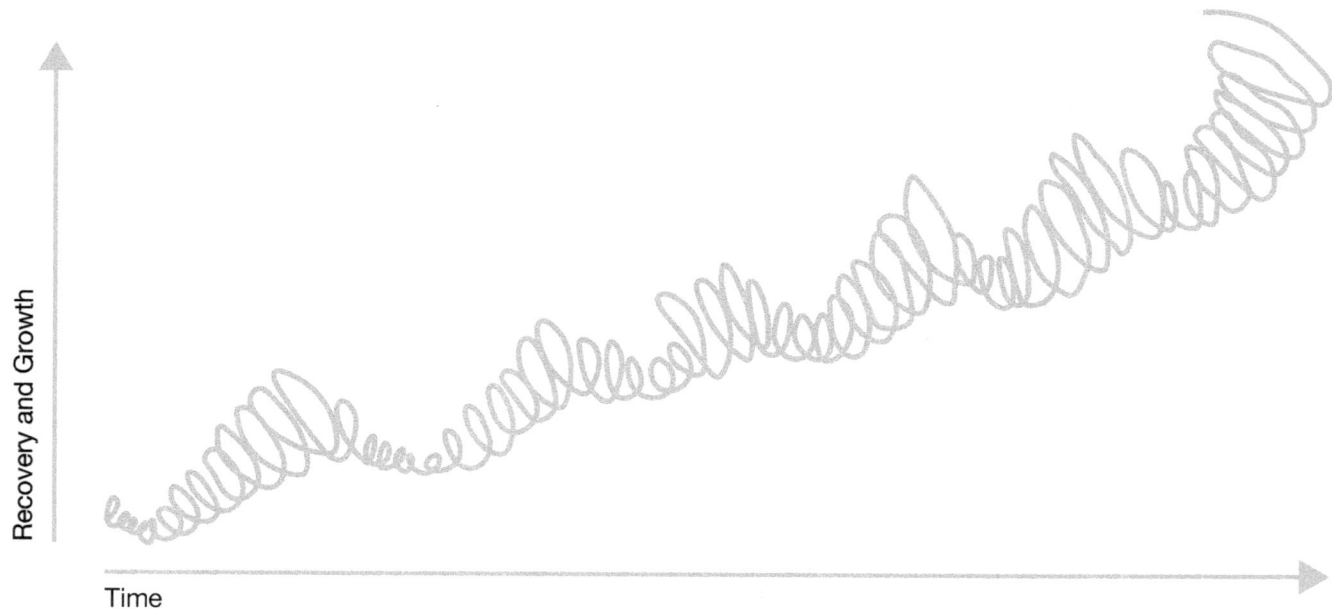

FIGURE 5. Recovery & Growth Through Experiencing, Telling Our Story and Observing It All

---

2. Whitfield, Charles L. *Healing the Child Within: Discovery and Recovery for Adult Children of Dysfunctional Families.* Deerfield Beach, FL: Health Communications, 1989. Print.

HERE IS OUR DOUBLE BIND:

We avoid true vulnerability in relationships through seeking to control the circumstances and people who potentially threaten us, yet it is through giving up control and being vulnerable we come into the light and find healing.

Your attempt at controlling or manipulating people and circumstances is a byproduct of trying to protect your wounds and prevent yourself from being hurt again. Hopefully, you are seeing with more clarity what you have been protecting. Emotional wounds don't have to be a big event or a huge whack to affect us. The neglect of a parent's time and affection can have an even bigger impact on you than the whack of the death of a family member. The wounds of neglect can lie concealed when the wounds of whacks can attract all your attention.

How do we see if we are still affected by the emotional wounds of our past and deal with them? Great question. Let's look in the rear view mirror of your life. Take a few minutes and walk through this checklist and circle "Yes" or "No" if the question is or has ever been true in your life. This is simply a list of questions to understand the depth of what you are dealing with.

EMOTIONAL WOUNDS CHECKLIST

1. Yes No I had medical problems or was hospitalized early in life.
2. Yes No I get easily lost in my work.
3. Yes No I have periods of sleeplessness.
4. Yes No At times, I feel bad about myself because of shameful experiences in my past.
5. Yes No There are actions I have trouble stopping even though they don't help me and are destructive.
6. Yes No My relationships are the same story over and over again.
7. Yes No I was adopted.
8. Yes No I am unable to recall details of painful experiences.
9. Yes No I avoid mistakes at all costs.
10. Yes No Unsettling thoughts or memories about something in the past have come to mind out of the blue.
11. Yes No Sometimes I have outbursts of anger or irritability.
12. Yes No Sometimes I spoil opportunities for success.
13. Yes No There is something destructive I do over and over that started early in my life.
14. Yes No I have difficulty concentrating.
15. Yes No Growing up I was separated from one or both parents or my siblings for a lengthy period of time.
16. Yes No My parents fought a lot verbally and/or physically.
17. Yes No We moved a lot when I was growing up.
18. Yes No I am a risk taker.
19. Yes No I stay in conflict with someone when I could have walked away.
20. Yes No I often feel sexual when I am lonely.
21. Yes No I feel loyal to people even though they have hurt me.
22. Yes No I feel I must avoid depending on people.
23. Yes No I use TV, reading, eating, and hobbies as a way of numbing out.
24. Yes No I have a problem with putting off certain tasks.
25. Yes No I need lots of stimulation so that I don't get bored.

HOW MANY ITEMS DID YOU MARK "YES"? _____

This is not a clinical test or a test that has been scientifically evaluated, but I have noticed that individuals who answer "Yes" to four or more items have emotional wounds in their life that are still affecting them. In most cases, these individuals have no idea that their life has been impacted by the event or circumstance. If you scored eight or more, it is likely that you have been significantly affected by these wounds. In that case, I recommend you seek additional help from a trained clinical counselor. I have seen men that work as hard as anyone else in group, but are unable to find lasting freedom. After getting professional help sorting through their emotional wounds, these same men make amazing progress toward living a life of freedom. If this is your battle, too, talk with your group leader who can help you get connected to a local counselor.

RESOLVING EMOTIONAL WOUNDS

So, what can you do about this now? Becoming vulnerable with a safe group of friends and allowing the Holy Spirit to revisit these emotional wounds with you will be a process over time. This is not something that will happen in one week. Remember the messy spiral from the beginning of the lesson and take faith steps throughout your week to follow the Lord where He wants to take you. It will be at His pace and He won't give you anything you can't handle.

> *Owning our story can be hard but not nearly as difficult as spending our lives running from it. Embracing our vulnerabilities is risky but not nearly as dangerous as giving up on love and belonging and joy—the experiences that make us the most vulnerable.*[3]
> Brené Brown

All of us must go through stages or steps of healing despite the fact that each story and experience is totally unique. You've already begun to do this work in past lessons.

1. ACCEPTANCE

This is where the battle is usually won or lost. You can tell when someone is losing the fight because they live in the opposite of acceptance…denial. It can range from minimizing to fantasy. Sexual addicts tend to have a well-developed fantasy life because they live in denial about their reality. They learned at an early age to escape the pain through fantasy. Denial protects us from unbearable loss and pain, but it also puts us in a mental prison and throws away the key. Acceptance always results in a paradigm shift away from fighting or running from pain to looking it square in the face and dealing with it.

Acceptance will continue to grow as you learn to follow the Lord's lead in your life. He'll take you back to parts of your story that you think you've already processed only to discover He has something more for you to work through. This is the messy spiral at work again. Breaking through denial and accepting reality is at the heart of every spiral God will take you through. The sooner you stop fighting against God and accept where He wants to take you, the quicker you will experience the fullness of life God has for you. You began the work of breaking denial and accepting reality in Lessons Two and Three, but this will be an ongoing process as you continue to walk with God.

---

3. Brown, Brené. *The Gifts of Imperfection: Let Go of Who You Think You Are Supposed to Be and Embrace Who You Are* (Center City: Hazelden, 2010).

① How have you seen God breaking through denial and getting your attention since you started *Living Free*?

_____
_____
_____
_____
_____
_____
_____
_____

② How have you been affected by allowing God to break through your denial so far?

_____
_____
_____
_____
_____
_____
_____
_____
_____
_____

2. INTEGRATION

The next step is integrating a new sense of self and revising your life story based on God's perspective and not your own. Restoration begins when you start to dream the dreams of God at the very point of the past wounds in your life. We can't change our past history, but we sure can reframe it. For example, I cannot change the fact that I experienced suicidal depression, but I can reframe that experience by realizing that God has called me to be a "mighty warrior with a tender heart." The enemy took advantage of my sensitive heart and drove me toward suicide. But, like David, I am a mighty warrior who trusts God with how He has made me and my tender heart is vital in a ministry of setting men free. Lesson Six on Personal Promises gave you the foundation for seeing your life from God's perspective and catching the vision He has for you. God says it best through Paul:

> *Blessed be the God and Father of our Lord Jesus Christ, the Father of mercies and God of all comfort, who comforts us in all our affliction, so that we may be able to comfort those who are in any affliction, with the comfort with which we ourselves are comforted by God. For as we share abundantly in Christ's sufferings, so through Christ we share abundantly in comfort too.*
> 2 Corinthians 1:3-5 (ESV)

1 How has God been reframing your story so you can see yourself from His perspective instead of your own?

_____
_____
_____
_____
_____
_____
_____
_____
_____

2 How have you been able to see God present in your story that you couldn't see before starting this workbook?

_____
_____
_____
_____
_____
_____
_____
_____

3 What might God want to do through your story in the lives of others?

_____
_____
_____
_____
_____
_____
_____
_____

3. REBOOTING

Rebooting is about realizing what pain we have endured and identifying how it still gets triggered. Many people who are stuck in the past need to take the first step of recognizing the shock that has taken place in their life. That is what you did in Lesson Twelve by identifying the pain in your life. If you neglect to do this work, you can get stuck for years because you are not aware of what triggers your reactions to life, which you've been medicating. You will end up stuck on an emotional merry-go-round, endlessly circling your pain and never resolving it. Lesson Fourteen helped you begin to get off that merry-go-round by identifying the ways you fight, flee or freeze.

Let's explore how your wounds still get triggered. A trigger can be anything that pushes your buttons and is mentally paired with a past wound whether you remember it or not. The truth of what you experienced is stored in your body, which is exactly why mapping your triggers is so helpful. Triggers inform you about what wounds you have experienced, even if you do not remember the original wounding event. Understanding your triggers will certainly help you get a handle on working on your overreactions and help you to keep your limbic system from overpowering you. Since triggers often lead to the body re-experiencing the feeling of the original wound, it is little wonder that we avoid them both consciously and unconsciously.

MAPPING YOUR TRIGGERS IN LIFE

Triggers fall into six categories: the five senses of taste, touch, smell, sight, and hearing, plus states of feeling. Let's dive deeper into the anger and worry you began to identify and work through in Lesson Fourteen.

List four things that really upset you or make you angry:

1. _____
2. _____
3. _____
4. _____

List four things you really avoid or worry about in life:

1. _____
2. _____
3. _____
4. _____

Write out a significant memory (good or bad) that is so strong that a taste, touch, smell, sight, or sound brings it vividly back to your mind.

_____
_____
_____
_____
_____

② When have you recently overreacted? What event, situation, or circumstance from your past caused you to overreact, to not be present?

_____
_____
_____
_____
_____
_____
_____
_____
_____
_____

③ Now back up and look at your responses so far. List any common wounds from your past that you still struggle with in the present and find yourself reacting to. Are any of these wounds listed on your 10 Most Painful Experiences in My Life exercise in Lesson Twelve?

_____
_____
_____
_____
_____
_____
_____
_____
_____
_____
_____

You need to pay close attention to anything that you listed in question three. These may not resolve quickly and may require you to bring them to Jesus, safe friends, and trusted counselors many times before you stop overreacting when they are triggered. The breathing technique outlined on the following pages will help you stay present when your wounds get triggered. This will need to become a normal part of your recovery habits as you walk into restoration.

4. RESTORATION

The final step is experiencing restoration to your new way of life; life free from addiction and fulfilling God's vision for you. It is when you finally can live in the present moment instead of the regret from the past or the fear of the future. You live in the here and now and have the ability to take life as it comes, asking for help when needed and living life in the light. There is no need to keep secrets because you are coming to truly believe that no sin can separate you from the love of the Father and you've got a safe group of trusted friends that prove the Father's love to you.

1 In what ways do you see yourself becoming more emotionally present and engaged?

_____
_____
_____
_____
_____
_____
_____
_____
_____
_____
_____

2 In what areas of life are you experiencing restoration? What areas are you still trusting God to see restoration take place?

_____
_____
_____
_____
_____
_____
_____
_____
_____
_____
_____

> It is impossible for me to consistently be fulfilling God's purpose and calling in my life unless I am training my mind to think about myself the way that God does.

NOTES

FUELING RESTORATION—PRACTICING THE PRESENCE OF GOD

Frank Laubach was a man who began an amazing spiritual quest. On January 20,1930, as a missionary to the Philippines, he made a decision.

> *I have started out trying to live all my waking moments in conscious listening to the inner voice, asking without ceasing, "What, Father, do you desire said? What, Father, do you desire done this minute?" It is clear that this is exactly what Jesus was doing all day every day. But it is not what His followers have been doing in very large numbers.*[4]

Frank Laubach made a commitment to bring Christ to mind at least one second of each and every minute of his day. My initial reaction to his quest was, "That is fine if you have nothing to do in life!" Yet, I discovered Laubach wasn't someone who just sat around in life. He was a missionary to the fierce Moros, an Islamic tribe on Mindanao. There, in the village of Lanao, he set about his inspiring quest to experience God, and simultaneously developed a technique for bringing the Moro language to writing. This not only made it possible to teach them to read, but also permitted them immediately to teach others. The famous "Each One Teach One" program was born, which laid the foundation for his worldwide efforts to promote literacy, beginning with India in 1935. During the last thirty years of his life, Laubach was an international presence in literacy, religious, and governmental circles.

After discovering this about his life I was challenged to join him in the quest of practicing the presence of God, but I failed miserably. As we have discovered, our minds don't easily stay focused. My "monkey mind" was jumping from tree to tree mentally and I quickly lost sight of my commitment. Paul's challenge to renew our minds isn't some spiritual quick fix response to our struggles in life. I realized I needed to develop more "mind muscles" – some strengthened neurological connections to walk this path of practicing the presence of Christ.

Read these amazing observations Laubach made after watching the sunset sitting atop Signal Hill, a knoll just outside the town he ministered to in the Philippines.

> *This concentration upon God is strenuous, but everything else has ceased to be so. I think more clearly, I forget less frequently… Even the mirror reveals a new light in my eyes and face. I no longer feel in a hurry about anything. Everything goes right. Each minute I meet calmly as though it were not important. Nothing can go wrong except one thing. That is that God may slip from my mind.*[5]

> *Having had this experience, which comes to me several times a week, the thrill of filth repels me, for I know its power to drag me from God. And after an hour of close friendship with God my soul feels as clean as new-fallen snow.*[6]

I hungered for that. So how does that happen? He was experiencing the reality that God is the Great I Am. We so frequently agonize over our past mistakes or worry about future problems. I need to learn how to be present spiritually, emotionally, and mentally. In other words, I need to learn how to practice the presence of God.

---

4. Frank Laubach, *Letters by a Modern Mystic* (Colorado Springs: Purposeful Design Publications, 2007) 3.
5. Ibid. 23.
6. Ibid. 23.

> *This book of the law shall not depart from your mouth, but you shall meditate on it day and night, so that you may be careful to do according to all that is written in it; for then you will make your way prosperous, and then you will have success.*
> Joshua 1:8 (NASB)

Meditating on the promises of God is something we are called to do as believers. I don't know about you, but I have thoughts in my head that I am sure God doesn't have in His. I need to replace my thoughts with His. It is impossible for me to consistently be fulfilling God's purpose and calling in my life, unless I am training my mind to think about myself the way that God does. I need to learn how to see myself the way heaven sees me!

One of the best skills I practice daily that helps me keep my limbic reactions from taking over is deep breathing. In other words, when I start to "power up" or "power down" and get lost in over or under reactions, it enables me to be present. We introduced deep diaphragmatic breathing in Lesson Six, but now I want to take it deeper.

> *Your adversary the devil walks about like a roaring lion, seeking whom he may devour.*
> 1 Peter 5:8b (NKJV)

I underlined the word "like" because as a follower of Christ, you have been given authority over the enemy. The problem is, until you renew your mind and become present, he frequently convinces you he has authority over you when you are under stress.

It will take time and attention to continually process the wounded parts of your life and you'll need this skill to help your brain stay engaged when these wounds get triggered. Here's why it works. Rapid, short breaths are part of your fight or flight reaction. Slow, deep breathing stimulates the reaction that calms you down. Shallow breathing is like stepping on the accelerator of a high powered car. Deep breathing engages the brakes.

Learning to program your mind for deep diaphragmatic breathing is one of the most basic skills to renew your mind in our stress filled world. I have lost count of the number of times I have been amazed at the effectiveness of deep breathing for helping me walk in faith.

EXERCISE YOUR BRAIN! TRY IT!

1. Get comfortable in your chair and place your feet flat on the floor.
2. Place one hand on your chest and the other on your stomach.
3. Take three deep breaths.

How did you do? Which hand moved? The hand on your chest, the hand on your stomach, or both? If you are like most people, the hand on your chest moved the most or both did. To do this right, only the hand on your stomach should move.

Now, I want you to spend five full minutes in a deep breathing exercise. Set a timer on your phone and walk through the following progression:

1. Start with simply noticing your breathing pattern. Don't fret if it is initially hard to breathe from your diaphragm. Be gracious toward yourself! You are learning a new skill.
2. Next take a short scriptural phrase. Use it as a centering prayer/focus. Here are some favorites:
   A. The joy of the Lord is my strength.
   B. The peace of God
   C. Have mercy, Lord Jesus.
   D. By His stripes I am healed.
   E. I can do all things through Christ.
   F. I am precious in God's eyes.
   G. Fear not, for I am with you.
3. Speak the phrase mentally to yourself in time with your breathing. Speak it when you breathe in and again when you breathe out. It becomes especially powerful when you find a scriptural phrase that uniquely applies to your situation and begin to deeply meditate on it or when you meditate on your Personal Promises.
4. After one minute of meditating on the phrase you chose, focus on taking deep breaths that fill your belly and not your chest. Quiet your mind and allow God to speak to you in imagery or words. If you find yourself becoming distracted (and you will!) just return to the phrase you chose for one minute before focusing on your breathing again.
5. When you focus on your breathing let your belly fill with air through your mouth over five seconds. Hold your breathe for three to five seconds before slowly exhaling through your nose over seven seconds.
6. Take a moment to write down anything God might have said to you during this time.

If you will be faithful to practice deep diaphragmatic breathing as suggested, there will be a neurological reprogramming that will be built into your brain. When you sense your limbic system is firing up and trying to take over your prefrontal cortex or higher reasoning, you now have the ability to engage deep diaphragmatic breathing. Just stop what you're doing and take a few short minutes to breathe and let God speak to you.

It is a choice you can make and it is amazing in its ability to calm you down so you can think straight. Your Personal Promises are excellent truths to meditate on while you breathe. If you diligently apply these biblical responses in stressful situations, you will truly be able to walk confidently into a life of full restoration.

ASSIGNMENTS FOR NEXT TIME

① Be prepared to share your answers to the test and the questions in this lesson at your next group meeting.

② Start every day this week with five minutes of deep breathing before doing any sort of prayer, devotional, or Bible study. Listen for God's voice before starting your day.

③ If you find yourself stressed during the week or overreacting in any way, respond with three minutes of deep breathing. Even taking just three deep breaths can help in a moment of stress.

LESSON SIXTEEN
GET UP OFF THE FLOOR

1 And David said, "Is there still anyone left of the house of Saul, that I may show him kindness for Jonathan's sake?" 2 Now there was a servant of the house of Saul whose name was Ziba, and they called him to David. And the king said to him, "Are you Ziba?" And he said, "I am your servant." 3 And the king said, "Is there not still someone of the house of Saul, that I may show the kindness of God to him?" Ziba said to the king, "There is still a son of Jonathan; he is crippled in his feet." 4 The king said to him, "Where is he?" And Ziba said to the king, "He is in the house of Machir the son of Ammiel, at Lo-debar." 5 Then King David sent and brought him from the house of Machir the son of Ammiel, at Lo-debar. 6 And Mephibosheth the son of Jonathan, son of Saul, came to David and fell on his face and paid homage. And David said, "Mephibosheth!" And he answered, "Behold, I am your servant." 7 And David said to him, "Do not fear, for I will show you kindness for the sake of your father Jonathan, and I will restore to you all the land of Saul your father, and you shall eat at my table always." 8 And he paid homage and said, "What is your servant, that you should show regard for a dead dog such as I?"

9 Then the king called Ziba, Saul's servant, and said to him, "All that belonged to Saul and to all his house I have given to your master's grandson. 10 And you and your sons and your servants shall till the land for him and shall bring in the produce, that your master's grandson may have bread to eat. But Mephibosheth your master's grandson shall always eat at my table." Now Ziba had fifteen sons and twenty servants. 11 Then Ziba said to the king, "According to all that my lord the king commands his servant, so will your servant do." So Mephibosheth ate at David's table, like one of the king's sons. 12 And Mephibosheth had a young son, whose name was Mica. And all who lived in Ziba's house became Mephibosheth's servants. 13 So Mephibosheth lived in Jerusalem, for he ate always at the king's table. Now he was lame in both his feet.
2 Samuel 9:1-13 (ESV)

In 2 Samuel 9, we see the amazing encounter between a man named Mephibosheth and King David. Prior to this encounter, Mephibosheth had been in line to be the next king of Israel. His grandfather, King Saul, had died, and his father, Jonathan, was killed in combat against the Philistines and God did something only God could do; He reached right over Mephibosheth without violating him in the process and put a relative unknown on the throne, which was King David. The news that David had become the new king spread like a wildfire throughout Israel. It was terrifying news to the household of Saul because, if you became king and your father had not been the king before you, you could end up dead. It was a cultural norm for a new king to hunt down and kill every member of the previous king's family. If he didn't, they could rise up against him and reclaim the throne.

In 2 Samuel 4:4, we see how Mephibosheth became crippled. He wasn't born that way, but became that way as a result of someone else's carelessness. Mephibosheth's nurse didn't know Da-

> Through Christ's work on the cross, you have been forgiven, restored and adopted into the King's family.

NOTES

vid's heart, so she ran for her life in panic when she heard he was king. In her haste to save herself, she dropped Mephibosheth, and as a result, he was crippled in both feet.

Years after David took the throne, he sought out someone to bless from the household of Saul. That was a countercultural and radical move because Saul had hunted him down like a dog for over a decade. The man sought every means possible to kill David. Yet, David was responding with such graciousness in seeking to bless someone from the household of Saul. So, the servant, Ziba, informed him there was one grandson left named Mephibosheth.

Mephibosheth was living in a place called Lo Debar, which means "pastureless," a place of desolation and loneliness. When Ziba knocked on Mephibosheth's door in Lo Debar, he may have thought that David finally found out where he was, and was going to kill him. At that point, Mephibosheth may have had two options. He could stay in Lo-debar and continue on a path of negative intimacy by retelling himself the story of how he got a raw deal in life. Had he rehearsed the story over and over he would have never gotten out of Lo-debar. Instead, at great personal risk to himself, he got up off the floor and came to the palace and discovered the goodness of God in a way he never dreamed possible.

What was the greatest challenge Mephibosheth faced and what is yours? Obviously, this is a loaded question. But I am hoping you see that you both face a very similar challenge. You both have experienced a damaging blow in life. This could have been a result of your moral failures or the addiction that grew out of an instinctive response to medicate the pain in your life. You may differ in the fact that your crippledness is internal, not external. But you don't differ in the fact that it affects how you operate in life. Your relationships with others, your view of yourself, and your view of God are all affected by your sexual bondage. Like Mephibosheth, you have been lifted up by the grace of God and brought to a place of blessing. Through Christ's work on the cross, you have been forgiven, restored, and adopted into the King's family.

You're moving on, but the pain still affects you. It hinders the way you deal with others and it affects your ability to relate and trust. Of course, the answer is not to blame other people for your sexual struggles or the pain in your past. But you can't deal with the present unless you first understand the wounds of the past and how the gospel can transform and heal you.

➲ Where have you noticed some crippling in your life? Use the categories below to make some observations about your struggles.

1. Dealing with conflicts and differences in relationships:

2. Dealing with family relationships:

3. Dealing with personal wounds and hurts:

4. Dealing with struggles at school or work:

5. Dealing with women/dealing with men:

> For freedom to grip your life, you will have to choose to identify the pain from your past and to deal with it head-on.

NOTES

Mephibosheth didn't deserve what he received from David and you don't deserve what you have received from Jesus either. It is called grace. God has given you second chances without end. One of the reasons you are reading this workbook and are part of this unique group of men is because of the grace of God. Change and healing can happen once you begin to understand how scandalous God's love is for you and that He will never give up on you, despite how many times you have given up on yourself. God's grace can give you the courage to look at your crippledness within, which you have done in a number of the workbook exercises so far. It is then that you can have the courage to get up off the floor.

Mephibosheth had to get up off the floor—and so do you! Getting up off the floor is not easy, but you can't stay down there because God has a place set for you. He has a place of blessing at his table. He has a plan to use your pain in life for good. So whatever it takes, you need to get up. Even if you have to crawl hand over hand.

Getting up off the floor can be such a frustrating experience because it takes time and daily choices that keep you headed in the right direction. A common misunderstanding is that there are quick fixes. So many men are praying for God to cast out of them things that are not demons. They are trying to get something out of them that is, quite frankly, not coming out. That part of their life has to be discipled, not delivered. God will not take away your flesh this side of eternity. For freedom to grip your life, you will have to choose to identify the pain from your past and deal with it head on. Otherwise, you'll continue to react and medicate the pain and wonder why you just can't stop certain harmful behaviors.

When I came to college, I was very isolated, closed off, and angry. I didn't trust many people, but I didn't really know why. As a result, I treated many people poorly, was very selfish, and viewed myself as being better and more important than others. Over the years, I gradually began to open up to people, trust more, and become less reactive. I still dealt with all of those behaviors to some extent and didn't know why until I experienced one of the biggest moments in my life; I decided to get up off the floor. This happened when I first began going to a Pure Desire sexual addiction recovery group. For the first time in life, I realized that I didn't just have a moral struggle with pornography and masturbation, I had a severe addiction. I was faced with the fact that it was going to take a lot of hard Spirit-filled work to

> You must make the choice to get up off the floor and walk in all that God has for you.

NOTES

see lasting freedom. I was going to have to identify and face the pain in my past that I had been medicating for years. I was going to have to implement a lifestyle change, including many disciplines and recovery tools that were foreign to me. But rather than turning away and giving up because it was time consuming and difficult, I made one of the best decisions of my life. I chose to get up off the floor and go through intensive recovery for several years.

Along the way, I learned that many of my sinful reactions and behaviors were a way of coping with the pain that I had experienced growing up. Subconsciously, I had learned that if you let people close to you, they will hurt you. I had many experiences which led to this defense mechanism. I was also very angry and reactive due to the high amount of rejection I faced in life. Anger became a way of protecting myself. I was afraid of being hurt again, so I compensated with anger to keep people away. Understanding and facing all of these things helped me heal, because you can't change what you don't understand.

Through this choice to get up off the floor, I was able to realize God's call on my life and purpose at His table. As I worked through my own addiction and pain, I realized what God had called me to do with my life. He called me to be a Restorer of Men, as He began to lead men to freedom through me. He had sovereignly allowed me to experience the pain in life that I faced so that I would walk through healing myself and be equipped to help many other men find healing. Sure, I still have some crippling, but I am continuing to work through my past pain as I enjoy my seat at the King's table.

God can use your temporary crippledness for good in the lives of so many others. But just like Mephibosheth, you must make the choice to get up off the floor and walk in all that God has for you. Your miracle is that you get to sit at the table of God's blessing right now as if you had never been dropped. There is a place at the table for you. The amazing thing about walking with God is that it doesn't matter who you are or how you have been dropped or how you may have messed up in life. If you get up off the floor and yield to Christ's desires for you, you will experience the abundant life that He promised.

As you have identified and began working through some intense pain in the past few weeks, it is common to feel defeated and discouraged. Just like Mephibosheth, you must make a decision to move forward despite the pain you have faced in life. The exercises in this lesson will help you draw on past times when you faced challenges and saw God move in your life. Seeing the bigger picture and what God wants to do in your life as a result of your pain will help you put things into perspective and find encouragement when you feel discouraged.

❓ Where do you need to get up off the floor in life?

In answering that question, let's start with a review of your past places of victories.

» Think back over your history and identify those times where you made good decisions, where you got up by the grace of God.

» Remember those commitments you made, followed through on, and how they affected your life?

» List in the following chart: the decision; the time or circumstance; action steps you took; resulting in long-term change. Most important of all, note what you discovered or learned in the process.

PAST "GET UP OFF THE FLOOR" VICTORIES IN MY LIFE

"Get Up Off The Floor" Decisions	The Time or Circumstance	Specific Steps Taken	Resulting Change	What I Learned or Discovered
Example: Didn't take it personally when a girlfriend dumped me.	March of last year	1. I worked through the anger and the hurt by talking to and seeking advice from friends and mentors. 2. I didn't isolate myself or try to outrun the pain. 3. I started dating another girl.	1. I realized dating teaches me how to relate to women. 2. I learned a lot about myself, and what I want and don't want in a relationship.	I discovered I can learn from rejection and that I have what it takes to face the pain in my life.

1.

2.

3.

"Get Up Off The Floor" Decisions	The Time or Circumstance	Specific Steps Taken	Resulting Change	What I Learned or Discovered
4.				
5.				

Where do you need to get up off the floor in your life right now? What decisions do you need to make today, this month, this year? What decisions must you make to get you to the place God has set aside for you?

1. List the decisions you must make to get up off the floor and move forward.
2. List the steps you need to take to get going.
3. What will be the results in your life if you get up?
4. How much courage is it going to take? Use a rating scale from 1 (not much) to 10 (the most possible).
5. Finally, rank the places where you need to get up off the floor in order of importance. Use a rating scale from 1 (not that important) to 10 (absolutely necessary).

"GET UP OFF THE FLOOR" DECISIONS FOR ME RIGHT NOW

"Get Up Off The Floor" Decisions	Steps I Need to Take	The Results if I Get Up	Amount of Courage	Importance of the Decision
Example: Stay relapse free.	1. Keep up the skills I learned and implemented after our group finishes the workbook. 2. Fight hard and reach out for help when I want to quit or relapse. 3. Take more steps toward healing (i.e. counseling, trauma therapy).	1. Have a healthy marriage and family. 2. Develop closer friendships. 3. Be able to help others get free.	10	10

1.

2.

"Get Up Off The Floor" Decisions	Steps I Need to Take	The Results if I Get Up	Amount of Courage	Importance of the Decision
3.				
4.				
5.				

1 **Now look back over your responses in both charts.**

» What is true about your relationship with yourself?

Example: I don't trust that I'll actually follow through on doing what I need to do. I flip flop between being confident and being fearful, so I don't trust my decision making abilities. I really like who I am most of the time, except for this one aspect of myself.

___

» How do you tend to view yourself, especially under pressure?

___

2 **Look at the times in the past where you decided to get up off the floor.**

» How did you get further than you ever thought possible?

___

» How was God faithful to you?

___

» How was the change positive?

___

» What does this say to you with respect to the tough decisions you listed in the "right now" get up off the floor decisions, those with high courage and importance factors?

_____
_____
_____
_____
_____

③ What patterns do you see in your life from these charts? Be specific.

A. _____

B. _____

C. _____

D. _____

E. _____

④ In light of your past challenges, future challenges, and the ways you have been crippled in life, how do you think God wants to use those experiences for good in the lives of others?

Example: God sovereignly allowed me to experience the pain in life that I faced, so that I would walk through healing in my own life and that I would be equipped to help many others experience healing.

A. _____

B. _____

C. _____

⎯⎯ ASSIGNMENTS FOR NEXT TIME ⎯⎯

① Complete all the charts in this lesson and respond to the accompanying questions.

② Choose one of the current Get Up Off The Floor decisions you are facing right now and implement it as your Commitment To Change this week.

LESSON SEVENTEEN
AROUSAL TEMPLATE—PART ONE

> *15 For I do not understand my own actions. For I do not do what I want, but I do the very thing I hate. 16 Now if I do what I do not want, I agree with the law, that it is good. 17 So now it is no longer I who do it, but sin that dwells within me. 18 For I know that nothing good dwells in me, that is, in my flesh. 19 For I have the desire to do what is right, but not the ability to carry it out. For I do not do the good I want, but the evil I do not want is what I keep on doing. 20 Now if I do what I do not want, it is no longer I who do it, but sin that dwells within me.*
>
> *21 So I find it to be a law that when I want to do right, evil lies close at hand. 22 For I delight in the law of God, in my inner being, 23 but I see in my members another law waging war against the law of my mind and making me captive to the law of sin that dwells in my members. 24 Wretched man that I am! Who will deliver me from this body of death? 25 Thanks be to God through Jesus Christ our Lord! So then, I myself serve the law of God with my mind, but with my flesh I serve the law of sin.*
>
> *1 There is therefore now no condemnation for those who are in Christ Jesus.*
> Romans 7:15-8:1 (ESV)

In this passage, Paul speaks so clearly of a struggle with habitual sin. He speaks of wanting to do one thing, but doing another. He speaks of setting his mind on doing what God wants him to do, but returning to sin over and over again despite his greatest efforts to stop. While we don't know the exact nature of Paul's struggle, we can certainly identify with the frustration of returning to sin and not being able to walk in the ways Christ desires for us and that we desire for ourselves.

For most, that may be the reason you are going through this workbook. You have felt the frustration and burden of struggling with the same habitual sin, and have tried everything to stop. You may have made promises to yourself and to God to stop looking at porn, acting out sexually with your girlfriend, or masturbating, but you keep returning to it. You may resonate with Paul's statement in verse 15 where he says, "I do not do what I want, but I do the very thing I hate."

Before going through *Living Free*, you may have felt like things were pretty good most days. You may have made it several weeks, or even several months without relapse, but then you returned to the very place you promised you would never return. You couldn't understand why you kept relapsing when it seemed like you were finally free. It appeared as though things were going fine, then in a moment of weakness, you relapsed.

Throughout college, I didn't understand why I kept returning to porn and masturbation. I thought I just kept making one immoral choice after another, but I didn't understand why I kept doing what I was doing and that I had developed a sexual addiction. I wanted to stop and made continual promises to God that I would, but I couldn't seem to kick the habit no matter what I tried.

> On your best days and on your worst days, this is a promise, there is no condemnation for you.

NOTES

I often thought that I just ended up in Relapse after making a split second decision. Of course, I kept returning to sin over and over due to my inherent sinfulness and fallen condition, but I had no idea that there were also other factors at work. There were many subconscious things happening in life that I allowed, which continually set me up for relapse. I'll expand upon what those things were in a moment, but let's not miss one of the most powerful truths we learn from this passage about those who follow Christ.

We see in Romans 8:1 that there is no condemnation for us. Positionally, we have been made whole and complete in Christ. We have been given His righteousness and perfect obedience, and have been made children of God. But, conditionally, we continue to struggle to obey Christ, to overcome addictions, and to be transformed. It is so crucial that the struggle with sin that Paul speaks of ends with the truth of the gospel. It gives us the freedom to enjoy our relationship with Christ, rather than living each day concerned about how He views us or if we are going to mess up one too many times and lose His love. On your best days and on your worst days, this is a promise, there is no condemnation for you, there is no wrath left from God toward you.

This truth gives us the freedom to strive, in the power of the Holy Spirit, to become more like Christ with no fear of failure because our souls need to be transformed continually. The term "soul" is described in Scripture as our will, intellect, and emotions. And here is a key truth: the hardware or gateway of your soul is your brain.

So, say you lived eighteen or so years before you decided to follow Christ. That means you were making decisions for eighteen years out of your soul. You were relating to God completely out of soul-ish wisdom. Now you might say, "But I came to Christ and that solved the problem, right?" I wish it were that simple. Your spirit was made whole, and positionally you are righteous due to Christ's work on the cross, but your soul needs to be transformed. And over time it becomes more and more obvious to you as you realize the depth of your sinfulness and the depth of Christ's love for you.

I remember reading statements like these in the Bible:
- » I can do all things in Christ.
- » I am more than a conqueror in Christ.
- » All things have passed away behold all things have become new.

Those promises in Scripture used to frustrate me. They were frustrating because initially I didn't understand that my soul and my brain needed to be renewed if I was ever going to fully experience them. This is not a simple process because our brains are such incredible gifts from God. One of the recent discoveries about the brain is the concept of neuroplasticity. Science has discovered that Paul was right in what he wrote two thousand years ago when he said "Do not be conformed to this world, but be transformed by the renewal of your mind…" in Romans 12:2 (ESV).

A human mind can be renewed. It can change and adapt to the environment.[1] Previously, science believed that your brain was hardwired and fixed in its structure. Now scientists realize that is totally false. For example, recent research has revealed that Braille reading individuals have a larger portion of their brain devoted to their index fingers. In fact, the seeing portion of their brain (the occipital lobe) was being used to process the sensations of touch. The human brain will devote larger and larger areas to repeated behaviors. This explains precisely why bad habits can be so hard to unlearn. Most of us think of our brains as a mental container. Learning just means putting something new into it, so when we are trying to break a bad habit we will do things like read more Scripture or pray more. Those things obviously are good, but just those things alone will usually not break the deep sinful patterns that you have repeated for years.

Why is that true? Because each time we repeat the behavior or see it repeated, the use of that space is not available for good habits. As one neuroscientist put it, "It is best to get it right early before bad habits get the competitive advantage."[2]

Where our brain begins to react in the old survival patterns we have established, we, like Paul in Romans 7, will find ourselves doing the very thing we don't want to do.

At this point in your healing journey, you've been exposed to many great tools and concepts that have helped you identify and address the underlying factors that set you up for relapse. From the FASTER Scale, identifying your Top 10 Most Painful Experiences, to understanding your Matrix of Addiction, you have grown in self-awareness.

In this lesson and the next, I want to introduce you to one of the most powerful tools we have discovered in this battle of helping men break free from sexual addiction. It is called the Arousal Template (AT).[3] The AT is something that everyone has, and it isn't inherently bad or good. It is simply part of how our brain has become wired as a result of who we are and our experiences in our lives. The AT operates at a subconscious level, until it is identified, which is why it keeps leading men back into sexual sin. In short, The AT is a compilation of everything that an individual finds arousing. The AT is specific to each individual.

So, let me illustrate something. Go ahead and close your eyes for a couple of minutes and think about the last time you were really angry or afraid. Picture the scene and re-experience the emotions you felt.

Now, let's debrief and make some observations. What happened to your heart rate and breathing during this exercise? What happened to your blood pressure and your field of vision? Did you notice your heart rate increasing and your breathing getting quicker? You just experienced a non-sexual form of arousal. Arousal is an automatic, neural physiological experience of tension and energy related to what is happening in your limbic system.

> Previously, science believed that your brain was hardwired and fixed in its structure. Now scientists realize that is totally false.

NOTES

---

1. Coon, Dennis & Mitterer, John O. *Introduction to Psychology: Gateways to Mind and Behavior*, 12th ed. (Belmont, CA: Wadsworth Cengage Learning, 2010) 48.
2. Norman Doidge, *The Brain that Changes Itself*, (New York: Viking, 2007) 60.
3. The concept of the Arousal Template comes from Dr. Patrick Carnes and Anna Valenti. Many men I have counseled through the years have been set free to win the battle through the brilliance of their therapeutic insight.

AROUSAL TEMPLATE—PART ONE

> **If you have tried to stop your sexual behavior and haven't been able to, this could be the critical weapon to turn the tide in your battle.**
>
> **NOTES**

During sexual arousal, our bodies respond in similar ways to what you just experienced. Understanding your specific Arousal Template will help you understand what triggers you and sets you up for wanting to turn back to sexual sin. The AT is an unconscious decision tree of how we have become wired sexually. It is what guides us to what we respond to as being erotic or arousing.

This is crucial for you to grasp: you will have minimal success in stopping your compulsive behavior without understanding your Arousal Template.

The AT organizes all that we have learned about respect, trust, safety, dishonesty, domination, objectification, power, and control into a mental map. It has synthesized what we fundamentally believe about value, worth, excitement, desire, and what to avoid. The limbic beliefs, ideas, and responses become associated with triggers or cues for arousal. Almost anything can become an arousal trigger, and a lot of times, things that aren't sexual will be a trigger. Below are some examples and categories of arousal triggers that make up part of an individual's Arousal Template.

- » **Locations:** hotel rooms, cars, computer lab, restrooms
- » **Sensations:** perfume, drugs, certain smells
- » **Body Types & Features:** tall, blonde, athletic body, soft voice
- » **Personality Types:** vulnerable, professional, flirty, dominant
- » **Feelings:** pain, loneliness, fear, anger, shame

You will begin one of the most challenging exercise in this workbook when you write responses to the Arousal Template that follows and share it with your group.

If you have tried to stop your sexual behavior and haven't been able to, this could be the critical weapon to turn the tide in your battle. We have seen men who have struggled for decades, been to every type of Christian counselor, and tried everything they could think of, but couldn't break free. But once they walked through this exercise, the lights turned on for them and they understood what kept setting them up for relapse. They were able to let go of the one thing they had kept returning to for comfort that was also the thing that was destroying them.

Sharing your Arousal Template with your Living Free group will be a test of courage and vulnerability due to its detailed and specific nature. Sharing your responses and feeling accepted by guys in your group will be a great opportunity to break free from the shame you may feel from your behavior.

Things are about to get real. Spend as much time as possible this next week filling out the following chart and thinking through the categories because almost anything can become a trigger. Try to come up with at least 10 items for each category. The more things and details you can list, the better. It's crucial to understand the specific things that trigger you personally. Next week, we will explore why these specific things trigger you. When you share the results of the Arousal Template with your group, be sure to stop and pray if someone feels triggered from what is shared. Because sharing this exercise takes a huge amount of courage and transparency, be sure to encourage and thank one another after sharing.

AROUSAL TEMPLATE—PART ONE

MY AROUSAL TRIGGERS OR SIGNALS

Locations (Example: beaches during the summer, being home alone, my room, bathrooms, the shower, the gym)

Sensations (Example: perfume, the sound of the computer modem, being buzzed or drunk, being sweaty)

Body Types & Features (Example: tall, short, blonde, athletic body, large breasts, tan)

Personality Types (Example: unavailable, vulnerable, dominant, loud, outgoing, flirty, quiet)

Feelings (Example: danger, shame, pain, aggression, exhaustion, rage, risk)

Culture (Example: older women, schoolgirls, Asian, teachers)

False Beliefs (Example: sex=love, sex=happiness, sex=life)

ASSIGNMENTS FOR NEXT TIME

1. Spend several hours completing the Arousal Template: Part One.

Please note: Do not share any illegal sexual activity that occurred after the age of 17 before first consulting the Memo Of Understanding in addition to the section about illegal activity in the Frequently Asked Questions Section of the "Leader's Guide."

2. What is your reaction to completing the Arousal Template: Part One in this lesson?

» Write a response below. Be prepared to share with the group.

LESSON EIGHTEEN
AROUSAL TEMPLATE—PART TWO

For the moment all discipline seems painful rather than pleasant, but later it yields the peaceful fruit of righteousness to those who have been trained by it. Therefore lift your drooping hands and strengthen your weak knees, and make straight paths for your feet, so that what is lame may not be put out of joint but rather be healed.
Hebrews 12:11-13 (ESV)

Throughout this process, you have taken great strides in implementing discipline and have worked hard in the power of the Holy Spirit. You have made countless phone calls to other group members to break isolation, spent hours each week on recovery homework, and implemented a lifestyle of recovery and surrendering to God on a daily basis. You may feel weary and frustrated with all of the discipline you have put into place throughout this process. A picture from the past might help at this point in your journey. In the 1980s, a movie came out about a skinny kid by the name of Daniel, who runs into an old Japanese gardener by the name of Mr. Miyagi. That's right—I am referring to the movie, *The Karate Kid*.[1]

There is a scene in the movie that is an absolute classic. Daniel is being bullied by some local kids who are being taught karate by a sadistic leader at a local dojo. Mr. Miyagi shows up out of nowhere and rescues Daniel from a beating. Mr. Miyagi is a reserved character who quickly dispatches the arrogant bullies with some incredible martial arts moves. Daniel then asks Mr. Miyagi to teach him karate. Out of that request, an incredible friendship develops between them.

Daniel shows up on the first day of instruction raring to get involved in some sparring. Instead, he finds himself polishing cars. You may remember the routine…wax on…wax off! This is followed the next day with another mundane job, painting both sides of a six-foot fence with Mr. Miyagi pointing out spots that Daniel had missed. As if things could not get more boring for him, soon after he finds himself sanding the floor.

The young man is rapidly approaching the limits of his patience. He wants to learn karate, not sand the floor or paint a fence. He wants to throw a few punches—anything except this mind-numbing routine he keeps going through. Nearly a week has passed and Daniel shows up at Mr. Miyagi's house only to be greeted by a letter instructing him to paint the house. Daniel works all day fuming over the senselessness of the tasks he has been asked to do. He finishes painting the house only to be greeted by his mentor returning from a relaxing trip. Mr. Miyagi stoically, once again, points out a spot Daniel had missed.

That was more than the young man could take. He storms off slinging vindictive one-liners at Mr. Miyagi as he exits. Mr. Miyagi commands him to return. The totally frustrated youngster

---

1. *The Karate Kid*. Columbia Pictures, 1984.

> God is at work transforming us and renewing our minds as we yield to His work in our lives and implement discipline in the power of the Holy Spirit.

NOTES

comes back and stands before his future mentor ready to explode. Suddenly Mr. Miyagi throws a karate punch his way and Daniel instinctively blocks the blow with the same hand motion he has been repeating all day long as he painted the house. Then in rapid-fire succession, Mr. Miyagi calls out "sand the floor," "paint the fence," and "wax on—wax off!" Each motion of Daniel's hands turns out to be the perfect counterpunch to block the various karate blows Mr. Miyagi is throwing his way. It is an amazing scene, as Daniel's eyes light up with the realization that Mr. Miyagi has been teaching and training him the entire time. He thought he was in exile from his dream of learning karate.

What a profound portrayal of our difficulties with God at times, especially as we slug through the process of coming out of our sexual struggles. It feels as if all we are doing is just putting one foot in front of the other. You may have even said to yourself, *What is the purpose of all these exercises of looking at my feelings and wounds within? This doesn't make any sense to me. Why do I need to do it this way instead of another way?* All great questions, but they are only answered as you realize...You *are* in training!

It's in times like these that you must remember what God tells us about discipline in Hebrews 12. It seems more painful, rather than pleasant in the moment, and we often don't see all that God is doing through it. But later, it yields the peaceful fruit of righteousness to those who have been trained by it. God is at work transforming us and renewing our minds as we yield to His work in our lives and implement discipline in the power of the Holy Spirit.

For the assignment in this lesson, you will complete the Arousal Template: Part Two. The Arousal Template has brought more men, who struggle with sexual bondages, to what I call a "Mr. Miyagi Moment" than anything else I have them do. So frequently, I have watched the lights turn on for a guy who has been perplexed by his sexual behavior for years. Suddenly, he understands how to block the enemy's punches against his soul.

I doubt that you will see the battle clearly until you pause at the end of this exercise and allow the Holy Spirit to open your eyes to what has been going on in your life. Therefore, it is critical that you answer the questions in each category with the utmost diligence and detail. I am sure it will feel like a "sand the floor" experience as you answer some of the questions. These are not easy questions to answer. They can be difficult to deal with, but you have come this far by the grace of God. Now is the time to walk into a real breakthrough regardless of the emotional effort required. You have been in training for such a time as this.

This exercise will help you think through how you may keep falling back into the same trap or intense temptation or relapse. Once you are sexually aroused, you can't think straight because you are limbically driven and your higher reason ability usually drops to near zero. We have to do our critical thinking before we get sexually aroused and the Arousal Template enables you to do exactly that. It enables you to deal with the subconscious triggers and patterns that have influenced your battle with sexual bondage.

Please note: There may be legal ramifications for any information about inappropriate sexual contact or behavior that involves minor children that is shared within your Living Free group. Please review the Memo of Understanding.

AROUSAL TEMPLATE—PART TWO

Steps One through Five should take several hours to complete. At minimum, use all of the space provided on the following pages for your responses to each step. You may need to use an extra sheet of paper. Your responses should be extremely specific and extensive.

STEP ONE

1. List ALL sexual behaviors that are arousing for you and have become problematic for you.
i.e. Compulsive masturbation, pornography, one night stands, acting out sexually with another person, voyeurism, anonymous sex, seduction, adult bookstores, exhibitionism, flirtation, role playing, rape, S & M, marital affairs, high risk sexual behaviors, or _____.

YOUR LIST:

___

2. Now, let's get into the specifics of the above behaviors.
i.e. What type of porn sites do you visit? What type of women or men do you like to view (tall, short, young, old, red hair, blonde, muscular or heavy)? What specific sexual acts do you find exciting (couples having intercourse, more than two people, rape, violence, school girls, older women, gay men, gay women, voyeuristic sites)?

What do the individuals you view have in common? Do you pursue them or like to be pursued? Do you see yourself dominating the individual or being dominated? Do you like to exhibit images of yourself? Do you like to watch "hidden camera" views of sexual images? Do you view minors, elderly, or physically/mentally handicapped individuals?

ANSWER THE ABOVE QUESTIONS IN DETAIL HERE:

STEP TWO

⊃ List all early painful sexual and relational experiences in your life. Pay particular attention to traumatic, abusive, and neglectful experiences. List your age of the experiences if you can remember. You'll want to refer back to other exercises like your Top 10 Most Painful Experiences and list them all below.

i.e. Rigid or disengaged family experiences, age 8: inappropriate exposure to sexually explicit information in your home, ages 10-14: parents having affairs, multiple marriages.

Boundary violations, spanked while naked, punished for normal childhood sexual exploration, failure to respect privacy when dressing or in the bathroom, ridiculing your body's development, exhibitionism by parent or parents.

YOUR LIST:

STEP THREE
⊙ **Identify childhood feelings and emotions or any themes related to abuse or neglect. Pay close attention to sexual or romantic themes.**

i.e. Being violated or having sexual boundaries intruded upon, getting something only when you were good (performance orientation), seeing sexual images prematurely (voyeurism), being flirted with (seduced), being subjected to abuse by a powerful parent (exploitive), experiencing abuse from a stranger (anonymous), being spanked while naked (pain), having no privacy (intrusive).

Remember trauma or pain, either a huge one-time experience or numerous small experiences, can become a hyper accelerator for sexual arousal. This is why individuals who have experienced abuse or neglect exhibit altered brain function.

YOUR LIST:
_____
_____
_____
_____
_____
_____
_____
_____
_____

STEP FOUR
⊙ **Try to come up with at least 10 items for each of the below categories.**

1. Identify emerging overall themes and core beliefs:

2. List possible coping skills (i.e. disassociation, control, perfectionism, being passive, narcissism, porn, masturbation, silence, anger/rage).

3. How have these coping skills become embedded themes or patterns in your life (i.e. I get angry when I feel rejected, I get angry at myself often)?

4. How have these patterns expressed themselves sexually in your life (i.e. I want to be sexual when isolated or angry, I make my dating relationships about trying to get my unmet childhood needs met)?

5. What beliefs or feelings trigger you to react sexually?

STEP FIVE

Now let's put the pieces together. Take your responses from Step One through Step Four, and identify your arousal patterns, triggers, and recovery strategies.

What are the patterns and triggers you see in your sexual arousal? What pain, unmet needs, or past experiences may cause this to be sexually arousing for you? What recovery strategies must you have in place when you get triggered?

➡ **List out at least five patterns you see and answer the above three questions for each one.**
i.e. A pattern of attraction to sexually aggressive women or the fantasy of someone else calling the shots in a sexual experience. This may be a way I have sexualized my desire to be pursued or affirmed due to the rejection I faced a lot growing up from friends and family. I am triggered when a woman flirts with me, compliments me, is loud and outgoing, talks about or jokes about sexual things, acts like she desires me. As a recovery strategy, I need to avoid these women or situations at all costs, remind myself I am sexualizing my need for affirmation and being wanted and this is a fantasy, make a phone call to a group member immediately, and remind myself of my Personal Promises.

YOUR LIST:

After you have completed Step One through Step Five, be prepared to share your responses in your next group meeting. It will probably take two weeks for everyone to share their responses with the group. After you share, ask them to see if there are any themes or patterns you might have missed. Remember to be very attentive while someone is sharing, and thank them for sharing.

I don't think anyone can understand an addict quite like a fellow addict. Try not to get defensive if they question the conclusions you have come to; you desperately need an outside observer you can trust. You need such input to help you get clarity because you have been battling the problem at such close range for so long that, at times, you cannot see the forest for the trees.

ASSIGNMENTS FOR NEXT TIME

1. **Complete Steps One through Five of the Arousal Template: Part Two.**

2. **Meditate on Hebrews 12:11-13 daily.**

LESSON NINETEEN
WHAT'S NEXT?

You have made it to the last lesson of the Living Free process. You have worked hard in the power of the Holy Spirit, processed significant pain from your past, and developed a new lifestyle of responding to pain and stress in life in healthy ways. What an achievement! You have taken steps of faith that many men will never take as a result of your desire to get free from sexual addiction and honor Christ with your life. Although you have made significant progress and completed months of recovery work, your journey to freedom is not over, and in some sense it has just begun. Pursuing sexual health is a lifestyle change that must continue the rest of your life. The concepts you have learned and implemented in this process must be continued daily, in the power of the Holy Spirit, to continue on in healing and freedom. As discussed earlier in this process, it usually takes two to five years to see healing from sexual addiction, although ceasing to act out sexually can happen instantly.[1]

So, now that you have just about completed this workbook, you may be asking what to do next. We will address that toward the end of this lesson, but first, let's take some time to think about what God may want to do through you in the lives of others as a result of your journey.

GOD DESIRES TO USE YOU AND YOUR STORY TO GIVE YOU A MINISTRY THAT WILL SET OTHER GUYS FREE FROM THEIR SEXUAL STRUGGLES.

The thief comes only to steal and kill and destroy.
I came that they may have life and have it abundantly.
John 10:10 (ESV)

In John 10, Jesus tells us that He is the Good Shepherd and that He came to bring us abundant life. He came to set us free from the condemnation we deserve as a result of our sin. He came to bring us true satisfaction through having a relationship with Him and living life the way He designed it to be lived. He came to bring us true life, to live life on His terms, surrender to Him rather than trusting our coping mechanisms, and to be set free from sexual addiction.

I believe that God intends to use you and your story to give you a ministry that will set other guys free from their sexual struggles. Right now, there are so many out there who are trapped in the bondage you're leaving behind with the help of your Living Free group, this workbook, and God's grace. God is calling you to stand alongside them. In the midst of their pain, shame, and bondage you'll tell them, "There was a time in my life when I was exactly where you are now. But the Lord's done amazing things for me and He can do that in your life, too."

---

1. Patrick Carnes, ed., *Clinical Management of Sex Addiction* (New York: Brunner-Routledge, 2002) 14-18.

> Your performance didn't determine whether or not you were a sinner, so it can't determine whether or not you're a saint.

NOTES

The beauty of your story lies in the fact that you can help more than one person. One wouldn't be sweet enough. You'll have the opportunity to minister to a bunch of guys, possibly hundreds, maybe even thousands. So many men just like you love God, but can't seem to stop their shameful sexual behavior no matter how hard they try.

You could be their answer. You could be their gift from God to find freedom. God intends you to reach beyond victory to getting sweet revenge against the enemy. You must understand that a significant part of your healing lies in learning how to give back to those in need, those men struggling with the same bondage you once battled in secret. The shame associated with sexual sin makes openness about your victory a real challenge. Many may not want to hear about sexual bondage, especially not among Christians. For those trapped in a behavior they hate but can't seem to stop, ignoring the problem only makes it worse. They need God's answer, and you can be part of that.

In order to take this kind of bold step, you must have a correct view of your relationship with God. Are you are a sinner who struggles to love him or a God-lover who struggles with sin? Your performance didn't determine whether or not you were a sinner, so it can't determine whether or not you're a saint. Paul makes that clear in Romans 5:

> *Therefore, just as sin came into the world through one man, and death through sin, and so death spread to all men because all sinned...But the free gift is not like the trespass. For if many died through one man's trespass, much more have the grace of God and the free gift by the grace of that one man Jesus Christ abounded for many.*
> Romans 5:12a,15 (ESV)

The reason we're sinners is not because we sin. We sin because we're sinners. Some may ask, "How is it fair that I was born a sinner?" While that is a legitimate question, I think a better question is, "How is it fair that I was made righteous in Christ alone?" You see, if you've surrendered your life to Christ, He has already forgiven every sin you've committed in the past, are committing now, and will ever commit. Again, your performance didn't determine whether or not you were a sinner, so it can't determine whether or not you're a saint. Only the perfect life of Jesus and His atonement on the cross for your sins can do that.

God has a fixed and determined love toward you. It's a covenantal faithfulness. It's God's faithfulness, not ours, that makes the covenant work in the first place. Most people don't realize that in the New Testament, Christ is the covenant maker. The covenant in the New Testament is an agreement between the Father and the Son, not between you and God. You see, Jesus is the covenant maker and the Holy Spirit is the covenant keeper. This incredible truth is clearly stated in Hebrews: "This makes Jesus the guarantee of a far better way between us and God—one that really works! A new covenant." (Hebrews 7:22 MSG)

The Father and the Son made a covenant together to deal with our sin. The Father kept His promise of blessing you by putting you in Christ—the one place the covenant couldn't be broken. And that's why Jesus declared, "No one comes to the Father except through me." (John 14:6 ESV)

He wasn't making an arrogant comment about His perceived self-importance. Instead, He was underlining His identity as covenant maker and keeper. This is also why He says, "I will never leave you nor forsake you." (Hebrews 13:5 ESV) That is both a promise and a threat. Christ is telling us, "If you think you can ever escape love, you'd better think again." Let this truth of His love sink in.

- He loves you during and after you're viewing porn and masturbating.
- He loves you even when the shame of what you've done caused you to turn from Him. You can't escape His love.
- He loves you even when you've given up on yourself because you've tried so many times to break your sexual bondage and failed—again, and again, and again.
- He loves you even though He knows all the dark secrets of your soul, the stuff you hope no one ever finds out.
- He loves you and will never, never, never, never, never give up on you.
- He loves you during your best moments and your worst moments. He loves you no matter what, period.

So, let's spend some time thinking through how God may want to use you and your journey to see other men set free. Who will you help in the year ahead? How do you plan to do it? Next, dream some big dreams in Christ. Plan out what you could do for others struggling with sexual addiction in the next five years. Don't think about all the reasons why you couldn't do something. Instead, make some serious plans to get sweet revenge against the enemy. Please remember that it is ideal that you see a minimum of six months of freedom from porn, masturbation, and sexual acts outside of marriage before leading a Living Free group, but there are other ways you can help individuals in the meantime.

① Who do I plan on helping in this year ahead?

_____
_____
_____
_____
_____
_____
_____
_____
_____

② How do I plan on doing it?

_____
_____
_____
_____
_____
_____
_____

③ What will I need to do to prepare?

MY FIVE-YEAR PLAN

① Who can I help over the next five years?

② What creative tools, concepts, or books could I develop in the next five years to help them?

3 What training or skills do I need to develop to make those dreams come true?

A. _____

B. _____

C. _____

D. _____

4 What will all of this look like and how will I feel once the dream comes true?

_____
_____
_____
_____
_____
_____

> *Therefore, since we are surrounded by so great a cloud of witnesses, let us also lay aside every weight, and sin which clings so closely, and let us run with endurance the race that is set before us...*
> Hebrews 12:1 (ESV)

Now that we've looked at what God may want to do through you in the coming years, let's look at how you can continue to allow Him to transform you in your own journey to freedom. I want to encourage you to continue to run the race set before you. This is a marathon, not a sprint. Following Jesus and pursuing sexual health is a lifelong endeavor. There are no quick fixes, and it is a journey that comes down to tons of little decisions you make on a daily basis. Continue to run this race with endurance in the power of the Holy Spirit and surrendering to Him.

One of the few times in Scripture that God clearly declares His will for our lives is in 1 Thessalonians 4:3-4 (ESV) which reads, "For this is the will of God, your sanctification: that you abstain from sexual immorality; that each one of you know how to control his own body in holiness and honor..." This is God's will for your life: your sanctification (the process of being conformed to the character of Christ). So often we ask, "What is God's will for my life?" This is an important question, but we must remember that God has spoken to us clearly about His desires for our lives in the Bible. 2 Peter 1:3 (ESV) says, "His divine power has granted to us all things that pertain to life and godliness..."

Maybe you don't yet know what He is calling you to do after you graduate college, and it's important to figure that out by seeking counsel from godly individuals, praying for God's leading, and looking at your skill set. Remember, His biggest concern for our lives is that we are growing more and more in love with Him and experiencing all that He has for us as a result of our relationship with Him on a daily basis. Pursue your relationship with Jesus daily and grow in sanctification.

So, what should your next steps be? At minimum, I would encourage you to do the following:

1. **Continue making a minimum of three phone calls per week to other group members.**
2. **Continue filling out a FASTER Scale Exercise weekly.**
3. **Continue meeting with your group weekly or every other week, in person, or on video chat, for an hour each meeting. During the meeting each week, spend the first 40 minutes going over your Check-in and the last 20 minutes going over your Commitment To Change.**
4. **Consider going through another resource such as *The Genesis Process* by Michael Dye, or if you haven't come to lasting sobriety, consider seeking out clinical treatment with a Certified Sexual Addiction Therapist through Pure Desire Ministries International (more information at puredesire.org).**
5. **If you have seen great freedom from porn, masturbation, and sexual acts outside of marriage, start another Living Free group and take other men through the healing journey!**

As you continue in your healing journey, you may experience new temptations or may even find yourself back in the trap of relapse. Don't give up, keep your eyes on Jesus, His calling on your life, and how He wants to use your journey in the lives of others. Continue to update your Battle Plan (Lesson Eight), create new Escape Plans (Lesson Ten), and update your Natural Consequences (Lesson Three). Keep identifying pain from your past and working through it with Jesus using the resources provided in Lessons Twelve, Fourteen, and Fifteen. Remember, the average recovery time runs two to five years,[2] so keep implementing things you've learned in this process daily.

The worst thing you could do right now is to give up and revert back to a lifestyle of isolation, shame, and sexual sin. Don't think for a minute that because you have seen growth, or haven't acted out in a while, that it's time to leave the skills you learned in this process behind. This is a lifestyle change, for life. Continue fighting this battle in the power of the Holy Spirit alongside the men in your life, while reminding yourself of who you are, Whose you are, and of Christ's love and view of you. Continue to run the race of following Christ with endurance, keeping up with the lifestyle change you have made as a result of this process.

ASSIGNMENTS FOR NEXT TIME

1. **Complete the questions in this lesson and share your responses with your group.**
2. **Make arrangements to keep meeting together weekly or every other week.**
3. **Continue making a minimum of three phone calls, filling out a Check-in and Commitment To Change, and completing a FASTER Scale Exercise weekly.**
4. **We also suggest creating an Escape Plan for the break ahead. Refer back to the Limbic Holiday Escape Plan from Lesson Ten for ideas.**

---

2. Patrick Carnes, ed., *Clinical Management of Sex Addiction* (New York: Brunner-Routledge, 2002) 14-18.

SEMESTER II COMMITMENT

The goal in this journey of restoration is not simply to walk through a book, but for the gospel to transform you at a deeper level. Therefore, it is of utmost importance that you actually incorporate into your life this information you have studied.

I have, to the best of my ability, completed all the exercises found in Semester II. By God's grace, in the power of the Holy Spirit, I will do everything I can to live these truths out in my life on a daily basis. Denial has stopped in my life!

My Name _____ **Date** _____

Signature _____

AFFIRMING WITNESSES

1 *I affirm the fact that* _____ *has grown in integrity and honesty in his life by the grace of God. Denial is no longer part of his life.*

My Name _____ **Date** _____

Signature _____

2 *I affirm the fact that* _____ *has grown in integrity and honesty in his life by the grace of God. Denial is no longer part of his life.*

My Name _____ **Date** _____

Signature _____

THE NEUROCHEMISTRY OF ADDICTION
BY DR. TED ROBERTS

PART ONE

The ultimate battlefield in your life is always located in your mind. The New Testament speaks of an internal battle that all of us face. Let's quickly look at a few incidents so you can have a clear understanding of the conflict in which you are involved.

> *For though we live in the world, we do not wage war as the world does. The weapons we fight with are not the weapons of the world. On the contrary, they have divine power to demolish strongholds. We demolish arguments and every pretension that sets itself up against the knowledge of God, and we take captive every thought to make it obedient to Christ.*
> 2 Corinthians 10:3-5 (NIV)

This is Paul's classic statement about the nature of the battle every man faces. Please notice that the fight is about pulling down mental bondages or strongholds of the mind. Notice that the focus is not on Satan's attacks, but rather on our minds and taking our thoughts captive for the glory of God.

> *Timothy, my son, I give you this instruction in keeping with the prophecies once made about you, so that by recalling them you may fight the battle well…*
> 1 Timothy 1:18 (NIV)

Paul is challenging his apprentice to stay in the fight and to be faithful to his calling. Once again the focus is not on Satan, but on Timothy's mind.

> *No one serving as a soldier gets entangled in civilian affairs, but rather tries to please his commanding officer.*
> 2 Timothy 2:4 (NIV)

Paul is calling Timothy to clear out the clutter in his life so he can be single minded. He is exhorting him to stay committed to the call of God regardless of the cost and to focus his mind.

> *What causes fights and quarrels among you? Don't they come from your desires that battle within you?*
> James 4:1 (NIV)

James is calling the reader not to be controlled by the self-orientated thinking that can so easily become part of our daily thought processes.

> *Dear friends, I urge you, as foreigners and exiles, to abstain from sinful desires, which wage war against your soul.*
> 1 Peter 2:11 (NIV)

The New Testament is vividly clear – the battlefield of our lives is in our mind. Therefore, it can be very helpful for us to understand more about our minds and how the battle with sexual sin affects our brains.

Let's begin by looking at the incredible gift of our mind. Take your right hand and curl it into a fist wrapping your fingers around your thumb. Next, do the same thing with your left hand. Now bring your two fists together with your knuckles touching. Look down at your two fists. This is a good approximation of the size of your brain.

Your brain is only about three pounds in weight. It makes up about 2% of your body mass, yet it uses up 20% of the oxygen and calories you consume on a daily basis. It is a very delicate organ composed of about 80% water with the consistency of butter at room temperature.[1] Yet, it is the most complex of God's creation. For example, it contains over 100 billion neurons or nerve cells. This is approximately the number of stars in our Milky Way galaxy. And that is not even counting all the supporting glia cells. Now, here is the fascinating news. Each of those individual neurons has upward of 10,000 connections with other neurons. This means your brain has more neurological connections than there are stars in our entire universe![2]

A TYPICAL NEURON

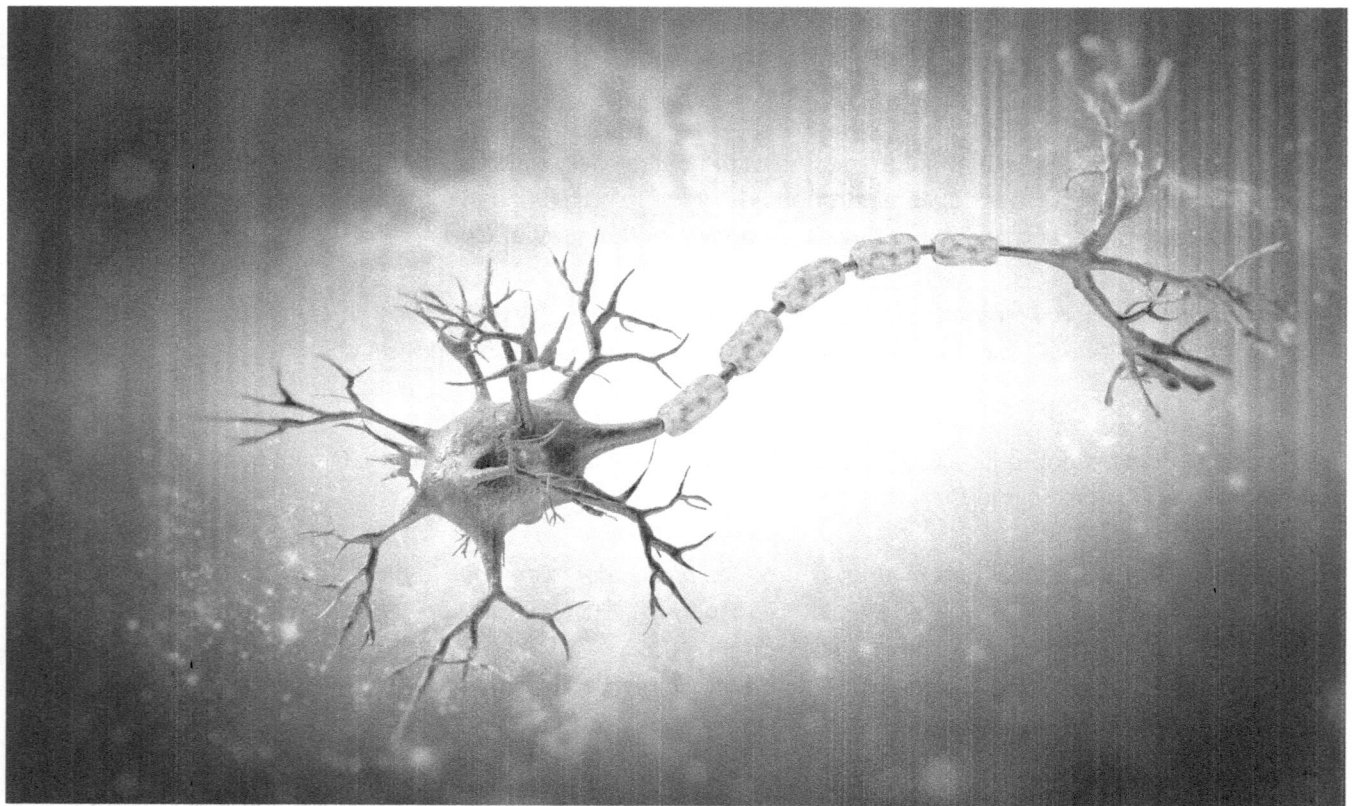

The way the individual neurons communicate with each other is intriguing. The signal initially travels down the length of the neuron electrically. Then the neuron sends a chemical signal across the gap between itself and the adjoining neuron. The neurons don't actually touch each other. The chemical nature of the signal sent across the gap or synapse gives you a hint as to why drugs like cocaine, meth, pot, and alcohol can so powerfully affect your brain.[3]

---

1. Coon, Dennis & Mitterer, John O. *Introduction to Psychology: Gateways to Mind and Behavior*, 12th ed. (Belmont, CA: Wadsworth Cengage Learning, 2010) 48.
2. Kurtz, Paul. *Science and Religion: Are They Compatible?* (Amherst, NY: Prometheus Books, 2003) 60.
3. Griggs, Richard A. *Psychology: A Concise Introduction*, 3rd ed. (New York, NY: Worth Publishers, 2012) 40.

We think our laptop computers are complex and sophisticated, but they are so primitive in comparison to the human brain. For example, your computer sends signals in binary form. In other words, the signal is either a "zero" or a "one," "on" or "off."

A BRAIN SYNAPSE

Scientists have been able to identify over 50 different types of neurotransmitter chemicals so far and have just begun to study the brain at this level. In other words, there are millions of unique signals that can be sent across the synapse of a single neuron with the various combinations of 50 different neurotransmitters. Your computer only has two options. Your brain is like an F-18 fighter and your computer is like a rock in comparison. And that is a severe oversimplification of the actual complexity of your brain.

So, let's take a tour of the battlefield. Below is a rough diagram of your brain and its primary structures.

THE HUMAN BRAIN

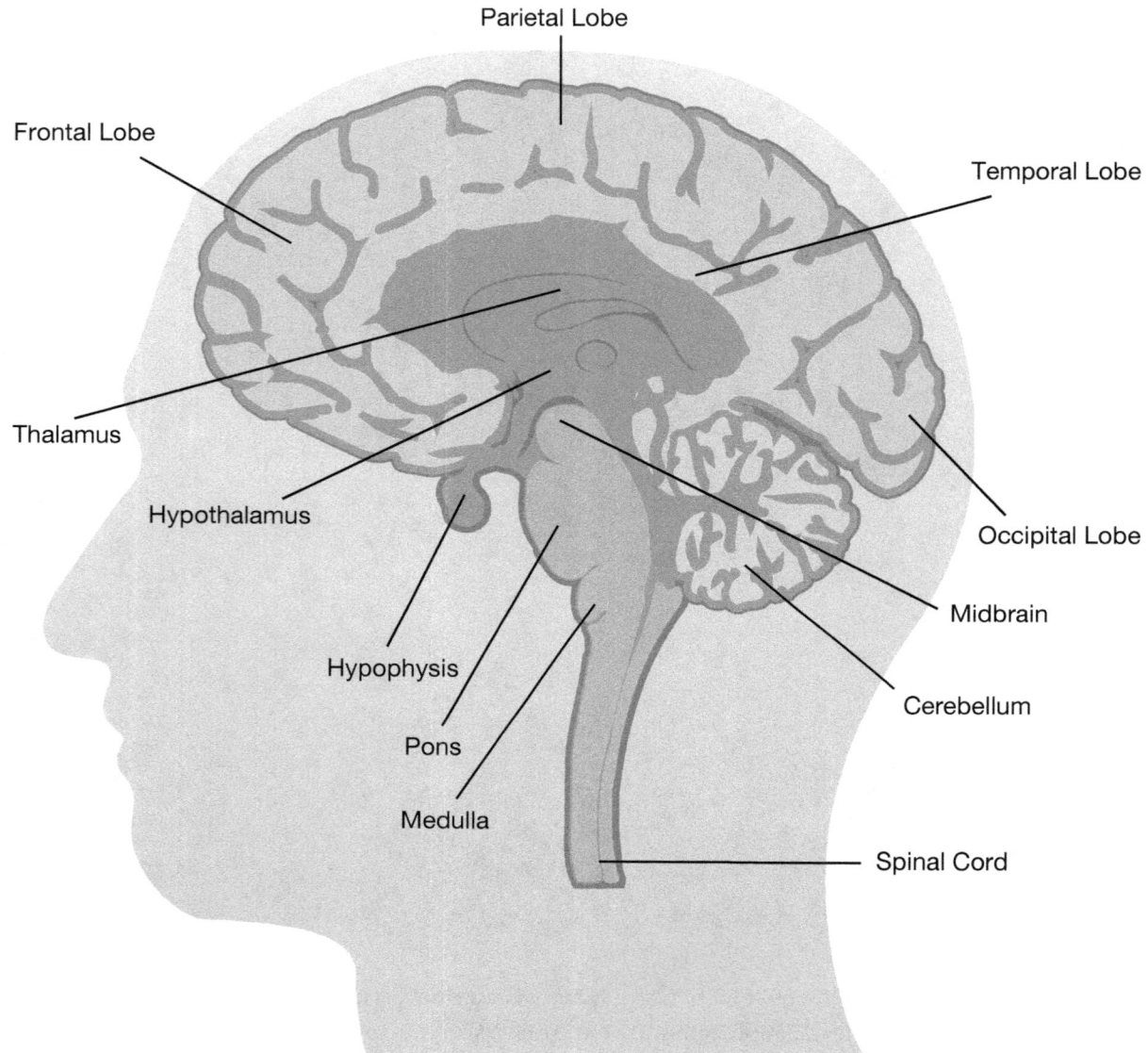

Starting up front is the frontal lobe, specifically the prefrontal cortex, which is the area of your working memory and concentration.[4] This is where executive planning, social awareness, and impulse control take place. This is the area of your brain that shuts down when you are acting out sexually.

Further back on the top of your head is the parietal lobe. This is where spatial awareness is created along with problem solving, and where attention and association take place.

---

4. John Demos, "Neurofeedback," (New York; W.W. Norton: 2005) 22-56.

The visual process occurs in the back of the brain in the region known as the occipital lobe. At the bottom and back of the brain is the cerebellum that controls voluntary muscle movements and processes information coming from muscles throughout the body. Our final stop in this general overview are the temporal lobes located on both sides of your head. These are an amazing part of your brain; they deal with word recognition, language, memory, music, face recognition, and your moods. If you struggle with frequent anger, you probably have some "hot temporal lobes."[5]

The brain doesn't come fully programmed, which is one of its great strengths, because of its infinite adaptability. The brain isn't fully developed until our mid-twenties. Specifically, your prefrontal cortex isn't fully matured until then, which means impulse control and judgment can be lacking.[6]

The first five years of growth in your brain are critical. Our brains are deeply social organisms. For example, from approximately six months to about a year and a half, the right side of your brain is rapidly developing. Some have termed this the "social side" of your brain. It is interesting to note that approximately 70% of the time a mom will carry her infant in her left arm.[7] Whether she knows it or not, this is so she can access the right side of the child's brain. In the constant interchange of comfort and care that occurs between an emotionally healthy mom and her child, a fascinating thing takes place. The mom's brain is serving as scaffolding for the formatting and construction of the child's social brain and affects regulation. Stick with me on this; it will explain why some men struggle so deeply with sexual addiction. "Affect regulation" is a fancy term for emotional stability. The child grows into a young man who can control and deal with the negative emotions of life. However, if there is abandonment, abuse, or lack of care in the family of origin, the brain can be set up for some profound struggles. I think you could sum up the impact of early neglect by saying the early childhood trauma in the form of emotional and physical abuse, sexual abuse, and neglect shape the structure and functioning of the brain in ways that negatively affect all stages of social, emotional, and intellectual development.[8]

If you have ever seen three-year-olds roaring around the kitchen getting into everything, you are seeing neurons making new connections like crazy. Their little brains are experiencing everything for the first time and it is exciting. Compare that to the jaded 17 year old standing in the kitchen responding to questions with one word cryptic answers, "nope" or "nothing" or the classic "whatever." One of the reasons for this extreme difference in behavior is that the teen has half the effective neurological connections of a three year old. They both have the same number of neuron connections, but the critical term is "effective."[9]

The teen has neurological freeways in his brain. Instead of thinking all over the place like a three year old, the teen has fixed ways of thinking. The neuron connections have pruned down the options. In the brain, the old phrase is true, "Use it or lose it." The neurons that fire together actually wire together. Some of the neurological connects a person had at three years old have atrophied, withered away due to lack of use.

Now for the critical question, "Where did those neurological highways come from? How were they constructed?" If you pause and think about it for a moment, the answer becomes glaringly obvious. Their family of origin taught them how to think either in a positive way or in reaction to the pain they experienced in their homes.

Here is an amazing fact: you really don't leave home; you take it with you in your brain. We carry our family of origin with us in our brains. This is where the biblical term "a generational curse" clinically comes from. I have never counseled a man struggling with sexual issues who wasn't carrying a negative family freeway around in his head.

---

5. Earl Henslin, "This is your Brain on Joy," (Nashville: Thomas Nelson: 2008) 172-192.
6. Amen, Daniel G., M.D. *Change Your Brain Change Your Life: The Breakthrough Program for Conquering Anxiety, Depression, Obsessiveness, Anger, and Impulsiveness.* (New York, NY: Three Rivers Press, 1998).
7. Dr. Louis Cozolino, Lecture Notes, IITP Symposium, Feb. 2008.
8. Louis Cozolino, "The Neuroscience of Human Relationships," (New York; W.W. Norton: 2006) 96.
9. Feinstein, Sheryl. *Inside the Teenage Brain: Parenting a Work in Progress.* (Lanham, MD: Rowman & Littlefield Education, 2009) 1-6.

Sexual addiction is frequently about medicating the family pain that the individual has carried around in his soul for years. The killer is, he usually can't even recognize it. It is like faulty software that was downloaded into his head as a kid. He has lived with it for so long, he thinks it's normal to have these thoughts and feelings. It's similar to the background music stores play as you shop; you don't even recognize it's playing. But stores go to the financial expense of having it because when you emotionally connect with the music, you buy more. The music is controlling you and you don't even know it. In much the same way, painful neurological freeways of the past can control us. And some of the most powerful ones originate from the home we were raised in, which is precisely why the Bible speaks so much about generational curses.

Your brain can also become vulnerable in another way. You may have grown up in a great family, but your teen years were very painful. The vast majority of men I have listened to throughout the years struggled with sexual battles that began in their early teen years. Recent research has clearly demonstrated that teens have very unique brains that are quite different than the brains of adults and children.[10] Teen brains are uniquely susceptible to risk-taking and the impact of such behavior. Their prefrontal cortex is not fully developed, thus reducing their ability to control impulses. Add to that the fact they are experiencing elevated levels of the neurotransmitter dopamine that is connected with thrill-seeking behavior.[11]

Here is the scene: A teen is driving a high-powered sports car with the accelerator to the floor, but the car only has the brakes of a go-kart. It is a recipe for disaster. Translate that illustration into sexual terms, and throw in the hyper-sexualized nature of our culture, and a sexual decision can be made as a teen that can affect someone for the rest of his life. The adolescent brain is distinctively sensitive to risky behavior. Studies have shown that teen brains form stronger connections to reward stimuli (drugs and sex) and that these associations last longer than they do for adults.[12]

The bottom line is that our history can be significantly affecting our present. This is especially true when it comes to sexual issues because they are such a foundational part of our identity. This is not to say we aren't responsible for our behavior because of our past. Instead, I am saying you will have little, if any, ability to move into a new beginning until you understand and redeem your past. And let me passionately add that if you had a difficult childhood, you are not blaming your parents for your struggles. Instead, reclaim what is yours in Christ. Your parents may have done the best they could, considering the family in which they were raised. But the curse stops with your generation. You will not pass on a sexually addictive mindset to your kids. Deal with your stuff, stop medicating the pain within, and learn how to walk in purity before your God and family!

PART TWO

I decide to do good, but I don't really do it; I decide not to do bad, but then I do it anyway.
Romans 7:19 (MSG)

I still remember the first time I read those jarring words of Paul. I thought, "That is me!" Those words so succinctly described the deepest frustrations of my life. I was totally committed to Christ trying to serve Him with all my heart, yet I kept being drawn to porn or _____. (You can put your area of sexual struggle in the blank).

---

10. Aron Fisher, (2005) "Reward, Motivation and Emotional Systems Associated with Early-Stage Intense Romantic Love," Journal of Neurophysiology 94 (1) 327-337.
11. Phillips, Sherre F. *The Teen Brain*. (New York, NY: Infobase Publishing, 2007) 54.
12. Emily Anthes, "Instant Egghead Guide to the Brain," (New York; St. Martin's Griffin: 2009) pg. 202.

"What is wrong with me?" I would ask. I thought that if I only tried harder, the problem would go away. But that only made it worse because as I kept driving myself and shaming myself, the relapses only became more painful and crippling to my soul. The turning point came when I understood that my brain had been hijacked. Like Paul in Romans 7, I was literally a double-minded man at war with myself.

The brain creates patterns and templates of action to help us deal more effectively with the demands of our day. Thus we don't have to decide which hand we will use to sign the check or which side of our face we will start shaving first in the morning. Have you noticed you always start with the same side of your face?

Your brain makes over three billion decisions per second, most of which are unconscious.[13] In fact, it has been estimated that 90% of the decisions you make on a daily basis are unconscious in nature. You are on autopilot most of the time, which frees up your prefrontal cortex to develop and analyze new situations. This isn't a problem—until the autopilot is hijacked. We all have had the experience of rushing around the house finding ourselves in a room and we can't remember why we are there. Then we remember we needed to go to the garage to find a screwdriver, but we end up standing in the living room because of our fatigue. We just walked into that room out of habit. Like Paul, we were headed one place and ended up in another. We ended up in the wrong place and we were under stress. More than likely we walked into the living room because that is where we frequently go when we want to relax.

Our autopilot was trying to help us, but instead, it ended up hijacking us from our desired destination. This is a common experience of someone struggling with sexual bondages. Sexual addiction is driven by the fact that you are dealing with a hijacked brain. That doesn't mean you can't help yourself; instead, it means you are going to have to work hard at recalibrating and reprogramming your brain. You will have to purposefully restructure the neurological connections of your brain that are setting you up to spend your life in the wrong places.

Years ago, I was flying a long overwater flight and the refueling range of a fighter aircraft is notoriously short. Therefore, we had to engage in a number of rendezvous with tanker aircraft. This is normally not a challenging endeavor, but that day I had an autopilot that wouldn't easily disengage and it was pulling the plane off the correct headings. The autopilot should have been my best friend. Long overwater flights can be very boring because you have to navigate by the instruments. There are no ground references to tell you where you are, so you are glued to the instrument panel. The autopilot can save you a lot of work, but in this case, the autopilot was increasing my load. I flew for hours battling with the thing, anxious that I might miss the tanker. The Pacific Ocean can be a very lonely place when you are frantically looking for the refueling tanker as your fuel gauge rapidly drops to zero.

This illustration is a vivid picture of the mental battle the addict goes through because his faulty autopilot is trying to ignore the judgment or "common sense" of his input. When you are struggling with sexual bondages your prefrontal cortex commitment to Christ is usually being pulled off course by the autopilot of your limbic system deep within your brain. When you continue to make choices that don't make any sense in your life, when you repeatedly make destructive sexual decisions, mark it down as a limbic system problem.

Your limbic system is comprised of the amygdala, hippocampus, medial thalamus, nucleus accumbens, and basal forebrain, all of which connect to the anterior cingulate gyrus, which is the major gateway to the prefrontal cortex.[14] Don't let all those technical terms freak you out. We are going to look at just three parts of the limbic system that drive your addictive behavior.

---

13. *The Human Brain: God's Design.* Salem Web Network; Godtube.com.
14. John Ratey. *A User's Guide to the Brain.* (New York; Vintage Books: 2001) 227.

1. THE HIPPOCAMPUS

This part of your inner brain consolidates learning by converting working memory into long-term memory and storing it in various regions of your brain. The hippocampus is constantly comparing working memory with long-term memory, creating a sense of meaning in your thought process. For example, Alzheimer's disease progressively destroys neurons in the hippocampus resulting in memory loss.

2. THE AMYGDALA

This part of the brain works in association with the hippocampus. It is survival central. The amygdala is your early-warning system. It processes information even before the prefrontal cortex gets the message that something has happened. When you smile at the sight or sound of someone you love even before you consciously recognize her, the amygdala is at work. Some recent research indicates that of all stimuli, the brain (especially the male brain) codes erotic scenes 20% faster than anything else.[15] The amygdala defines what you see as being critical for your survival. It underlines in your memory what you should flee from or what you are willing to fight for so that you can survive. The amygdala identifies things so terrifying to you that you will just freeze, being unable to respond to the threat. It defines what food is critical for your survival and what is vital for you sexually.

An essential feature of brain anatomy is the fact that there are more connections running from the amygdala to the prefrontal cortex than the other way around.[16] That means that the amygdala will win the battle every time. That explains why Paul is in such despair in Romans 7. When these two parts of the brain are at war with one another it is a bit like Mike Tyson facing off with Woody Allen.

Fear, anger, sexual lusts, which all stem from the amygdala, are notoriously resistant to our ability to reason ourselves out of them. Once fearful reactions or traumatic memories (especially sexual ones) are burned into the amygdala, they tend to lock the mind and body into a recurring pattern of arousal. We have a great deal of difficulty restraining an excited amygdala. Noted neuroscientist Joseph LeDoux, author of *The Emotional Brain*,[17] states that all strong emotional memories are neurobiologically indelible. I would agree with that statement apart from the power of the Holy Spirit. But, if we allow the Holy Spirit's work to take place deep in our lives, our brains can be changed. I want to underline the fact that this process will not take place in a single prayer or Christian experience. It can only take place through the renewing of our minds. Much like a stroke victim, the addict has to re-grow various parts of his brain. You will have to renew your mind.

3. NUCLEUS ACCUMBENS

The third element of your limbic system we will look at is your nucleus accumbens. In 2005, *Discover Magazine* listed the discovery of the endogenous (which means internal) reward system as one of the greatest discoveries in the last 25 years of scientific research.[18] The reason it is so significant is the fact that all drugs and behaviors that are addictive appear to involve the nucleus accumbens.

The nucleus accumbens identifies a certain activity as one that needs to be repeated. The nucleus accumbens releases dopamine in the brain that floods across the synapse of the prefrontal cortex. This causes the "good feelings" from certain activities. But this reward system can be hijacked. For example, cocaine can flood the brain with a "super high" because it blocks the uptake pumps of the dopamine receptors in the brain. This results in a tidal wave of dopamine at the synapse, creating an abnormal firing pattern in the neurons. Over a period of time this literally rewires the brain. Brain scans of cocaine addicts clearly show a reduced overall brain function and specifically reduced prefrontal cortex activity.[19] This is precisely why addicts can make dumb decisions.

---

15. Patrick Carnes, *The 40-Day Focus: Book One* (Carefree, Arizona; Gentle Path Press: 2005), pg 20.
16. Punset, Eduardo. *The Happiness Trip: A Scientific Journey*. (White River Junction, VT: Chelsea Green Publishing Company, 2007) 45.
17. Joseph LeDoux, *The Emotional Brain* (New York: Simon & Schuster, 1996)
18. Discover Magazine, July 2005.
19. Doidge, Norman, M.D. *The Brain That Changes Itself: Stories of Personal Triumph from the Frontiers of Brain Science*. (New York, NY: Penguin Group, 2007) 106.

Here is the connection with sexual addiction. Brain scans of sex addicts and gambling addicts show that the mere thought of sexual activity or gambling lights up their nucleus accumbens like a Christmas tree, much like what happens with a cocaine addict. Sexual addiction and gambling are "process addictions." The high is created by the action, not a drug, because the individual's own brain creates the drug.[20]

This makes process addictions much more difficult to deal with for two reasons. First, the rationalization structures are harder to break through. If someone is taking a drug and has needle marks up and down his arms or his nose is being destroyed by snorting cocaine, it is harder for him to rationalize. A sex addict, however, can keep his activity hidden from view.[21]

Second, process addictions have the capacity to create the immediate onset of a high, similar to cocaine, through things like sexual fantasy. Your battle with sexual fantasy will lie at the core of your ultimate freedom.

Every time you act out, there is a surge of dopamine creating pleasure that triggers neurons and synapses in your brain. That sequence activates a set of beliefs and reinforces limbic dysfunctional experiences that may have begun in early childhood. Old destructive ways of coping with the pain in your life continue to be reinforced. Most of this takes place beyond the awareness of your conscious beliefs.

Paul wrote about this brain pattern in Romans 7:19, "I want to do what is right (conscious beliefs), but I keep doing what is wrong (unconscious dysfunctional beliefs and patterns)." We just keep repeating the old patterns of dancing with destruction. Just trying harder will not solve the problem because we are engaging conscious processes trying to solve unconscious destructive processes.

The ministry of the Holy Spirit is so important in our healing. He is the one who reveals Jesus to us (John 16) and He will uniquely reveal our unconscious processes that are entrapping us. (Romans 8:11-17,26-27)

All addictions, and especially sexual addictions, are deadly traps. Once you experience the dopamine spike of destructive sexual activity, the brain tries to balance itself. Being a sexual addict means your limbic system is "on" most of the time through your sexual fantasies. Therefore, the brain, in an attempt to balance things, reduces the production of dopamine that in turn weakens the reward system. Now the trap has been sprung because you are compelled to act out, not to feel high, but just to feel normal. This is why your sexual addiction has slowly been escalating over time. You have developed what is called "tolerance." What sexually excited you previously doesn't turn you on now. This is why most sex addicts experience a decreased enjoyment of sexual relations with their wife. Or the addict will pressure his wife to engage in sexual behavior he has observed in the pornography he has been viewing.

Your pain and shame level have only increased as you acted out because of your commitment to Christ, but your ability to medicate the pain through porn, voyeurism, masturbation, or strip clubs has continued to diminish. Welcome to insanity!

As the process continues, the brain is significantly changed. Dr. Eric Nestler of the University of Texas has recently discovered that a hijacked dopamine cycle will produce a protein called DeltaFosB[22] in the brain. It will accumulate in the neurons. As it accumulates it eventually throws a genetic switch that causes changes that persist long after the reward cycle has stopped.

---

20. Boleyn-Fitzgerald, Miriam. *Pictures of the Mind: What the New Neuroscience Tells Us About Who We Are*. (Upper Saddle River, NJ: Pearson Education, Inc., 2010) 41.
21. "Process Addictions: Approaches for Professionals" notes from seminar presented by Foundations Recovery Network, April 22-24, 2009.
22. Eric Nestler, (2001). "Psychogenomics: Opportunities for understanding addictions". Journal of Neuroscience, 21 (21), 8324-8327.

The addict is now far more prone to addiction because he experiences stronger cravings. His brain has become sensitized to the experience. Sensitization is different than tolerance. As tolerance develops, the addict needs more and more sexual acting out to get a pleasant affect. But, as sensitization develops, the addict needs less and less of the experience for the cravings to increase. There are two separated systems in your brain, one for excitement and the other has to do with the satisfying pleasure cycle. The man is caught in the vice of a vicious bondage. He is getting excited more and more easily, but experiencing less and less fulfillment. Welcome to total insanity!

Because your brain has literally been hijacked in battle, you need some incredibly powerful weapons to set you free. This workbook is based on the latest research in neurochemistry. I have used the exercises time and again and have seen the deepest levels of bondage broken in men's lives.

However, you can have the finest clinical advice in the world and still be hopelessly in bondage. Two commitments are essential if you are ever going to break free. Both of these attitudes are foreign territory for sexual addicts.

1. A COMMITMENT TO HARD WORK AND HONESTY

You may be a hard worker and deeply honest in many areas of your life, but with respect to your sexuality this hasn't been true for a long time. The hard work with respect to you breaking free is going to be especially difficult because you can't be in control, which is where the honesty comes in. Your Living Free group will be a place where your honesty will be tested. In answering the questions in the workbook you can hide if you want to, but I pray that your group becomes a place where nothing is hidden in your life. I pray that your group becomes a place where you finally open up about your life. Choose to totally trust some other men and be open to their feedback, even when it is painful and revealing.

2. A COMMITMENT TO TAKE UP THE SWORD OF THE SPIRIT IN YOUR LIFE

In Paul's description of the warrior God has designed you to become, he makes a critical observation.

> *Take the helmet of salvation and the sword of the Spirit, which is the word of God.*
> Ephesians 6:17 (NIV)

The sword is the only offensive weaponry Paul mentions in the complete description of armor for a Roman soldier; everything else enables the soldier to stand against the enemy's assaults. Therefore, you must have this spiritual weapon in your battle. What is Paul talking about? Fortunately, he makes it very clear. It is the Word of God that you need, but not just in a general sense. Paul uses the phrase, "the sword of the Spirit, which is the rhema of God." This structure is called a "genitive of origin," meaning that the sword was given to you by the Holy Spirit.[23]

God the Holy Spirit will be speaking promises to you as you walk through this workbook. When He speaks, write them down and review His promises every morning in your quiet time. You must have a God-given dream to make it through the battle. You need something with which you can cut into the enemy when you feel like quitting or when your "DeltaFosB" is driving you crazy with cravings. You need that God-given dream when you are feeling worthless and like a failure, or when your mind is sliding toward the cliff of relapse.

Take a stand with God's promise to you in your hand, His dream in your heart, and with your band of brothers in the Living Free group standing beside you.

---

23. Markus Barth, "Ephesians 4-6," (New York; Doubleday: 1974) 777.

TOOLS FOR RECOVERY

CHECK-IN

The Check-in is a set of questions that review each person's behavior and emotional state from the previous week. The purpose of the review is to help men become more aware of the addictive and healing processes that are at work in their lives. Prior to filling out the Check-in, be sure to fill out a FASTER Scale Exercise. These questions should be filled out within 24 hours before the weekly group meeting starts.

1. What is the lowest level you reached on the FASTER Scale this week? (If there was a relapse be sure to fill out a Relapse Analysis.)

2. What level did you find yourself predominantly living in?

3. What was the double bind you were dealing with in question one? In question two? How could you have practically implemented the harder choice? (Remember, there is always an easier choice and a harder choice. Moving toward health usually involves the harder choice. Check out Lesson Five for more info.)

4. Where are you on your Commitment to Change from our last meeting?

5. Have you lied to anyone this week either directly or indirectly? Why?

6. What positive things have you done to move toward relational and sexual health in your life this week?

COMMITMENT TO CHANGE

A Commitment to Change (CTC) is simply a commitment that is developed through answering a set of questions each week that helps one move toward health. A CTC puts laser focus toward responding to a challenge in the coming week. It could center around a stressful situation that needs to be resolved or that one will be facing, it could be steps that need to be implemented to get off the FASTER Scale, or it could be implementing a certain healthy activity into daily life like going to the gym to exercise several days a week. These questions should be filled out within 24 hours before the weekly group meeting.

1) What area do you need to change or what challenge are you facing next week?

2) What will it cost you emotionally if you do change?

3) What fear do you feel with what you have chosen to change?

4) What will it cost you if you don't change?

5) What is your plan to maintain your restoration regarding these changes?

6) Who will keep you accountable to this commitment? What are the details of your accountability for this week? What questions should they ask you?

THE FASTER SCALE[1]

RESTORATION: Accepting life on God's terms, with trust, vulnerability, and gratitude

- ☐ No current secrets
- ☐ Working to resolve problems, identifying fears and feelings
- ☐ Keeping commitments to meetings, prayer, family, church, people, goals, and self
- ☐ Being open and honest, making eye contact
- ☐ Reaching out to others
- ☐ Increasing in relationships with God and others
- ☐ True accountability

FORGETTING PRIORITIES: Starting to believe the present circumstances and move away from trusting God. Denial, flight, a change in what's important, how you spend your time and what you think about

- ☐ Secrets
- ☐ Less time/energy for God, meetings, church
- ☐ Avoiding support and accountability people
- ☐ Superficial conversations
- ☐ Sarcasm
- ☐ Isolating
- ☐ Changes in goals
- ☐ Obsessed with relationships
- ☐ Breaking promises and commitments
- ☐ Neglecting family
- ☐ Preoccupation with material things: TV, computers, other entertainment
- ☐ Procrastination
- ☐ Lying
- ☐ Over-confidence
- ☐ Bored
- ☐ Hiding money

Forgetting Priorities will lead to:

ANXIETY: A growing background noise of undefined fear; getting energy from emotions

- ☐ Worry, using profanity, being fearful
- ☐ Being resentful
- ☐ Replaying old negative thoughts
- ☐ Perfectionism
- ☐ Judging other's motives
- ☐ Making unrealistic goals and to-do lists
- ☐ Mind-reading
- ☐ Fantasy, co-dependent rescuing
- ☐ Sleep problems, trouble concentrating, seeking drama
- ☐ Gossip
- ☐ Using OTC medication for pain, sleep, or weight control
- ☐ Flirting

Anxiety then leads to:

SPEEDING UP: Trying to outrun the anxiety which is usually the first sign of depression

- ☐ Avoiding slowing down
- ☐ Feeling driven
- ☐ Can't turn off thoughts
- ☐ Skipping meals
- ☐ Binge eating (usually at night)
- ☐ Overspending
- ☐ Can't identify own feelings/needs
- ☐ Repetitive negative thoughts
- ☐ Irritable
- ☐ Dramatic mood swings
- ☐ Too much caffeine
- ☐ Over-exercising
- ☐ Nervousness
- ☐ Difficulty being alone or w/ people
- ☐ Difficulty listening to others
- ☐ Making excuses for having to "do it all"
- ☐ Super busy and always in a hurry (finding good reason to justify the busyness), workaholic, can't relax

---

1. Adapted from the *Genesis Process* by Michael Dye www.genesisprocess.org

Speeding Up then leads to:

TICKED OFF: Getting an adrenaline high from anger and aggression

- [ ] Procrastination causing crisis in money, work, relationships
- [ ] Increasing sarcasm
- [ ] Black and white (all or nothing) thinking
- [ ] Feeling alone
- [ ] Nobody understands
- [ ] Overreacting, road rage
- [ ] Constant resentments
- [ ] Pushing others away
- [ ] Increasing isolation
- [ ] Blaming
- [ ] Arguing
- [ ] Irrational thinking
- [ ] Can't take criticism
- [ ] Defensive
- [ ] People avoiding you
- [ ] Needing to be right
- [ ] Digestive problems
- [ ] Headaches
- [ ] Obsessive (stuck) thoughts
- [ ] Can't forgive
- [ ] Feeling superior
- [ ] Using intimidation

Ticked Off then leads to:

EXHAUSTED: Loss of physical and emotional energy; coming off the adrenaline high, onset of depression

- [ ] Depressed
- [ ] Panicked
- [ ] Confused
- [ ] Hopelessness
- [ ] Sleeping too much or too little
- [ ] Can't cope
- [ ] Overwhelmed
- [ ] Crying for "no reason"
- [ ] Can't think
- [ ] Forgetful
- [ ] Pessimistic
- [ ] Helpless
- [ ] Tired
- [ ] Numb
- [ ] Wanting to run
- [ ] Constant cravings for old coping behaviors
- [ ] Thinking of using sex, drugs, or alcohol
- [ ] Seeking old unhealthy people and places
- [ ] Really isolating
- [ ] People angry with you
- [ ] Self abuse
- [ ] Suicidal thoughts
- [ ] Spontaneous crying
- [ ] No goals
- [ ] Survival mode
- [ ] Not returning phone calls
- [ ] Missing work
- [ ] Irritability
- [ ] No appetite

Exhausted then leads to:

RELAPSE: Returning to the place you swore you would never go again

- [ ] Giving up and giving in
- [ ] Out of control
- [ ] Lost in your addiction
- [ ] Lying to yourself and others
- [ ] Feeling you just can't manage without your coping behaviors, at least for now
- [ ] Result is reinforcement of shame, guilt, and condemnation, and feelings of abandonment and being alone

FASTER SCALE EXERCISE

1. **Check all the behaviors on the FASTER Scale that you identify with.**
2. **Circle the most powerful one in each section. Write it in the corresponding heading below.**
3. **Answer these three questions:**
   - **A.** How does it affect me? How do I act and feel?
   - **B.** How does it affect the important people in my life?
   - **C.** Why do I do this? What is the benefit for me?

RESTORATION: _____
A. _____
B. _____
C. _____

FORGETTING PRIORITIES: _____
A. _____
B. _____
C. _____

ANXIETY: _____
A. _____
B. _____
C. _____

SPEEDING UP: _____
A. _____
B. _____
C. _____

TICKED OFF: _____
A. _____
B. _____
C. _____

EXHAUSTED: _____
A. _____
B. _____
C. _____

RELAPSE: _____
A. _____
B. _____
C. _____

ACCOUNTABILITY PHONE CALLS

As part of recovery, you must commit to initiating at least three phone calls, not text messages, with other people in your group on different days throughout the week to break isolation and Check-in about your current status on the FASTER Scale, double binds (Lesson Five), and current status on fulfilling your Commitment to Change. Since sexual addiction happens in secrecy, it's crucial for you to develop a lifestyle of constant vulnerability throughout the week. Phone calls are a great opportunity to process what's going on in life and ask for help in living a life of restoration.

If you call another member and they don't pick up, leave a voicemail sharing what is going on. Take the opportunity to begin to process and break isolation, but don't count this as one of your three calls for the week.

Phone calls typically last anywhere from five minutes to thirty minutes depending on time available and what is going on in each others' lives. If you're limited by time, be sure to tell the other person how much time you have to talk. If your conversation is cut short and you need to process more that is going on in life, call another group member. Use the following five questions to check in with one another.

1 Where are you on the FASTER Scale?

2 What double bind are you facing? How can you practically make the harder choice?
(Remember, there is always an easier choice and a harder choice. Moving toward health usually involves the harder choice.)

3 Where are you on your Commitment to Change you made at the end of our last meeting?

4 What challenges are you facing this week? Who will help you as you face these challenges?

5 What is your plan to maintain restoration regarding these additional challenges? Is the plan you chose at group still applicable? If not, what do you need to pay attention to right now?

RELAPSE ANALYSIS

DESCRIBE IN DETAIL YOUR LAST RELAPSE BELOW:

What was the relapse?

_____

When did the relapse happen?

_____

Where did the relapse happened?

_____

Did you make a phone call to a group member for help when you were thinking about relapsing? If not, why not? (This is a key step to preventing relapse.)

_____

❓ **What were the actions/interactions/reactions that led up to the relapse (people/places/things involved)?**

_____
_____
_____
_____
_____

❓ **How long were you in relapse and reacting in your addiction (exhaustion > trigger > relapse)?**

_____
_____
_____
_____
_____

❓ **What were your last five days on the FASTER Scale?**

_____
_____
_____
_____
_____

➡ **Provide an emotional analysis leading up to relapse:**

_____
_____
_____
_____

➡ **Provide a spiritual analysis leading up to relapse:**

_____
_____
_____
_____

◯ **Provide a physical analysis leading up to relapse:**

_____
_____
_____
_____
_____
_____
_____

◯ **What was the double bind with the relapse? How could you have practically implemented the harder choice?**

_____
_____
_____
_____
_____
_____
_____
_____

◯ **What was your level of accountability leading up to relapse?**

_____
_____
_____
_____
_____
_____
_____
_____

◯ **What must you implement to avoid a future relapse?**

_____
_____
_____
_____
_____
_____
_____
_____

CLINICAL TESTS

FAMILY OF ORIGIN — FACES II: FAMILY VERSION[1]

DESCRIBE THE FAMILY IN WHICH YOU GREW UP:

① Almost Never   ② Once in a While   ③ Sometimes   ④ Frequently   ⑤ Almost Always

___ 1. Family members were supportive of each other during difficult times.
___ 2. In our family, it was easy for everyone to express his/her opinion.
___ 3. It was easier to discuss problems with outside people than with family members.
___ 4. Each family member had input regarding major family decisions.
___ 5. Our family gathered together in one room.
___ 6. Children had a say in their discipline.
___ 7. Our family did things together.
___ 8. Family members discussed problems and felt good about the solutions.
___ 9. In our family, everyone went his/her own way.
___ 10. We shifted household responsibilities from person to person.
___ 11. Family members knew each others' close friends.
___ 12. It was hard to know what the rules were in our family.
___ 13. Family members consulted other family members on personal decisions.
___ 14. Family members said what they wanted.
___ 15. We had difficulty thinking of things to do as a family.
___ 16. In solving problems, the children's suggestions were followed.
___ 17. Family members felt very close to each other.
___ 18. Discipline was fair in our family.
___ 19. Family members felt closer to outside people than to other family members.
___ 20. Our family tried new ways of dealing with problems.
___ 21. Family members went along with what the family decided to do.
___ 22. In our family, everyone shared responsibilities.
___ 23. Family members liked to spend their free time with each other.
___ 24. It was difficult to get a rule changed in our family.
___ 25. Family members avoided each other at home.
___ 26. When problems arose, we compromised.
___ 27. We approved of each other's friends.
___ 28. Family members were afraid to say what was on their minds.
___ 29. Family members paired up rather than do things as a total family.
___ 30. Family members shared interests and hobbies with each other.

---

[1]. David H. Olson, Joyce Portner & Richard Bell

DIRECTIONS FOR OBTAINING CIRCUMPLEX TYPE SCORE[1]

FOR COHESION:

1. Sum items 3, 9, 15, 19, 25 and 29. _____
2. Subtract that figure from 36. 36 - _____ = _____
3. Sum all other odd numbers plus item 30. + _____
4. Add the figure from step two and step three to obtain a total cohesion score. _____

FOR ADAPTABILITY:

1. Sum items 24 & 28. _____
2. Subtract that figure from 12. 12 - _____ = _____
3. Sum all other even numbers except item 30. + _____
4. Add the figure from step two and step three to obtain a total adaptability score. _____

LINEAR SCORING & INTERPRETATION

	COHESION			ADAPTABILITY			FAMILY TYPE
8	74-80	ENMESHED	8	65-70	CHAOTIC	8	EXTREME
7	71-73		7	55-64		7	
6	65-70	CONNECTED	6	50-54	FLEXIBLE	6	MODERATE TO HIGH
5	60-64		5	46-49		5	
4	55-59	SEPARATED	4	43-45	STRUCTURED	4	LOW TO MODERATE
3	51-54		3	40-42		3	
2	35-50	DISENGAGED	2	30-39	RIGID	2	EXTREME
1	15-34		1	15-29		1	

_____ + _____ = _____ /2 = _____
Cohesion   Adaptability   Type

1. **Find your total Cohesion score and your total Adaptability score in the chart above. Then look at the number (1 through 8) associated with that range. Write that number (1 through 8) in the space provided.**

Example: If you score a 59 on Cohesion, put a 4 above Cohesion. If you score a 30 on Adaptability, put a 2 in the blank above Adaptability.

2. **Then add your Cohesion and Adaptability numbers and divide by 2 to get your Family Type.**

---

1. C.H. Olson, C.S. Russell, & d. H. Sprenkle, *Circumplex model: Systemic Assessment and Treatment of Families*, (The Haworth Press, New York, NY, 1988). Used with permission.

③ Next, look at the Linear Scoring and Interpretation diagram pictured here to understand what this Type shows about your family of origin.

LINEAR SCORING AND INTERPRETATION DIAGRAM

Family Type is determined through the combined Cohesion and Adaptability scores. Extreme forms of family functioning are evident in very high and very low scores: enmeshed/chaotic and disengaged/rigid. Moderate to high scores correlate with connected and flexible family functioning; whereas, low to moderate scores correlate with separated and structured family functioning. The 16 possible variations of Family Type are displayed in the following diagram.

	Disengaged (1–2)	Separated (3–4)	Connected (5–6)	Enmeshed (7–8)
Chaotic (7–8)	Chaotically Disengaged	Chaotically Separated	Chaotically Connected	Chaotically Enmeshed
Flexible (5–6)	Flexibly Disengaged	Flexibly Separated	Flexibly Connected	Flexibly Enmeshed
Structured (3–4)	Structurally Disengaged	Structurally Separated	Structurally Connected	Structurally Enmeshed
Rigid (1–2)	Rigidly Disengaged	Rigidly Separated	Rigidly Connected	Rigidly Enmeshed

Cohesion: Low → High
Adaptability: Low → High

After taking the FACES test, you should have greater insight into the type of family you grew up in. If your family doesn't meet a Balanced Family Type, you have some significant pain to work through, which can fall into two categories. The first category could be referred to as "whacks," which are short moments of extreme intensity and impact. This type of trauma could include violent physical abuse, sexual abuse or other infrequent high intensity incidences. The second category, could be referred to as "lacks," which are frequent moments of low intensity. This could include constant criticism, a lack of affirming or loving words from parents, being bullied, being manipulated or made fun of, not getting certain emotional needs met growing up, and much more.

On the surface, the "lacks" may appear to be totally insignificant, but their cumulative effect can be as crippling as a massive traumatic event. Both kinds of trauma can lead to such high inner pain levels that they trigger compulsive behaviors to medicate. Lessons 12, 14, and 15 will help you begin to identify and work through this pain.

PTSI (POST TRAUMATIC STRESS INDEX)[1]

© Copyright Patrick J. Carnes, PhD, CAS 1999

The PTSI will help you to see any hidden wounds in your life. Please take time to walk through this analysis. It could be an open door to understanding the stealthy adversary you have been fighting for years. Pay close attention to the categories that you have moderate to severe trauma in and begin thinking through the therapeutic strategies.

The following statements typify the reactions trauma victims often have to child abuse.

- » Please check those that you believe apply to you.
- » Although the statements are written in the present tense, if the statements have ever applied to your life, then place a check next to that item.
- » Statements are considered false only if they have never been a part of your life. If in doubt, let your first reaction be your guide.
- » Given these guidelines, check the statements you feel apply to you.

☐ 1. I have recurring memories of painful experiences.
☐ 2. I am unable to stop a childhood pattern harmful to myself.
☐ 3. I sometimes obsess about people who have hurt me and are now gone.
☐ 4. I feel bad at times about myself because of shameful experiences I believe were my fault.
☐ 5. I am a risk taker.
☐ 6. At times I have difficulty staying awake.
☐ 7. I sometimes feel separate from my body as a reaction to a flashback or memory.
☐ 8. I deny myself basic needs at times like groceries, shoes, books, medical care, rent and heat.
☐ 9. I have distressing dreams about experiences.
☐ 10. I repeat painful experiences over and over.
☐ 11. I try to be understood by those who are incapable or don't care for me.
☐ 12. I have suicidal thoughts.
☐ 13. I engage in high-risk behaviors.
☐ 14. I eat excessively to avoid problems.
☐ 15. I avoid thoughts or feelings associated with my trauma experiences.
☐ 16. I skip vacations because of lack of time or money.
☐ 17. I have periods of sleeplessness.
☐ 18. I try to recreate an early trauma experience.
☐ 19. I keep secrets from people who have hurt me.
☐ 20. I have attempted suicide.
☐ 21. I am sexual when frightened.
☐ 22. I drink to excess when life is too hard.
☐ 23. I avoid stories, parts of movies, or reminders of early painful experiences.
☐ 24. I avoid sexual pleasure.
☐ 25. I sometimes feel like an old painful experience is happening now.
☐ 26. There is something destructive I do over and over from my early life.

---

1. Post Traumatic Stress Index Test & Analysis. Copyright Patrick J. Carnes, PhD, CAS 1999. Used by permission of Patrick J. Carnes.

- [ ] 27. I stay in conflict with someone when I could have walked away.
- [ ] 28. I have suicidal thoughts.
- [ ] 29. I often feel sexual when I am lonely.
- [ ] 30. I use depressant drugs as a way to cope.
- [ ] 31. I am unable to recall important details of painful experiences.
- [ ] 32. I avoid doing "normal" activities because of fears I have.
- [ ] 33. I have sudden, vivid or distracting memories of painful experiences.
- [ ] 34. I attempt to stop activities I know are not helpful.
- [ ] 35. I go "overboard" to help people who have been destructive.
- [ ] 36. I often feel lonely and estranged from others because of painful experiences I have had.
- [ ] 37. I feel intensely sexual when violence occurs.
- [ ] 38. My procrastinating interferes with my life activities.
- [ ] 39. I sometimes withdraw or lack interest in important activities because of childhood experiences.
- [ ] 40. I will hoard money and not spend money on legitimate needs.
- [ ] 41. I am upset when there are reminders of abusive experiences (anniversaries, places, symbols).
- [ ] 42. I compulsively do things to others that were done to me as a young person.
- [ ] 43. I sometimes help those who continue to harm me.
- [ ] 44. I feel unable to experience certain emotions (love, happiness, sadness, etc.)
- [ ] 45. I feel sexual when degraded or used.
- [ ] 46. Sleep is a way for me to avoid life's problems.
- [ ] 47. I have difficulty concentrating.
- [ ] 48. I have attempted diets repeatedly.
- [ ] 49. I have difficulty sleeping.
- [ ] 50. My relationships are the same story over and over.
- [ ] 51. I feel loyal to people even though they have betrayed me.
- [ ] 52. I have a dim outlook on my future.
- [ ] 53. I feel sexual when someone is "nice" to me.
- [ ] 54. At times I am preoccupied with food and eating.
- [ ] 55. I experience confusion often.
- [ ] 56. I refuse to buy things even when I need them and have the money.
- [ ] 57. I have difficulty feeling sexual.
- [ ] 58. I know that something destructive I do repeats a childhood event.
- [ ] 59. I remain a "team" member when obviously things are becoming destructive.
- [ ] 60. I feel as if I must avoid depending on people.
- [ ] 61. I sometimes feel bad because I enjoyed experiences that were exploitive of me.
- [ ] 62. I abuse alcohol often.
- [ ] 63. I tend to be accident prone.
- [ ] 64. I spend much time performing "underachieving" jobs.
- [ ] 65. Sometimes I have outbursts of anger or irritability.
- [ ] 66. I do things to others that were done to me in my family.

- [ ] **67.** I make repeated efforts to convince people who were destructive to me and not willing to listen.
- [ ] **68.** I engage in self-destructive behaviors.
- [ ] **69.** I get "high" on activities that were dangerous to me.
- [ ] **70.** I use TV, reading, and hobbies as a way to numb out.
- [ ] **71.** I go into a "fantasy" world when things are tough.
- [ ] **72.** I am "underemployed."
- [ ] **73.** I am extremely cautious of my surroundings.
- [ ] **74.** I have thoughts and behaviors repeatedly that do not feel good to me.
- [ ] **75.** I attempt to be liked by people who clearly were exploiting me.
- [ ] **76.** I engage in self-mutilating behaviors (cutting self, burning, bruising, etc.)
- [ ] **77.** I use drugs like cocaine or amphetamines to speed things up.
- [ ] **78.** I have a problem with "putting off" certain tasks.
- [ ] **79.** I use "romance" as a way to avoid problems.
- [ ] **80.** I feel very guilty about any sexual activity.
- [ ] **81.** I often feel that people are out to take advantage of me.
- [ ] **82.** I revert to doing things I did as a child.
- [ ] **83.** I am attracted to untrustworthy people.
- [ ] **84.** I endure physical or emotional pain most people would not accept.
- [ ] **85.** I like living on the "edge" of danger or excitement.
- [ ] **86.** When things are difficult, I will sometimes "binge."
- [ ] **87.** I have a tendency to be preoccupied with something else than what I need to be.
- [ ] **88.** I have a low interest in sexual activity.
- [ ] **89.** I am distrustful of others.
- [ ] **90.** Some of my recurring behavior comes from early life experiences.
- [ ] **91.** I trust people who are proven unreliable.
- [ ] **92.** I try to be perfect.
- [ ] **93.** I am orgasmic when hurt or beaten.
- [ ] **94.** I use drugs to escape.
- [ ] **95.** I use marijuana or psychedelics to hallucinate.
- [ ] **96.** I sometimes spoil success opportunities.
- [ ] **97.** I am startled more easily than others.
- [ ] **98.** I am preoccupied with children of a certain age.
- [ ] **99.** I seek people who I know will cause me pain.
- [ ] **100.** I avoid mistakes at any cost.
- [ ] **101.** I love to "gamble" on outcomes.
- [ ] **102.** I work too hard so I won't have to feel.
- [ ] **103.** I will often lose myself in fantasies rather than deal with real life.
- [ ] **104.** I go "without" necessities for periods of time.
- [ ] **105.** I get physical reactions to reminders of abuse experiences (breaking out in cold sweat, trouble breathing, etc.)

- [ ] 106. I engage in abusive relationships repeatedly.
- [ ] 107. I have difficulty retreating from unhealthy relationships.
- [ ] 108. I sometimes want to hurt myself physically.
- [ ] 109. I need lots of stimulation so I will not be bored.
- [ ] 110. I get "lost" in my work.
- [ ] 111. I live a "double life."
- [ ] 112. I vomit food or use diuretics to avoid weight gain.
- [ ] 113. I feel anxious about being sexual.
- [ ] 114. There is a certain age of children or adolescents that are sexually attractive to me.
- [ ] 115. I continue contact with a person who has abused me.
- [ ] 116. I often feel unworthy, unlovable, immoral, or sinful because of experiences I have had.
- [ ] 117. I like sex when it is dangerous.
- [ ] 118. I try to "slow down" my mind.
- [ ] 119. I have a life of "compartments" that others do not know about.
- [ ] 120. I experience periods of no interest in eating.
- [ ] 121. I am scared about sex.
- [ ] 122. There are activities that I have trouble stopping even though they are useless or destructive.
- [ ] 123. I am in emotional fights (divorces, lawsuits) that seem endless.
- [ ] 124. I often feel I should be punished for past behavior.
- [ ] 125. I do sexual things that are risky.
- [ ] 126. When I am anxious, I will do things to stop my feelings.
- [ ] 127. I have a fantasy life that I retreat to when things are hard.
- [ ] 128. I have difficulty with play.
- [ ] 129. I wake up with upsetting dreams.
- [ ] 130. My relationships seem to have the same dysfunctional pattern.
- [ ] 131. There are certain people who I always allow to take advantage of me.
- [ ] 132. I have a sense that others are always better off than me.
- [ ] 133. I use cocaine or amphetamines to heighten "high risk" activities.
- [ ] 134. I don't tolerate uncomfortable feelings.
- [ ] 135. I am a daydreamer.
- [ ] 136. At times, I see comfort, luxuries and play activities as frivolous.
- [ ] 137. I hate it when someone approaches me sexually.
- [ ] 138. Sometimes I find children more attractive than others.
- [ ] 139. There are some people in my life who are hard to get over though they hurt or used me badly.
- [ ] 140. I feel bad when something good happens.
- [ ] 141. I get excited/aroused when faced with dangerous situations.
- [ ] 142. I use anything to distract myself from my problems.
- [ ] 143. Sometimes I live in an "unreal" world.
- [ ] 144. There are long periods of time with no sexual activity for me.

STRESS INDEX ANSWER GRID

- On the grid below, place an "X" by all the questions that you checked as true for you.
- Next, add up all the Xs in each column and place the total in the space at the bottom of each.
- Explanations of your scores appear in the PTSI Overview.

1	2	3	4	5	6	7	8
9	10	11	12	13	14	15	16
17	18	19	20	21	22	23	24
25	26	27	28	29	30	31	32
33	34	35	36	37	38	39	40
41	42	43	44	45	46	47	48
49	50	51	52	53	54	55	56
57	58	59	60	61	62	63	64
65	66	67	68	69	70	71	72
73	74	75	76	77	78	79	80
81	82	83	84	85	86	87	88
89	90	91	92	93	94	95	96
97	98	99	100	101	102	103	104
105	106	107	108	109	110	111	112
113	114	115	116	117	118	119	120
121	122	123	124	125	126	127	128
129	130	131	132	133	134	135	136
137	138	139	140	141	142	143	144
TRT	**TR**	**TBD**	**TS**	**TP**	**TB**	**TSG**	**TA**
___	___	___	___	___	___	___	___

- Transfer your score for each category to the appropriate section in the PTSI Overview.

PTSI ANALYSIS OVERVIEW

Based on your scores for the Post-Traumatic Stress Index (PTSI), the following is a brief explanation of what the score measures. If you have been in recovery, then these are possible "vulnerable" areas of which to be aware.

- » If your score is **low (0-2)**, this is not an area of concern.
- » If your score is **moderate (3-6)**, you may wish to explore strategies that might help resolve the past or how to reduce your vulnerability in this area.
- » If your score is **severe (7-18)**, this is an area of potential intense focus or periodic significance.

Obviously, the higher the number, the more concern one has about the severity and chronicity of brain change. Please note that this screening instrument assists in beginning to think about the potential role of trauma or relational experiences in your life. Further assessment with your therapist will determine if these results "fit" and what protocols to consider.

TRT — TRAUMA REACTIONS: MY SCORE ____

Experiencing current reactions to trauma events in the past. This relates to post-traumatic stress disorder (PTSD) symptoms and a tendency to over-react or under-react. Most individuals who score in this area experienced some kind of anxiety (stress) in their family of origin, or growing up and feeling a sense of fear or terror (lack of safety). This sense of uncertainty may be acute or chronic and longitudinal. The general idea is that perceived trauma by an individual results in the release of stress hormones, which may actually damage (rewire) the brain when stress is sustained.

TYPICAL THERAPEUTIC STRATEGIES:
- » Study and write down your automatic "knee jerk" reactions and distorted thinking.
- » Write letters to those who facilitated less-than nurturing experiences for you, telling them of the long-term impact you are experiencing.
- » Also write amends letters to those you know you have harmed.
- » Decide with a therapist what is appropriate to send.
- » You may need to wait until you are further along in your individual and coupleship (if applicable) recovery before attending to amends.

TR — TRAUMA REPETITION: MY SCORE ____

Repeating behaviors or situations that parallel early relationally traumatic experiences. This relates to reenactment and the tendency to "do over." Individuals who score in this area often report OCD or OCPD features (hyper-focus, obsession, rumination).

TYPICAL THERAPEUTIC STRATEGIES:
- » Understand how history repeats itself in your life experiences.
- » Develop habits which help to center yourself (e.g., breathing, journaling, meditation, light exercise) so you are doing what you intend — not the cycles of old.
- » Work on boundaries, both external and internal. Boundary failure is key to repetition compulsion.

TBD — TRAUMA BONDS: MY SCORE ____

Being connected (loyal, helpful or supportive) to people who are dangerous, shaming or exploitative. People who score in this area tend to trust those they should not and mistrust those they should.

TYPICAL THERAPEUTIC STRATEGIES:
- Learn to recognize trauma bonds by identifying those in your life.
- Look for patterns.
- Use "detachment" strategies in situations and with people who "trigger" your codependence.

TS—TRAUMA SHAME: MY SCORE ___

Feeling unworthy, or helpless/hopeless/worthless; having self-hate because of trauma experience. This relates to a sense of self, self-esteem and the experience of thinking "I'm not enough" and "I'm not safe" (e.g., "I can't be myself and be enough, and I'm not safe in this world … being who I am"). Often, individuals will react to stress with extremes (under or overfunctioning, grandiosity or worthlessness, over-control or helplessness and avoidance or passive-aggressive behavior, excessive neediness or hopelessness).

TYPICAL THERAPEUTIC STRATEGIES:
- Understand shame dynamics in your family of origin and how those patterns repeat in your relationships today.
- To whom was it important that you feel ashamed?
- Write a list of your secrets.
- Begin reprogramming yourself with 10 affirmations, 10 times a day (in front of the mirror is best).

TP—TRAUMA PLEASURE NEUROPATHWAY: MY SCORE ___

This is one of the addictive neuropathways related to intensity. When the brain is triggered limbically, automatic reactions ensue and defenses (familiar coping mechanisms) result. Individuals who score in this area often find pleasure in the presence of extreme danger, violence, risk, or shame. Thoughts and behaviors primarily used to reduce pain and acted out with intensity, risk, danger, power/control.

TYPICAL THERAPEUTIC STRATEGIES:
- Write a history of how excitement and shame are linked to your past trauma.
- Note the costs and dangers to you over time.
- Write a First Step and relapse prevention plan about how powerful this is in your life.

HOW THIS NEUROPATHWAY FACILITATES BEHAVIORAL SYMPTOMS IN VARIOUS AREAS:

1. **Erotic (sexual):** All focus is on erotic behavior, excitement, sexual possibility and orgasm. High intensity, risk and danger are often associated. Trauma survivors may incorporate pain and trauma into behavior. Violent/Painful S&M. Voyeuristic Rape. Humiliation. Degradation. Anonymous. Prostitutes. One-night stands. Exhibitionism. Swinging/Swapping. Massage Parlors. Adult Bookstores. Frotterism. Masturbation w/or without porn or 900#.

2. **Romance (sexual):** Romance junkies turn new love into a "fix." They fall into love repeatedly or simultaneously. Roller-coaster romances are highly sexual, volatile, and dangerous. Partners are often unreachable, unavailable or unreadable. Seduction. Exploitation. Conquest. Flirtation. Fatal Attraction syndrome. Having sex with employees and professional "relationships." Office romances. Affair with neighbor. Affairs. Harassment. Swinging/swapping. Clubs/bars.

3. **Relationship (sexual):** Volatile, intense, controlling and often dangerous relationships. Traumatic bonding, stalking and codependency thrive in abandonment, fear-based or dangerous collaborations. Cycles of sex and breakups. High involvement with a stalker. Keep trying to "break it off." Seen in public with a lover. Domestic violence syndrome.

④ **Drugs/Money/Food:** Methamphetamine, Cocaine, Ecstasy, Violence. Craps, Race track. Over-eating. When facilitated in health (ability to self-soothe): life-enhancing, passion, advocacy.

TB—TRAUMA BLOCKING NEUROPATHWAY: MY SCORE ____

This is one of the addictive neuropathways related to numbing. When the brain is triggered limbically, automatic reactions ensue and defenses (familiar coping mechanisms) result. Patterns exist to numb and block out overwhelming feelings that stem from trauma in your life. The unconscious need is for satiation and trancing, which is used to soothe the anxiety and stress of daily life. Behavior is used to sleep, to calm down, or to manage internal discomfort. Anxiety occurs when highly ritualized behavior is frustrated or disturbed. Thoughts and behaviors primarily used to reduce anxiety.

TYPICAL THERAPEUTIC STRATEGIES:
» Work to identify experiences in which you felt pain or diminished.
» Re-experience the feelings in a safe place with the help of your therapist and make sense of them as an adult. This will reduce the power they have had in your life.
» Write a First Step if necessary.

HOW THIS NEUROPATHWAY FACILITATES BEHAVIORAL SYMPTOMS IN VARIOUS AREAS:

① **Erotic (sexual):** Sex is used to soothe the anxiety and stress of daily life. Sex is used to sleep, to calm down high-risk takers, or to manage internal discomfort. Anxiety occurs when highly ritualized behavior is frustrated or disturbed. Masturbation to sleep. Adult bookstores. Lounges. 900#. Internet. Voyeurism.

② **Romantic (sexual):** Romance becomes a way to manage anxiety. Person becomes anxious if not in love with someone or with the person loved. How you are and who the other is not as important as the comfort of being attached. The only goal is to be with someone. Avoid being alone/lonely at all costs. Serial or simultaneous dating/marriage. CoSA/S-Anon.

③ **Relationship (sexual):** Compulsive relationships include tolerating the intolerable – battering, addiction, abuse and deprivation. Person will distort reality rather than face abandonment. Domestic violence.

④ **Drugs/Money/Food:** Alcohol, valium, heroin. Slot machines. Over-eating. When facilitated in health (ability to self-soothe): reflective, calming, solitude.

TSG—TRAUMA SPLITTING NEUROPATHWAY: MY SCORE ____

This is one of the addictive neuropathways related to dissociation. Dissociation exists on a continuum from "simply spacing out sometimes when driving" to severe Dissociative Identity Disorder. When the brain is triggered limbically, automatic reactions ensue and defenses (familiar coping mechanisms) result. Ignoring traumatic realities by dissociating or compartmentalizing experiences or parts of the self. Flighting in to fantasy and unreality as an escape. Dissociation and OCD symptoms are typical. Obsession and preoccupation become the solution to painful reality. Fantasy is an escape used to procrastinate, avoid grief and ignore pain. The neurochemicals involved are typically estrogens and androgens that occur naturally for libido, lust and the drive to procreate. In terms of courtship disorder, this results in dysfunctional patterns of noticing, attraction, touching and foreplay. Thoughts and behaviors primarily used to reduce shame. Acting out with dissociation, compartmentalizing, escape, obsession.

TYPICAL THERAPEUTIC STRATEGIES:
» Learn that dissociating is a "normal" response to trauma.
» Identify ways you split from reality and the triggers that cause that to happen.

- » Cultivate a "caring" adult who stays present so you can remain whole.
- » Notice any powerlessness you feel and how you're drawn to control or having to know exactly what/how/why, or managing the outcome, and may experience difficulty with flexibility and trusting the process.

HOW THIS NEUROPATHWAY FACILITATES BEHAVIORAL SYMPTOMS IN VARIOUS AREAS:

1 Erotic (sexual): Obsession and preoccupation become the solution to painful reality. Fantasy is an escape used to procrastinate, avoid grief and ignore pain. Ultimate orgasm, Strip clubs. Swinging/swapping. Cruising. Cybersex. Porn. 900#. High ritualization.

2 Romance (sexual): Person avoids life problems through romantic preoccupation. Planning, intrigue and research fill the void. Emails and chats, magical romance and stalking are more real than family. Erotic stories. Sexual misconduct. Stalking. Internet "soulmate."

3 Relationship (sexual): Compulsive relationships are built on distorted fantasy. Charisma, role, cause, gratitude play role in cults, sexual misconduct and betrayal. Mystique is built on secrecy, belief in uniqueness, and "special" needs/wants. "Cosmic relationship."

4 Drugs/Money/Food: Cannabis, LSD. Internet lottery. Binge-purge. When facilitated in health (ability to self-soothe): focus(ed).

TA—TRAUMA ABSTINENCE: MY SCORE ___

As a result of traumatic experience, individuals who score in this area tend to deprive (also noted as Trauma Deprivation or TD) themselves of things that are wanted, needed or deserved. There is difficulty in meeting for, or asking for help in meeting, one's needs and wants. Trauma Aversion is used to reduce terror/fear by providing a false sense of control. Individuals will often experience or act out in extremes or binge/purge patterns. Thoughts/Behaviors used primarily to reduce terror/fear. Acted out with Control and Binge-Purge.

TYPICAL THERAPEUTIC STRATEGIES:
- » Understand how deprivation is a way to continue serving your perpetrators.
- » Write a letter to the victim that was you in the past about how you learned to tolerate pain and deprivation.
- » Work on strategies to self-nurture and protect/comfort your inner child.
- » Visualize yourself as a precious child of God.

HOW THIS NEUROPATHWAY FACILITATES BEHAVIORAL SYMPTOMS IN VARIOUS AREAS:

1 Erotic (sexual): Anything erotic or suggestive is rejected. Sex is threatening, mundane, tolerable; not pleasurable. Sex may be okay if the other person does not matter (objectified). Self-mutilation. Objectification of self, being used (prostitution).

2 Romance (sexual): Extreme distrust of romantic feelings or initiatives. At best person seeks "arrangement." Marriage without sex. Suspicious of kindness (seeks ulterior motives). Avoid and withdraw.

3 Relationship (sexual): Avoids. Isolated, lonely, restricted emotions, and poor or nonexistent communication skills. May be overly intellectual/analytical. Secret attachments (nobody can know that I care about …).

4 Drugs/Money/Food: Under-earning, Hoarding. When facilitated in Health (ability to self-soothe): Ascetic (for a higher purpose – as in choosing celibacy as a spiritual way of life, or abstinence for a specific period of time to promote self-awareness and healthy nurturing).

SEXUAL ADDICTION SCREENING TEST (SAST)[2]

SAST—R V2.0

© 2008, P. J. Carnes, Sexual Addiction Screening Test—Revised

The Sexual Addiction Screening Test (SAST) is designed to assist in the assessment of sexually compulsive or "addictive" behavior. Developed in cooperation with hospitals, treatment programs, private therapists and community groups, the SAST provides a profile of responses that help to discriminate between addictive and non-addictive behavior.

- » To complete the test, answer each question by placing a check next to it if it is true for you.
- » Although the statements are written in the present tense, if the statements have ever applied to your life, then place a check next to that item.
- » Statements are considered false only if they have never been a part of your life. If in doubt, let your first reaction be your guide.
- » Please complete the scoring, filling out the Core Item Scale, the Subscales and the Addictive Dimensions on the page that follows the test. Pay close attention to your results on the Core Item Scale as a score of 6 or more indicates an addiction may be present.

☐ 1. Were you sexually abused as a child or adolescent?

☐ 2. Did your parents have trouble with sexual behavior?

☐ 3. Do you often find yourself preoccupied with sexual thoughts?

☐ 4. Do you feel that your sexual behavior is not normal?

☐ 5. Do you ever feel bad about your sexual behavior?

☐ 6. Has your sexual behavior ever created problems for you/your family?

☐ 7. Have you ever sought help for sexual behavior you did not like?

☐ 8. Has anyone been hurt emotionally because of your sexual behavior?

☐ 9. Are any of your sexual activities against the law?

☐ 10. Have you made efforts to quit a type of sexual activity and failed?

☐ 11. Do you hide some of your sexual behaviors from others?

☐ 12. Have you attempted to stop some parts of your sexual activity?

☐ 13. Have you felt degraded by your sexual behaviors?

☐ 14. When you have sex, do you feel depressed afterwards?

☐ 15. Do you feel controlled by your sexual desire?

☐ 16. Have important parts of your life (job, family, friends, leisure activities) been neglected because you were spending too much time on sex?

---

2. Patrick J. Carnes. © 2008, P. J. Carnes, Sexual Addiction Screening Test – Revised. Test & Scoring information used by permission.

☐ 17. Do you ever think your sexual desire is stronger than you are?

☐ 18. Is sex almost all you think about?

☐ 19. Has sex (or romantic fantasies) been a way for you to escape problems?

☐ 20. Has sex become the most important thing in your life?

☐ 21. Are you in crisis over sexual matters?

☐ 22. The Internet has created sexual problems for me.

☐ 23. I spend too much time online for sexual purposes.

☐ 24. I have purchased services online for erotic purposes (sites for dating).

☐ 25. I have made romantic or erotic connections with people online.

☐ 26. People in my life have been upset about my sexual activities online.

☐ 27. I have attempted to stop my online sexual behaviors.

☐ 28. I have subscribed to or regularly purchased or rented sexually explicit materials (magazines, videos, books or online pornography).

☐ 29. I have been sexual with minors.

☐ 30. I have spent considerable time and money on strip clubs, adult bookstores, and movie houses.

☐ 31. I have engaged prostitutes and escorts to satisfy my sexual needs.

☐ 32. I have spent considerable time surfing pornography online.

☐ 33. I have used magazines, videos, or online pornography even when there was considerable risk of being caught by family members who would be upset by my behavior.

☐ 34. I have regularly purchased romantic novels or sexually explicit magazines.

☐ 35. I have stayed in romantic relationships after they became emotionally abusive.

☐ 36. I have traded sex for money or gifts.

☐ 37. I have had multiple romantic or sexual relationships at the same time.

☐ 38. After sexually acting out, I sometimes refrain from all sex for a significant period.

☐ 39. I have regularly engaged in sadomasochistic behavior.

☐ 40. I visit sexual bath-houses, sex clubs, or video/bookstores as part of my regular sexual activity.

☐ 41. I have engaged in unsafe or "risky" sex even though I knew it could cause me harm.

☐ 42. I have cruised public restrooms, rest areas, or parks for sex with strangers.

☐ 43. I believe casual or anonymous sex has kept me from having more long-term intimate relationships.

☐ 44. My sexual behavior has put me at risk for arrest for lewd conduct or public indecency.

☐ 45. I have been paid for sex.

SCALES	ITEMS	CUT-OFF	MY SCORE
Core Item Scale	1-20	6 or more	
SUBSCALES			
Internet Items	22-27	3 or more	
Men's Items	28-33	2 or more	
Women's Items	34-39	2 or more	
Homosexual Men	40-45	3 or more	
SUBSCALES			
Preoccupation	3, 18, 19, 20	2 or more	
Loss of Control	10, 12, 15, 17	2 or more	
Relationship Disturbance	6, 8, 16, 26	2 or more	
Affect Disturbance	4, 5, 11, 13, 14	2 or more	

RELATIVE DISTRIBUTIONS OF ADDICT & NON-ADDICT SAST SCORES

This instrument has been based on screenings of tens of thousands of people. This particular version is a developmental stage revision of the instrument, so scoring may be adjusted with more research. Please be aware that clinical decisions must be made conditionally since final scoring protocols may vary. A score of 6 or more on the Core Item Scale indicates an addiction may be present.